I0800256

THEN & NOW

HANCOCK COUNTY

FRONT COVER: The Sporting Goods store operated by A.A. Gappen was located on south side of Greenfield's Main Street *c.* 1920s. Bicycles were the early mode of transportation offered by the shop. As motorcycles developed they became the shops lead sales item. Harley-Davidson, a name that is recognized to this day, was the brand they offered for many years. Its interesting to note that their lineup of products is similar to that seen on car lots to this day.

THEN & NOW

HANCOCK COUNTY

Joseph L. Skvarenina and Larry L. Fox

ARCADIA PUBLISHING

Copyright © 2001 by Joseph L. Skvarenina and Larry L. Fox
ISBN 978-0-7385-1581-0

Published by Arcadia Publishing
Charleston, South Carolina

Printed in the United States of America

Library of Congress Catalog Card Number: 2001090072

For all general information contact Arcadia Publishing at:
Telephone 843-853-2070
Fax 843-853-0044
E-mail sales@arcadiapublishing.com
For customer service and orders:
Toll-Free 1-888-313-2665

Visit us on the Internet at www.arcadiapublishing.com

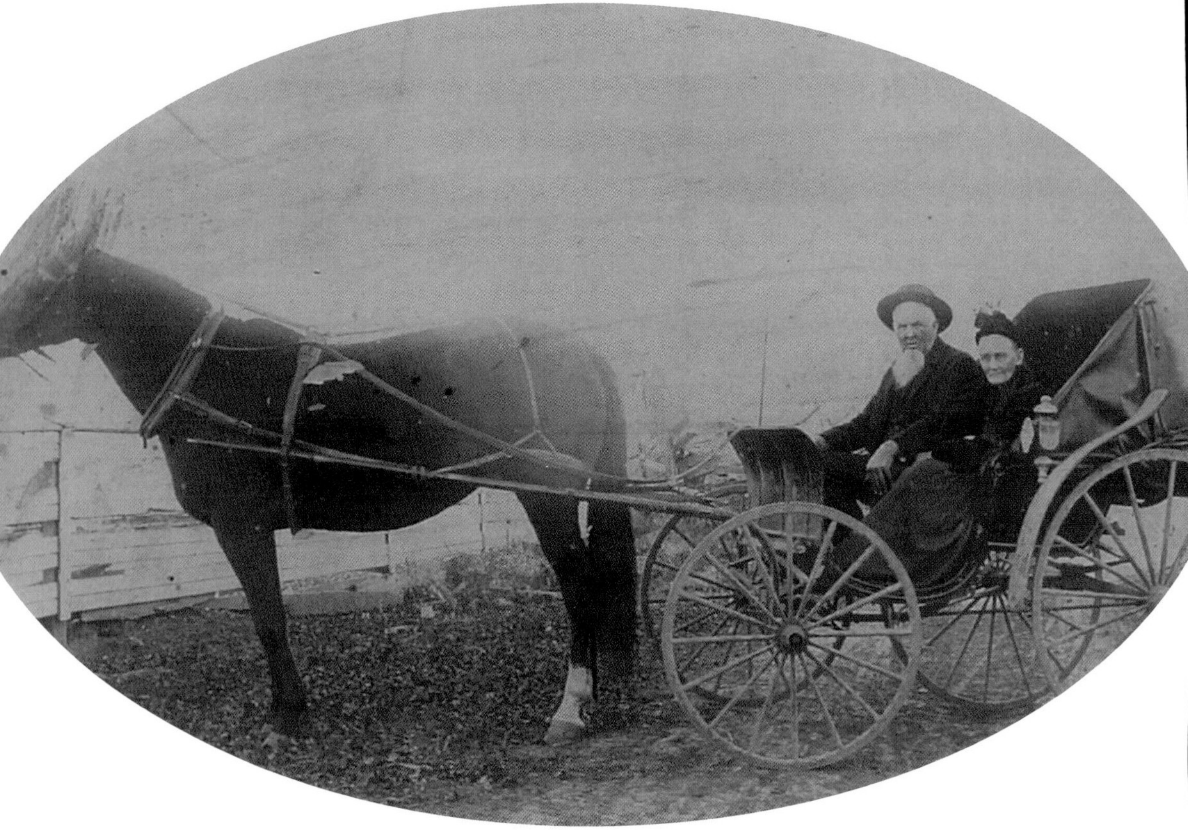

Brown Township farmer and wife Mr. and Mrs. Moses McCray are seen here out for an afternoon. The McCrays lived just north of Wilkinson, and to this day the McCray Cemetery is where many local people find their final rest.

Contents

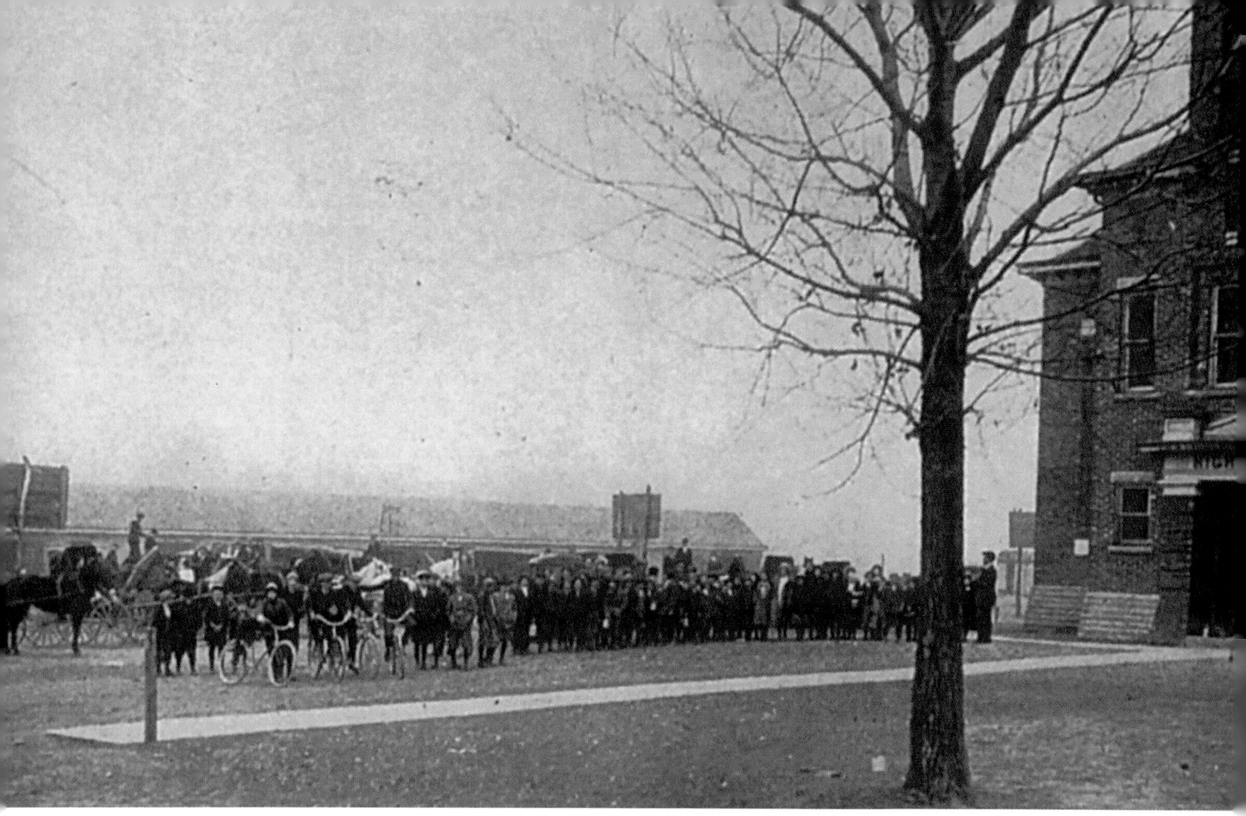

Blue River Township High School at Westland is seen here in 1914. In the background is a long barn set up to provide shelter for the horse or horse and buggy the student might drive to school.

ACKNOWLEDGMENTS

A special debt of gratitude goes to the many individuals who have shared their unique Hancock County pictures and stories with us.

We would like to thank the following individuals and organizations, past and present, who have assisted us in gathering information and photographs essential to the completion of this book: Ashley Carpet, American Legion Post 119, James and Sue Baker, Richard Bell and the Fortville Vernon Township Library, Darrell Deck, Bobby Dye, Lindsey Hendrix, Hancock County Public Library, Hancock County Historical Society, Ellen Landing, Marcia Hunt, Ed Ramsey, Randy Sorrell, Shirley Historical Society, Ruth Ann Smith, Sue A. Thompson, and Thomas E.Q. Williams.

This book is dedicated to the many people who have written to us or who have called us over the years to discuss county history. It is also dedicated to old buildings and their preservation. Lastly, this book is dedicated to our grandchildren.

INTRODUCTION

Author Thomas J. Schlereth gives interesting insight into the study of local history, which he labels landscape history. As a matter of explanation, Schlereth defines archaeology as the work of researchers "who usually excavate the material remains of past cultures and through such evidence, attempt to recreate the history of man from his earliest past, and to determine the nature of cultural systems at different times and place around the world." Schlereth goes on to tell us, "Above-ground archaeologists, unlike their below ground colleagues, dig into the past but usually on the surface; they examine what they find before it is buried by time and chance." Above ground archaeologists can also be called landscape historians. Landscape historians are "intent on looking at all objects, be they pot shards or service stations with an intense symptomatic and precise scrutiny that ultimately yields specific cultural information from single artifacts as well as braided cultural patterns..." But like tree rings, the evidence of the past comes easily enough to hand. Yet we still need to be taught to see it, read it, and explain it before it can be turned into a story—a narrative tradition or history.

This book is a landscape history and as such may be defined as an enormous jig saw puzzle with a lot of missing parts. For example, certain material and man made events have made a major impact on Hancock County's landscape. For instance *c.* 1834–1835, the National Road was opened in Hancock County and it ushered in a period of rapid growth. In 1839, the first great Greenfield fire occurred on the north side of Main Street between Mount and State Street, destroying several business blocks. In 1857, another fire occurred in the same district and also destroyed several buildings. In 1887, natural gas was discovered and Hancock County became a "boom" area for the next 20 years. On 15 September 1902, a sawmill exploded in Maxwell and killed several people. On 24 March 1913, it rained and flooded in Greenfield for 24 hours. In 1943 and 1963, there were two massive train wrecks. On 3 April 1970 and 17 March 1986, tornadoes touched down in Hancock County. All these events contributed to our landscape history which "Then and Now" attempts to highlight.

Acknowledgment and thanks must be given to earlier books and other authors. *The Binford and Richman History* and other books by Dorothy June Williams, Thomas E.Q. Williams, and Rosalie Richardson were extraordinarily useful. Their efforts contributed mightily to this volume and our understanding of the past.

Greenfield Indiana
1 July 2001

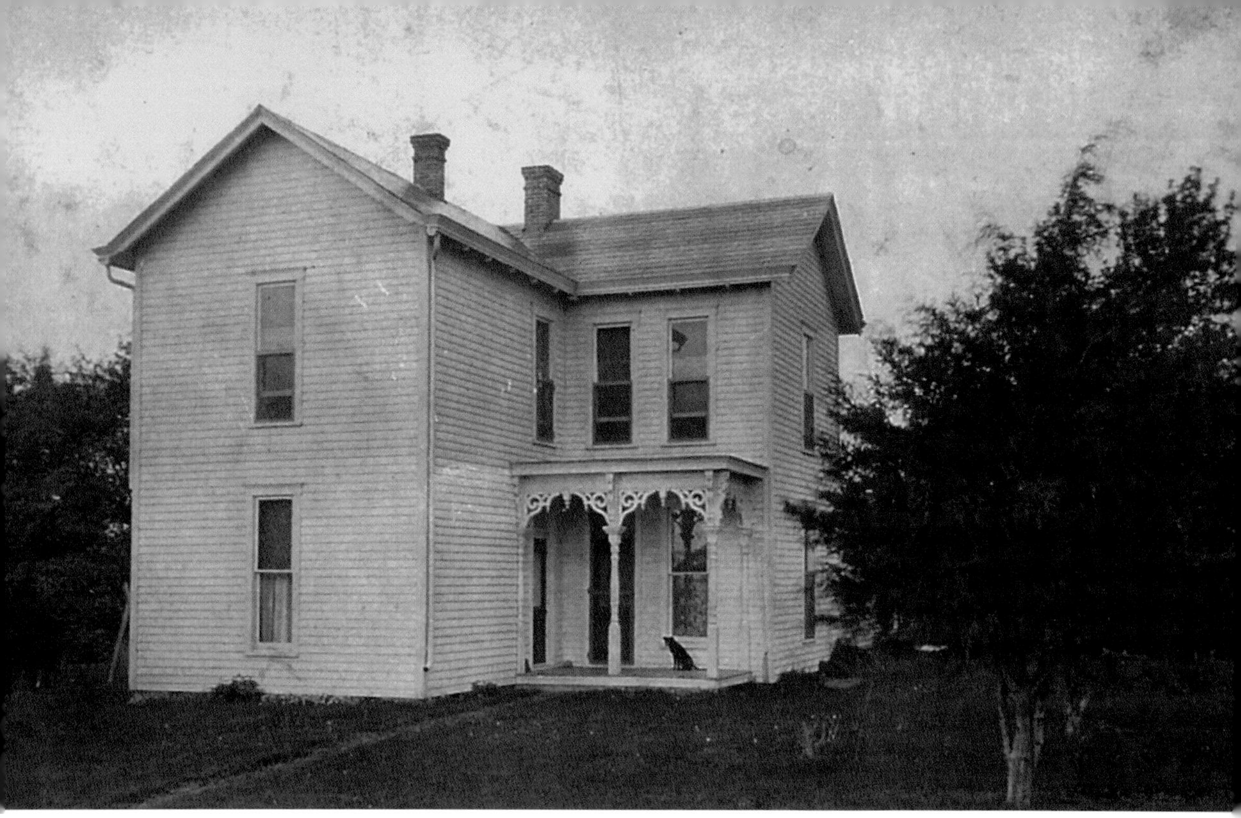

Elijah Clay Martindale's home in Brown Township, Hancock County, Indiana is an excellent example of the fine homes that were built in the area before 1890.

A group of ladies, maybe from a club in Greenfield, were photographed around the turn of the century. One of the groups was called the Ionic Club, named in honor of its founder, Mrs. Ione Brown Black. It started on 17 December 1888. The Club's motto was: "We taste an intellectual place twice, and with double the results when we taste it with a friend." The clubs only objective was the reading of new books. Women during the Victorian period were expected to add to the community's culture.

Chapter 1
People and Their Environment

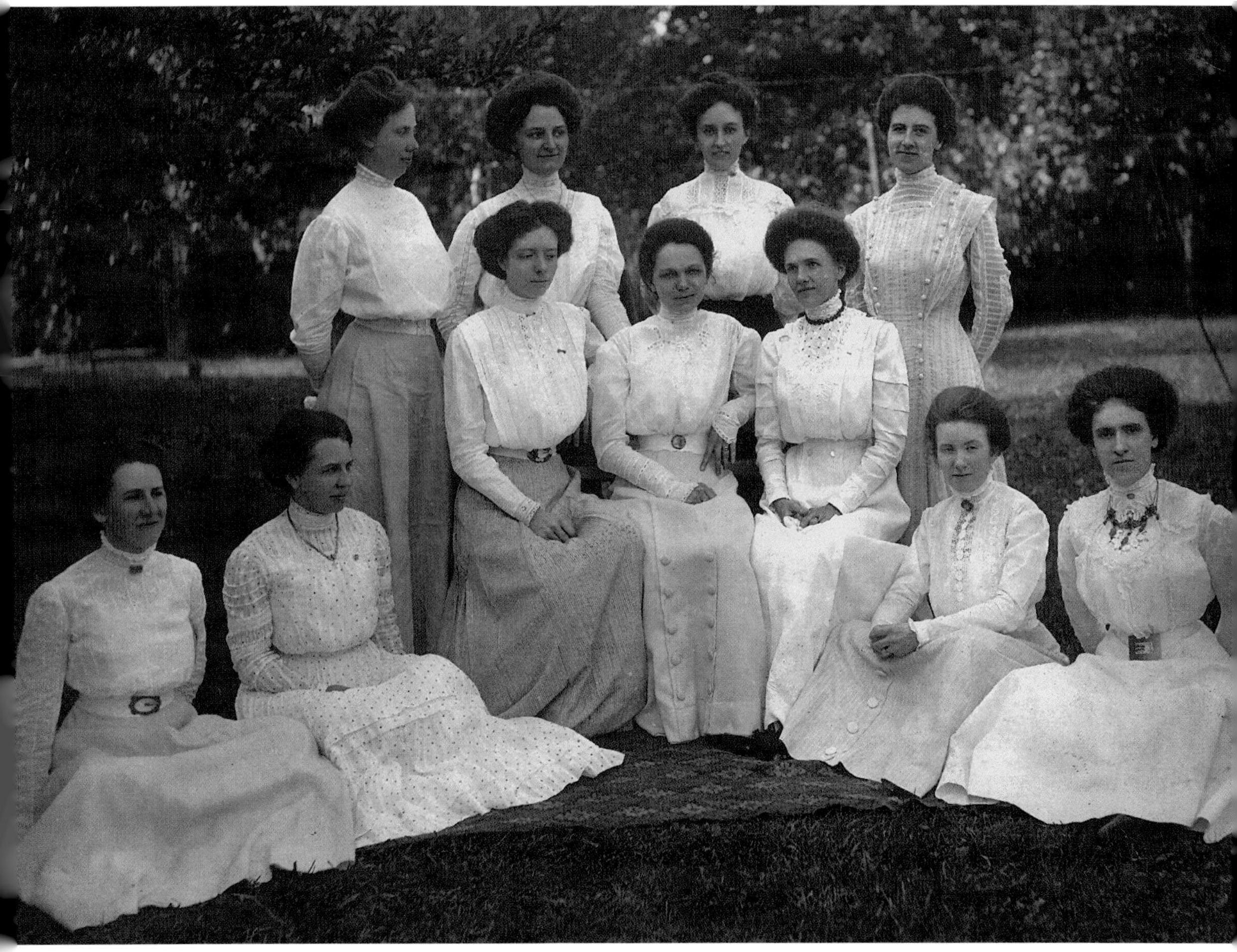

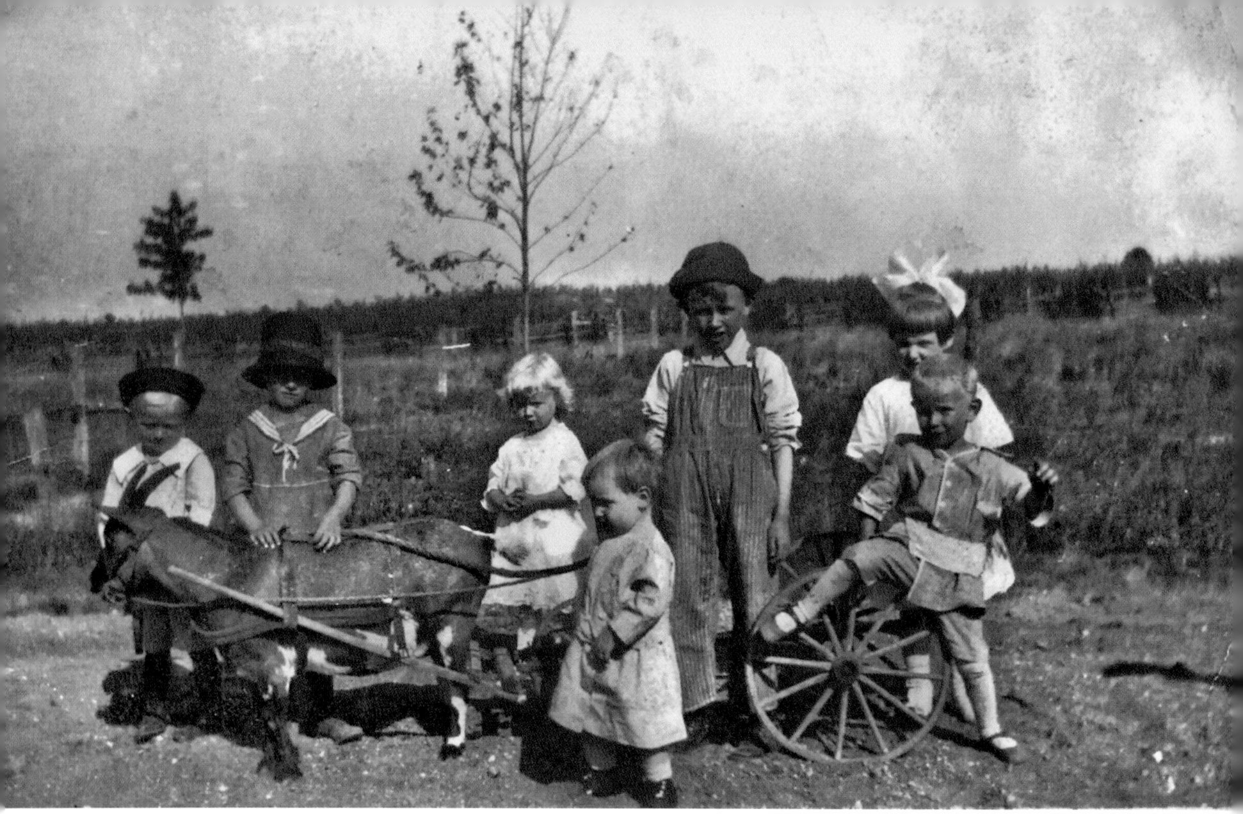

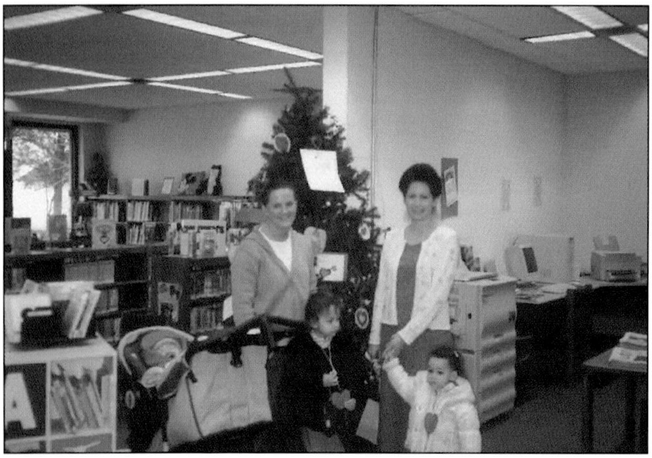

The children of Mr. and Mrs. Robert Vandenbark and Mr. and Mrs. Mose Vandenbark were long remembered for their goat and cart in the Nameless Creek neighborhood. They drove up and down the lane and out on the road in a day when fast traffic was largely unheard of in a rural community. In time, they all left the little community of their childhood for towns and cities not too far away, like Indianapolis, Anderson, Wilkinson, and Greenfield. The photo is dated *c.* 1920. The children of the "now" photograph will likely grow up to move across the country 500 to 1,000 miles or more, and could find themselves running a space station or walking on the moon. They are visiting the Fortville Vernon Township Library, and they are, left to right: Cole Worley, four months; Emily Ann Worley; Elaina, three years; Amy Olson; and Erica, one year.

The two boys and their dog are ready for outdoor fun in the "good old days." Pets and wagons are popular with children to the present day. The time period is *c.* 1910. Cindy and Sandy Nelson pose for the camera about 56 years later. They enjoy some lighthearted fun with a little game of dress up. Playing with pets and wagons as well as dress up games remain something both boys and girls seem to enjoy generation after generation.

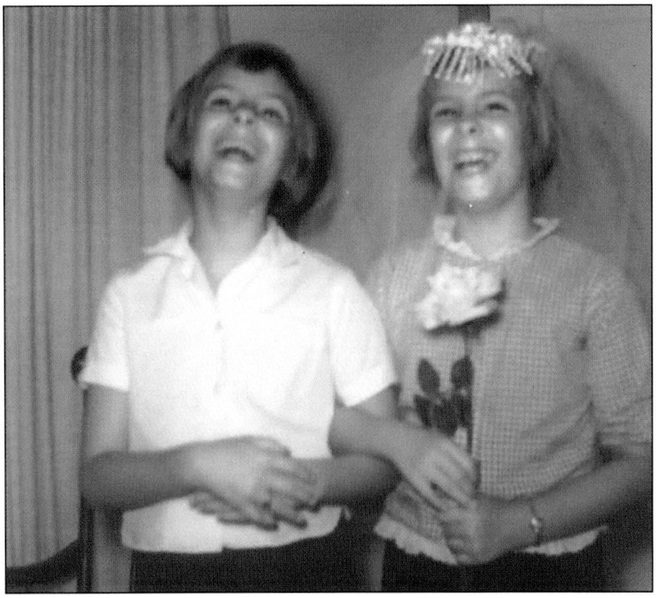

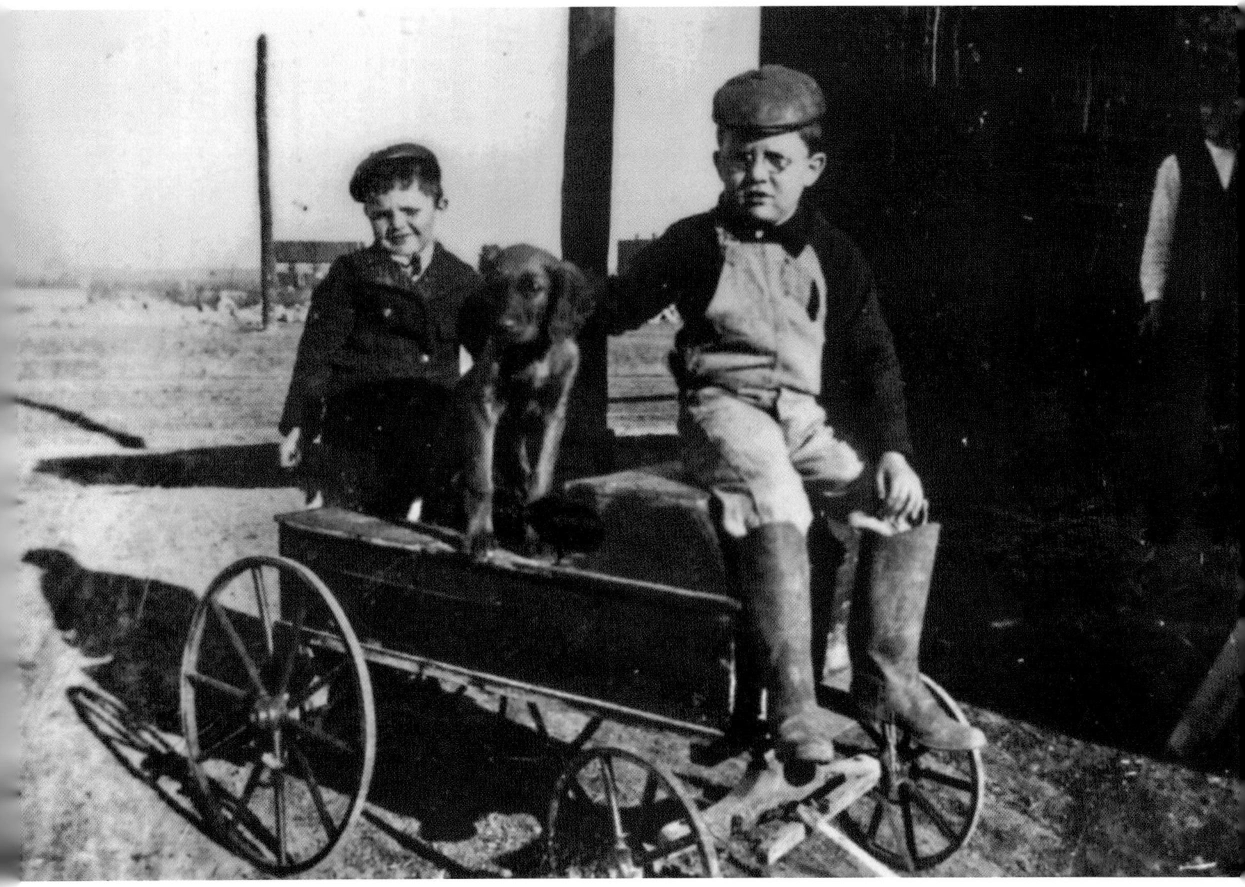

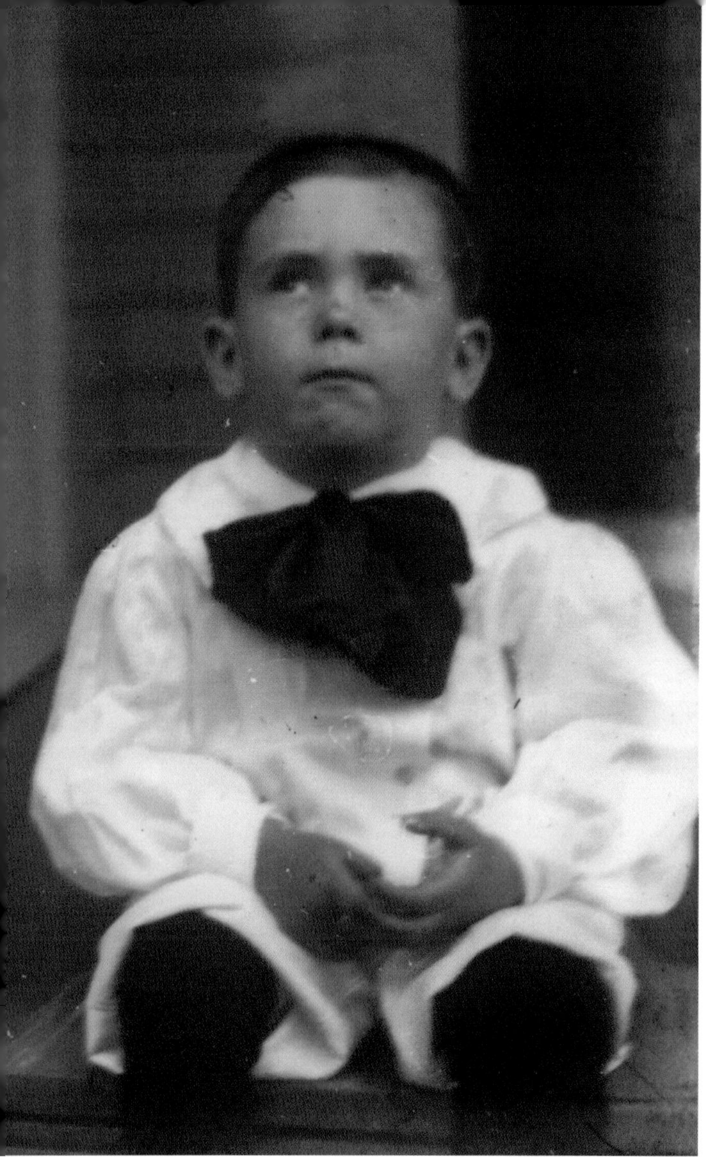

As you can see, children dressed differently in the "good old days." The child's picture dates *c.* 1915. The modern visitors to the Hancock County Library in Greenfield are Lori Chochran, Paul Chochran, and friend Joshua Cornet. Paul is 3 1/2 years old, and is making the most of the children's section. In earlier times, children were often relegated to play during their early years. Today a greater effort is made to include them in local facilities.

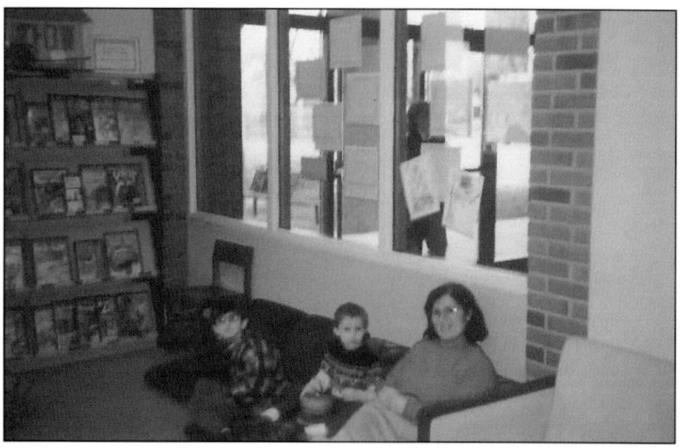

Young men quickly picked up on the value of a car, and by the 1920s they were well into automobiles.

This young man prepares for a spin around town, or perhaps a date at the downtown soda fountain. During the period 1920 to 1950, a fountain coke, a group of friends, and a date were the "in" thing. The 1950s brought drive-in restaurants, and the "in" scene changed as many young people had access to cars for running around and dating. The hangouts from the 1950s to 1980s were on the edge of town, and served burgers, fries, and a coke. Sports were especially important to the guys, and many like Alan Matsey, who is warming up for basketball, worked hard to be a member of the team. Matsey's picture is from the 1970s.

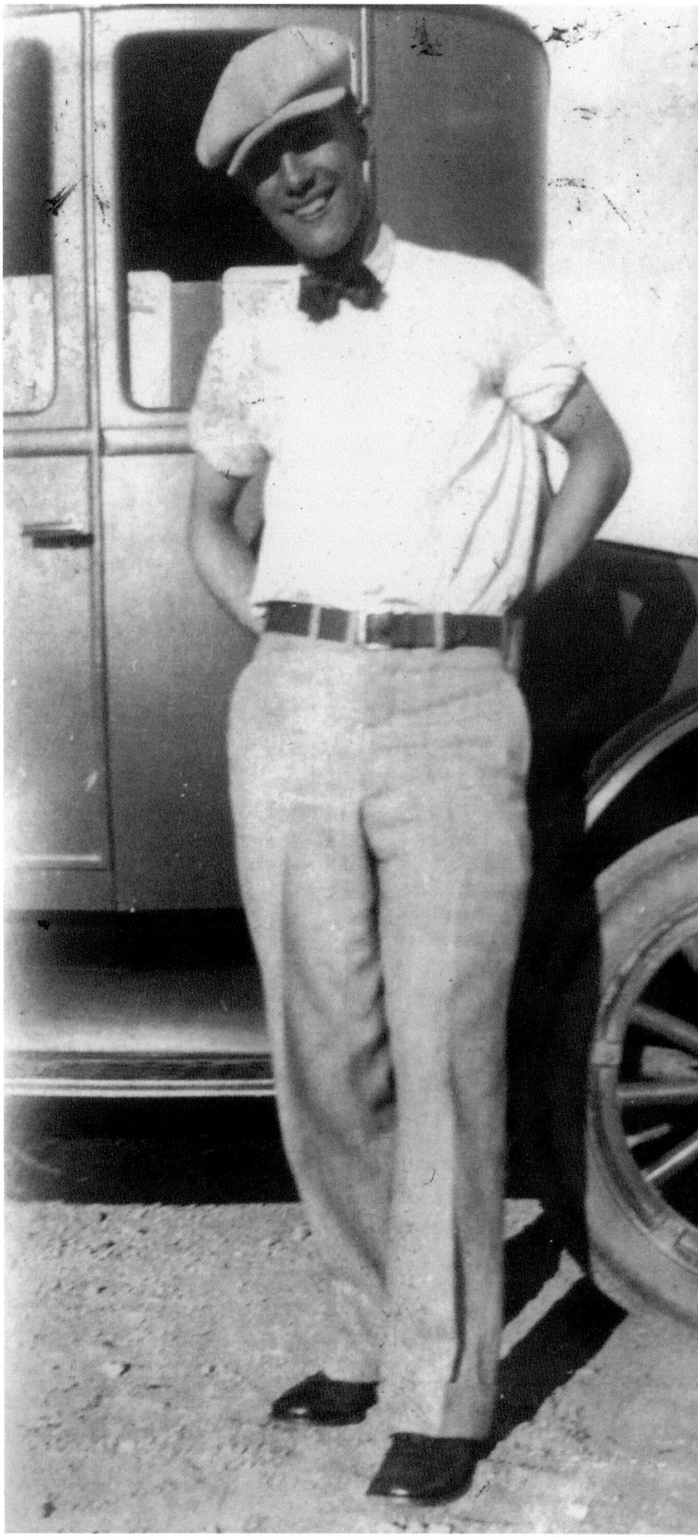

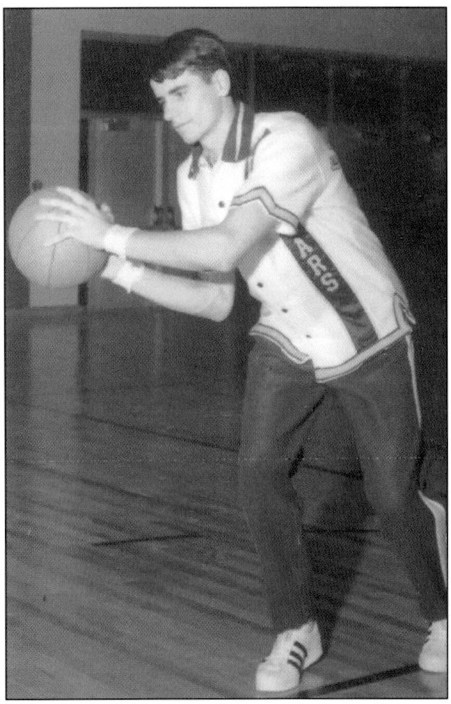

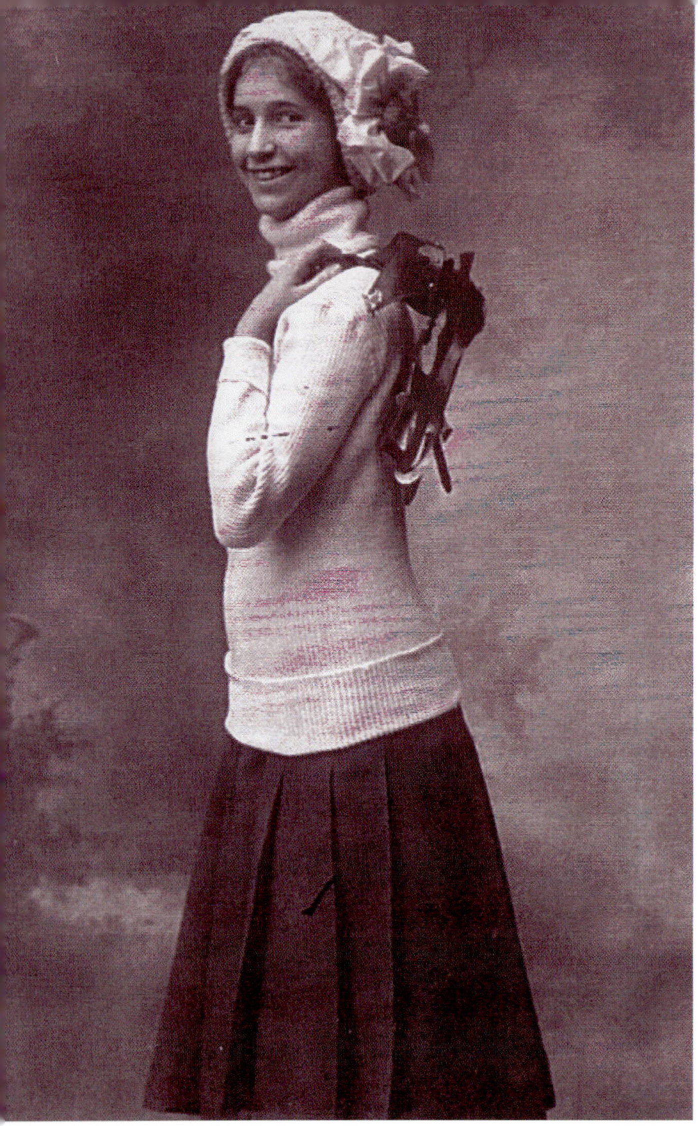

The young lady with skates was Gertrude Vaughn Gilpin, granddaughter of the famous evangelist John Hatfield who founded the Cleveland Campground. In her day around Hancock County you would ice skate at small ponds scattered here and there. Today children play on the courthouse square, where water is allowed to freeze in the winter for ice skating. In earlier times, South Street traveled the back of the square allowing for parking on both sides of the street. The business blocks around the courthouse were the center of Greenfield's downtown. Today, South Street has been closed for a plaza and a gazebo, planters, and flagpoles fill out the area. Here children are shown entertaining bystanders as they dance around a Maypole.

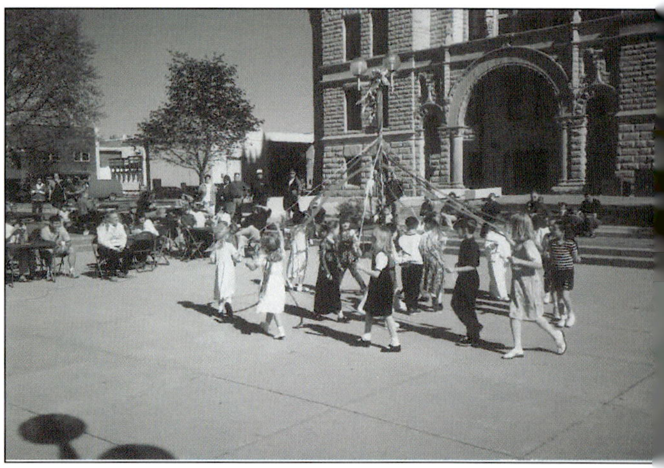

Sue Baker and her mother are seen in front of what is today the law office of Dean Dobbins on the south side of W. Main Street in Greenfield. In the background are the Rexall Drug sign and the clock just below. The picture was taken 7 July 1929. In those days, a big treat for the kids was a stroll downtown to shop with mom. The drug stores were where people went for a snack or a date. It might be after a movie that you would take a trip to the soda fountain of the local drug store for an orange ice cream soda or a Coca-Cola.

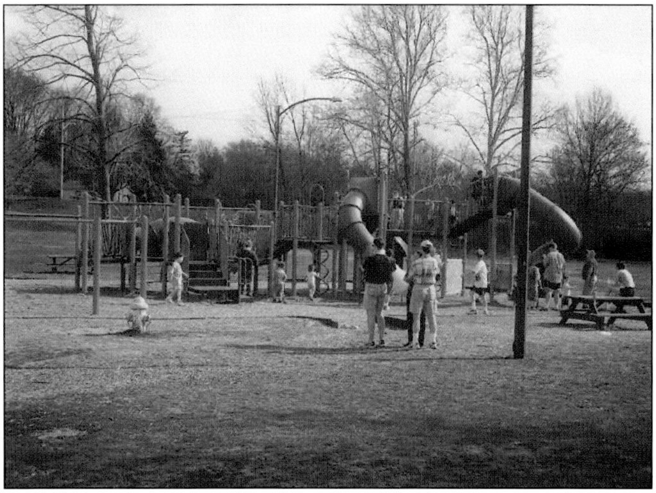

On 8 April 2001, the record high temperature for the day was shattered with a reading of 83 degrees. Many Greenfield parents were at Riley Park with their children to enjoy a wonderful Sunday afternoon. On this day, the park seemed the place to go for relaxation.

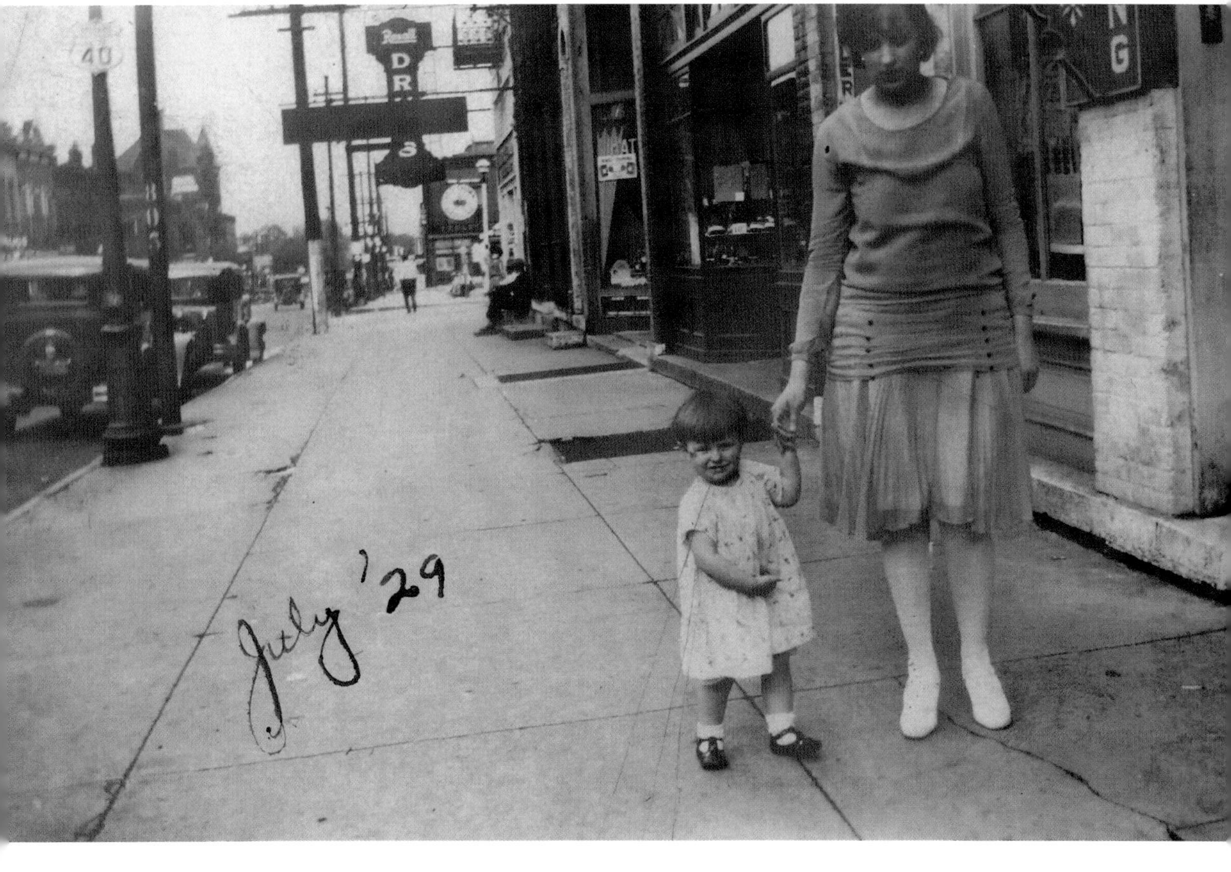

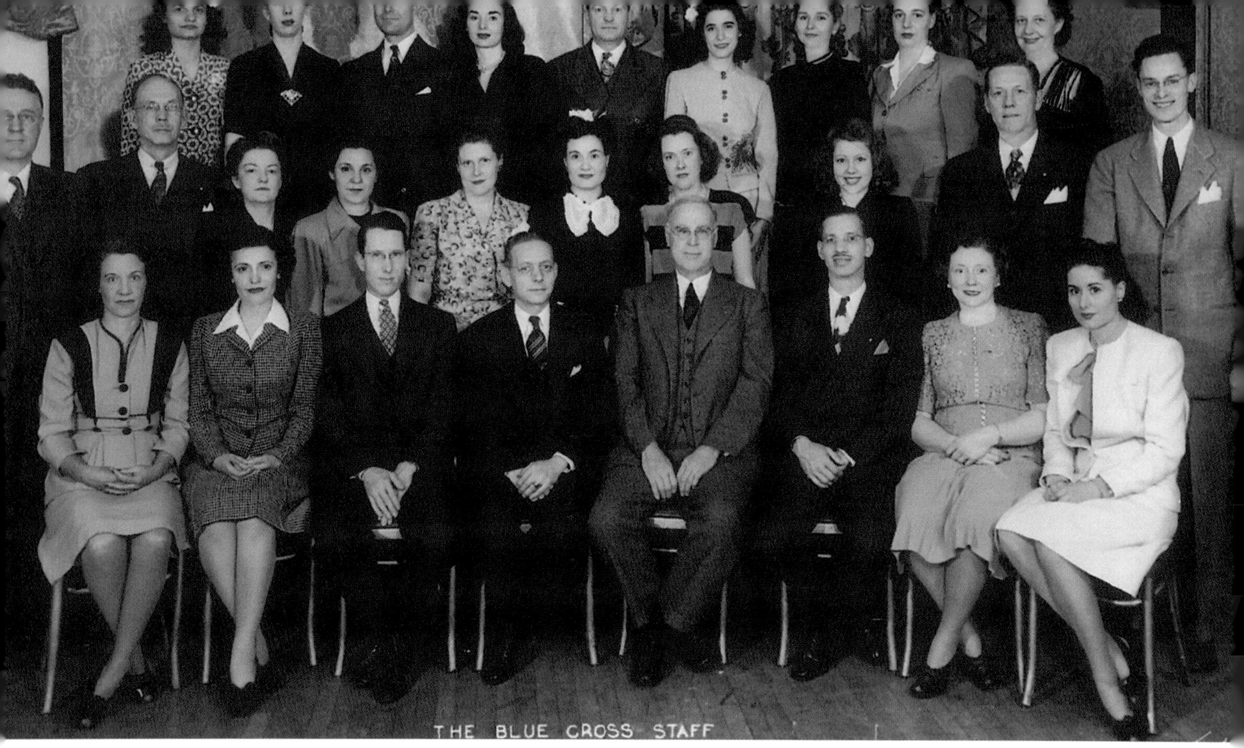

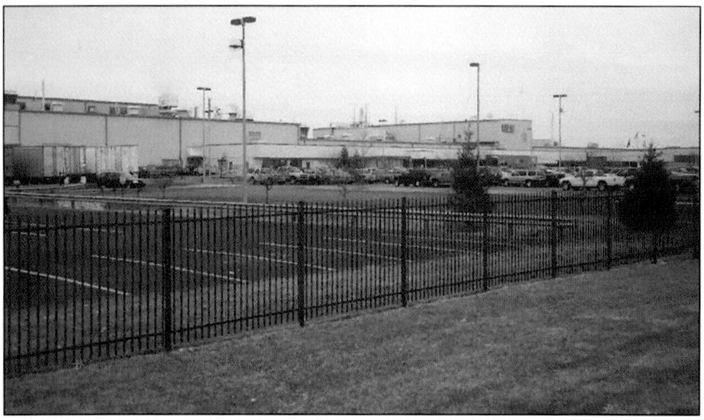

This is a Blue Cross-Blue Shield staff photo of the Indianapolis office from 1943. The person on the first row far right is from Hancock County and her name is Mercedes Russo. Her husband was overseas in World War II at the time the picture was taken. Many Hancock County people worked in Indianapolis from the 1920s to the present. In the earlier years, there were few high-paying jobs in Greenfield or Hancock County, so many local people sought work in the next county west. Many county manufacturing operations developed with natural gas from the 1880s to the 1920s, such as glass factories, canning factories, and numerous other industrial operations that rose and fell through the 1940s. The city and county began to realize by the 1960s that more industry was needed. They were looking for better pay and benefits without going to Indianapolis. The Roll Coater of Arvin Industries was one of the earliest that was attracted following the Korean War. The community continued to work to attract industry in the late 1980s and 1990s, and that led to the acquisition of a plant operated by Indiana Precision Technology for the Industrial Park at Indiana 9 and I-70. Since that time, Fasson and other operations have been attracted to nearby sites.

The Red Man's Lodge occupied the southeast corner of American Legion Place and Main Street. The Lodge was on the second floor, and was the scene of regular events including dances that were often heard across the courthouse square. The early photo is of the Red Man Lodge degree team *c.* 1920–1930. The "attire" was very colorful, but sadly the members names were not included. The later picture *c.* 1958 includes some names. The members are, from left to right: (front row) Earl Collier, Harry Marks, Billy Curry, Bill Welkins, Kenneth Curry, Homer Foxworthy, and Glen Trent; (back row) Kenneth Gift, John Banefield, Clarence Colestock, George Deck, Abe Marks, Harold Jack, unknown, Lon Craig, Mr. Colestock, and Glen Slifer.

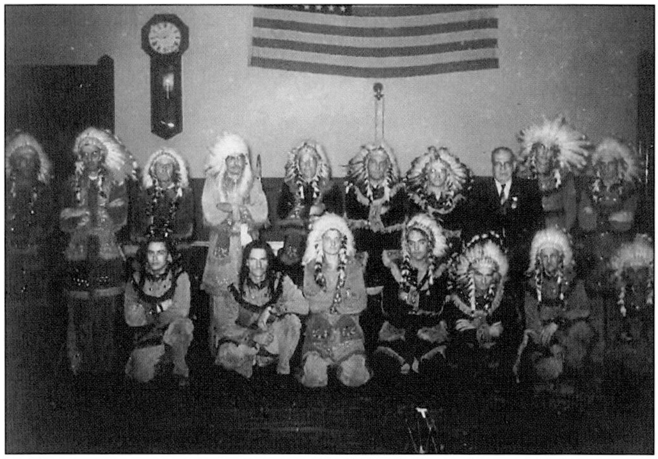

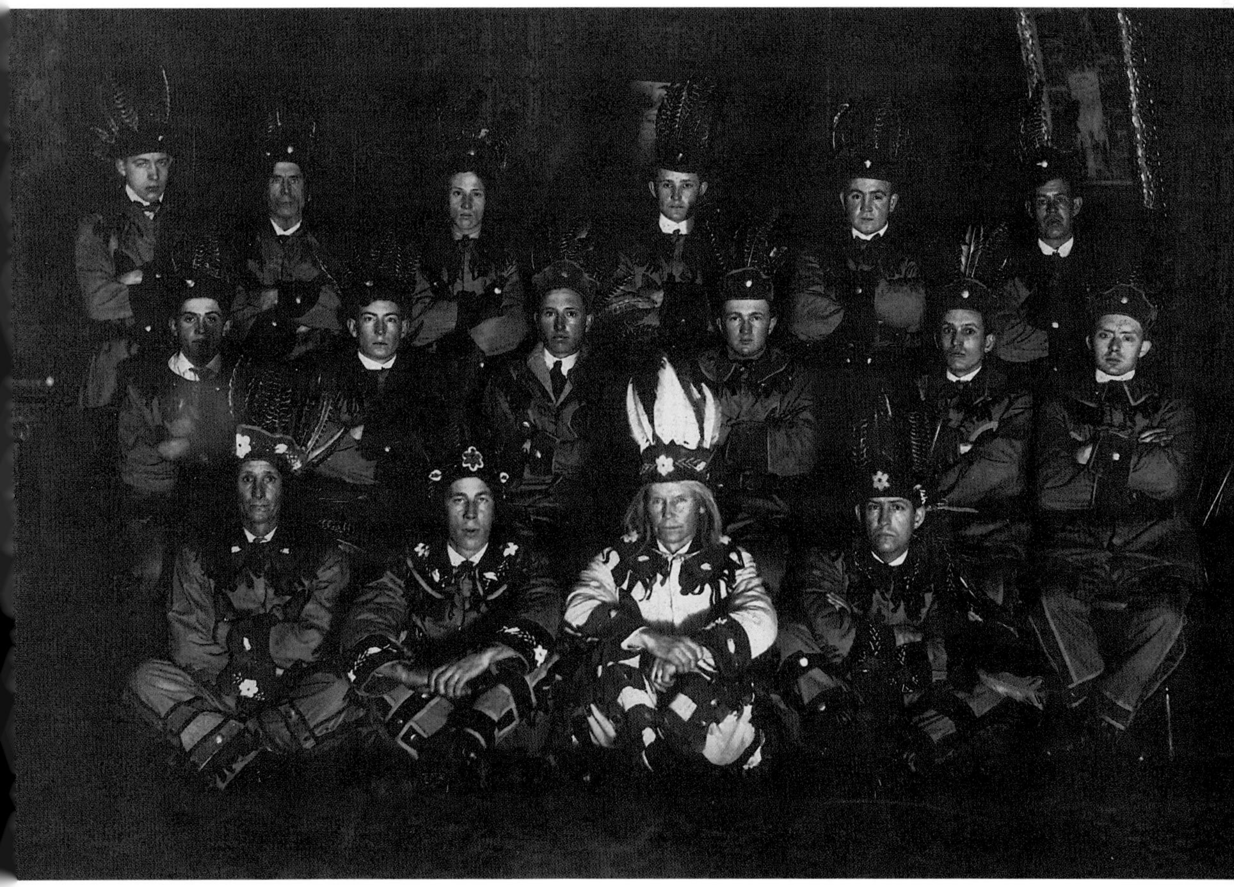

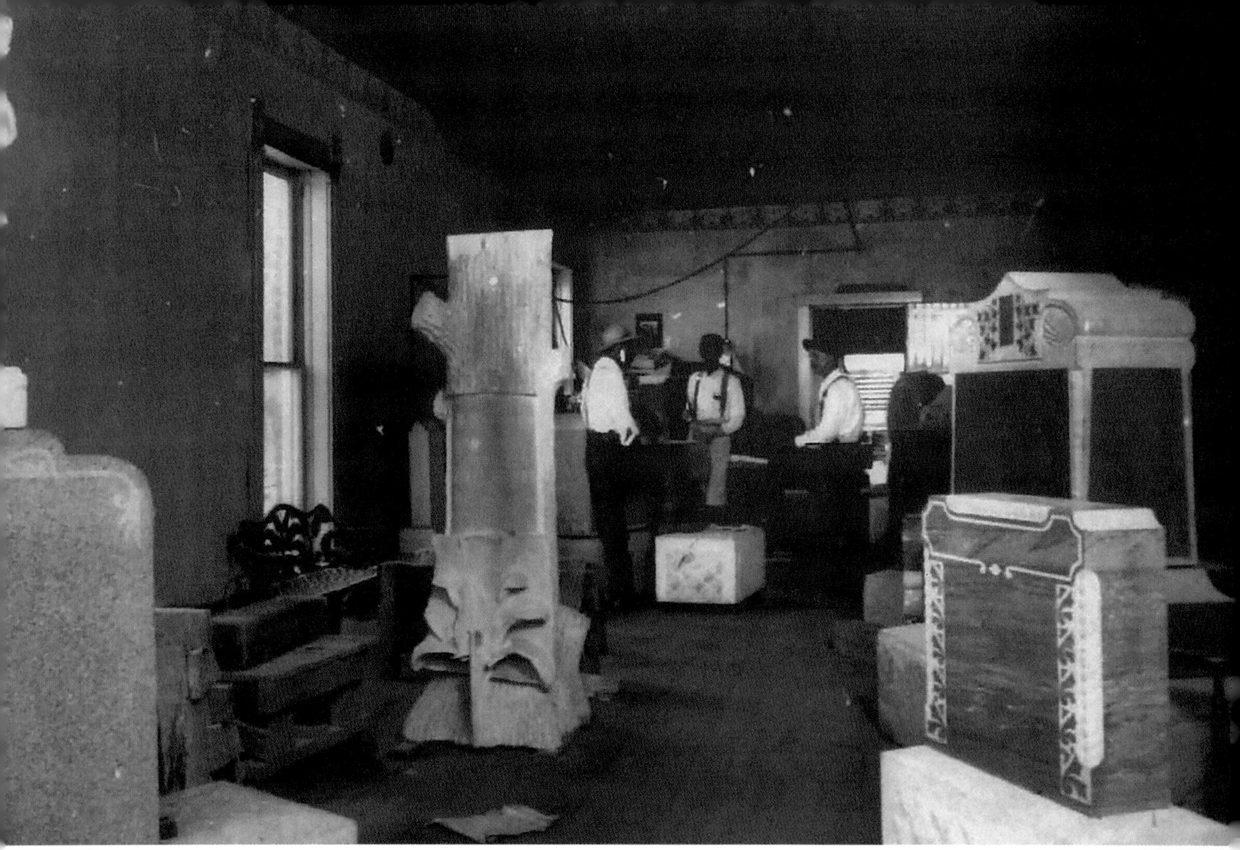

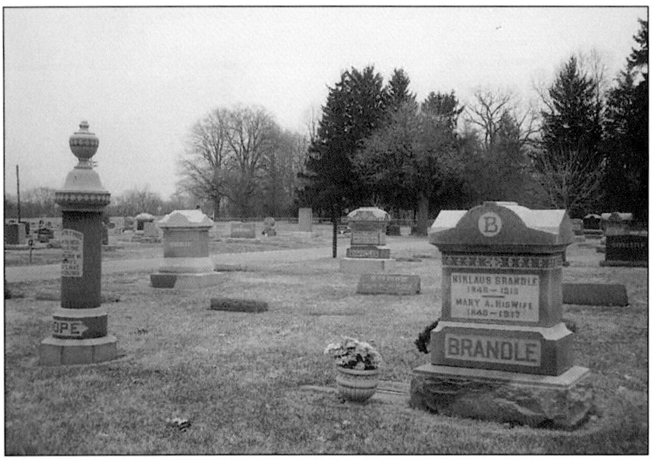

The late 1890s or early 1900s seem to have been the height of the stone cutter's art in cemetery monuments. The elaborate "tree" marker is an outstanding expression in unique form. The inscription on the tall marker is M. Wampler 1808–1905. The large monument in the background on the right is very similar to several that are found in Gravel Lawn Cemetery north of Fortville. Many local residents have been buried there for generations. Examples of turn of the century pieces can be found in cemeteries all over Hancock County, from Simmons Cemetery in Jackson Township to New Palestine Cemetery in Sugar Creek. The largest cemetery in Hancock County is Park Cemetery in Greenfield, which dates from the Civil War period. James Whitcomb Riley's family is buried there, including his beloved sister in-law whose ashes were returned from California. (Courtesy Vernon Township Library—Richard Bell.)

These people are some of the management and employees that contributed to the success of Jim Dandy in its early days in Greenfield. Being honored, left to right are: Julia Gray, 15 years; Harry Reasoner, president; Gerald "Whitey" Ware at 22 years, who created the "wet tenderloin;" and Kay Cain, 18 years. Their hard work along with that of others eventually built the successful business that gave rise to the new facility located on McKenzie Road. The change in the location was brought about in part due to the placement of I-70 as a major east-west highway just 1 1/2-mile north of the old Greenfield City limits.

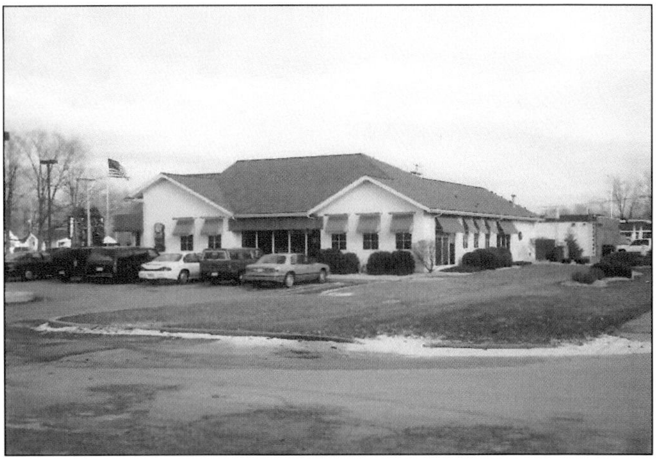

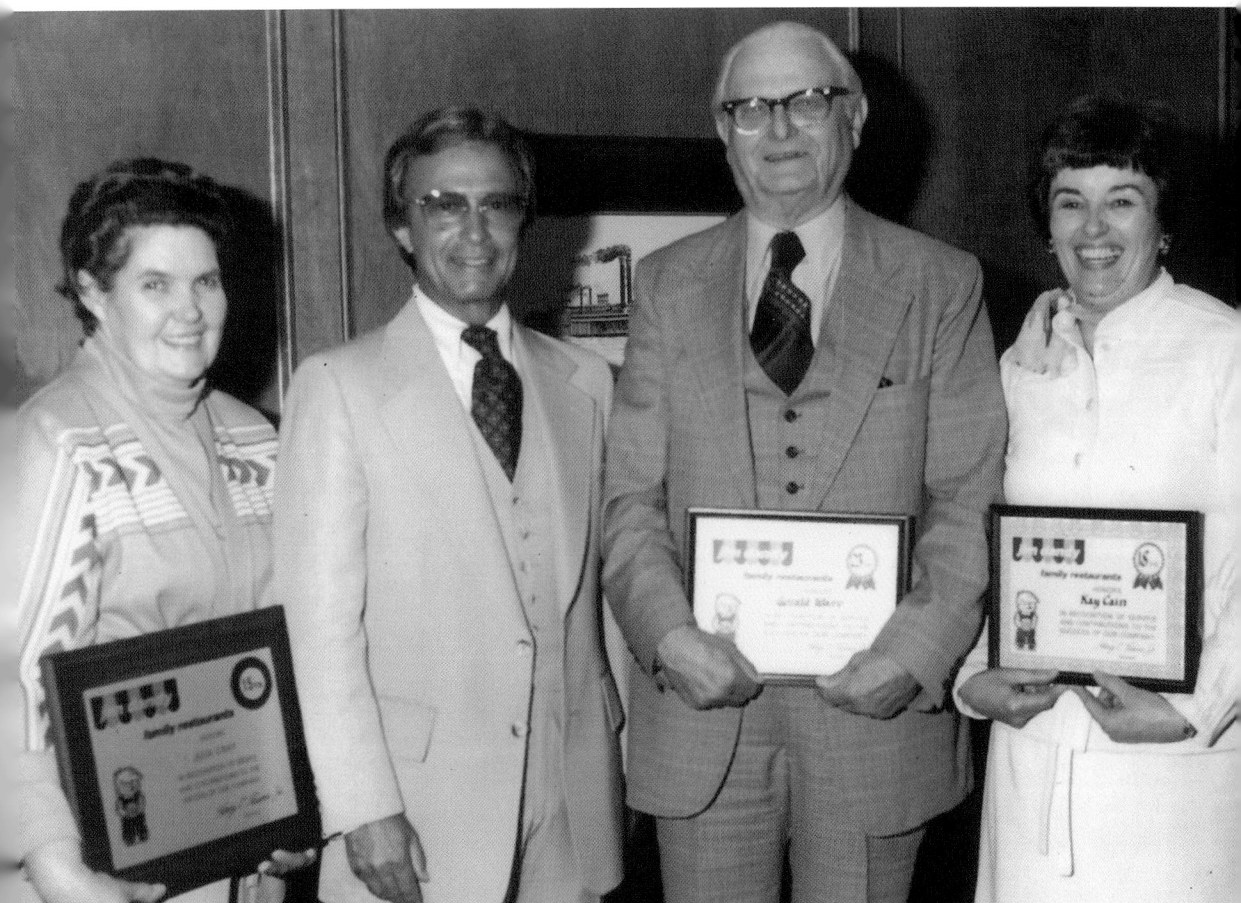

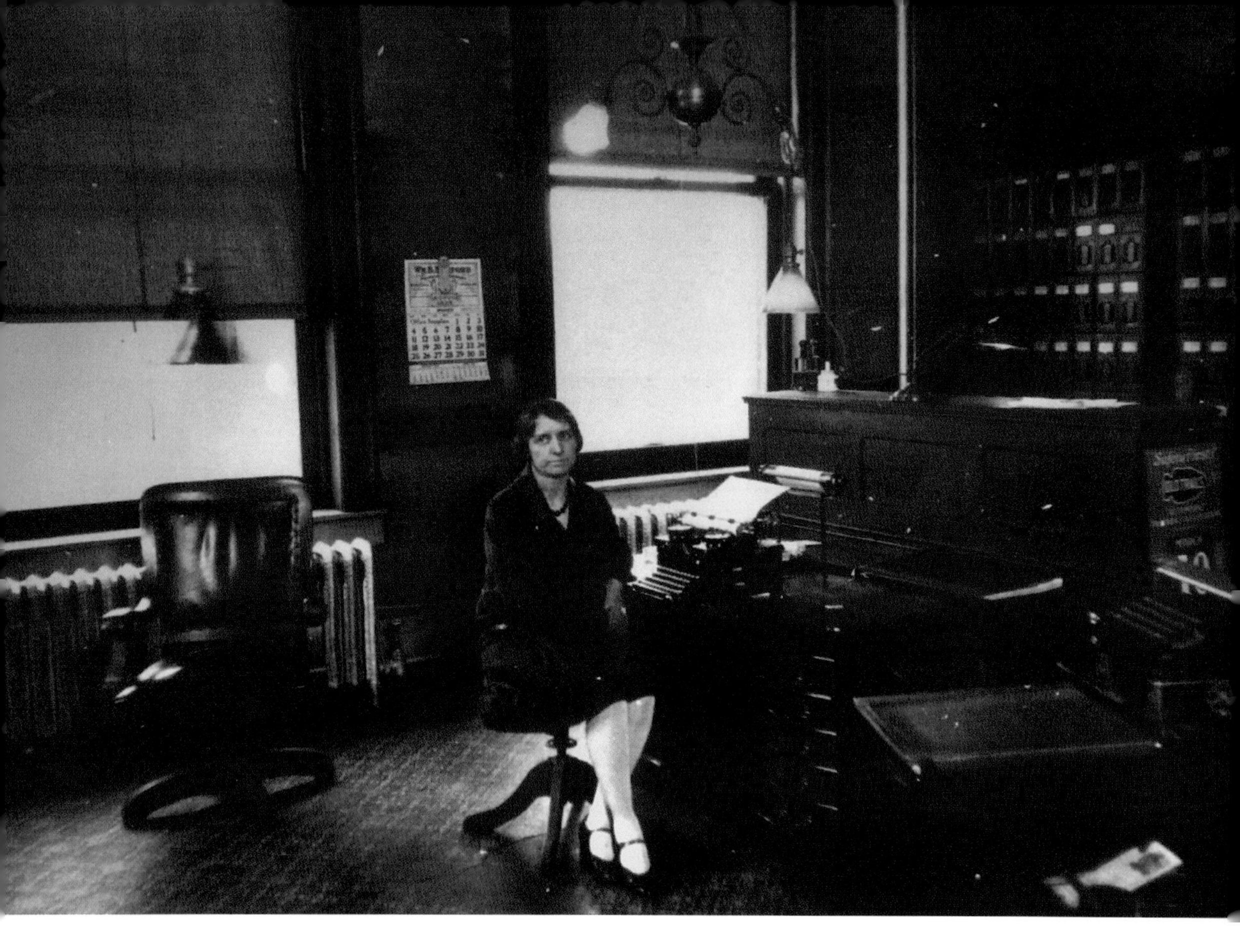

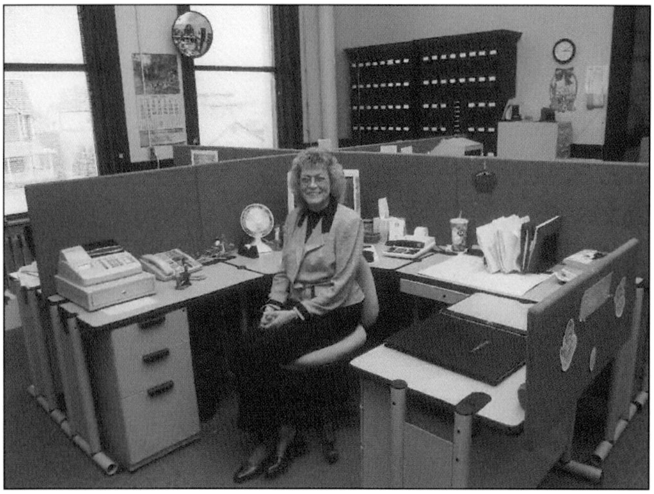

Hazel Moore Thompson served as the Hancock County recorder as a result of her nomination and election by the Democratic Party in 1929. She was the first women to hold such local office, and could be regarded now as one of the earliest to prepare the way for women in county and city offices in this area. Today Republican Carolyn Grass holds the Hancock County recorder's office. Carolyn has been involved in local politics for a number of years. Note the interesting similarities in the picture along with the contrast of a modern workstation.

Guy Westlake traveled some 750,000 miles, wore out 2 wagons and 18 automobiles to deliver the mail.

Westlake, like many rural free delivery carriers, made getting the mail out his life's work. They traveled thousands of miles in untold weather conditions and provided a service rural folk badly needed. In town, you could pick up your mail from a box at the post office or take delivery from a person on foot who traveled his route exposed to the weather. In the contrasting photo people are getting their mail from just such a carrier on N. Pratt Street in Greenfield. They are, left to right: Mr. and Mrs. Dubois and Postman Rob Goodin.

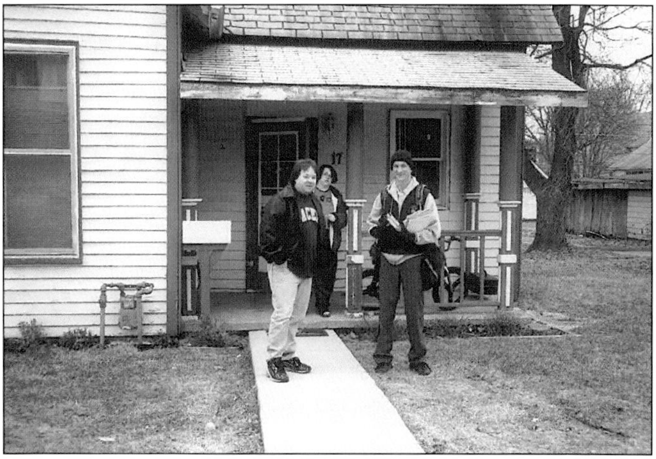

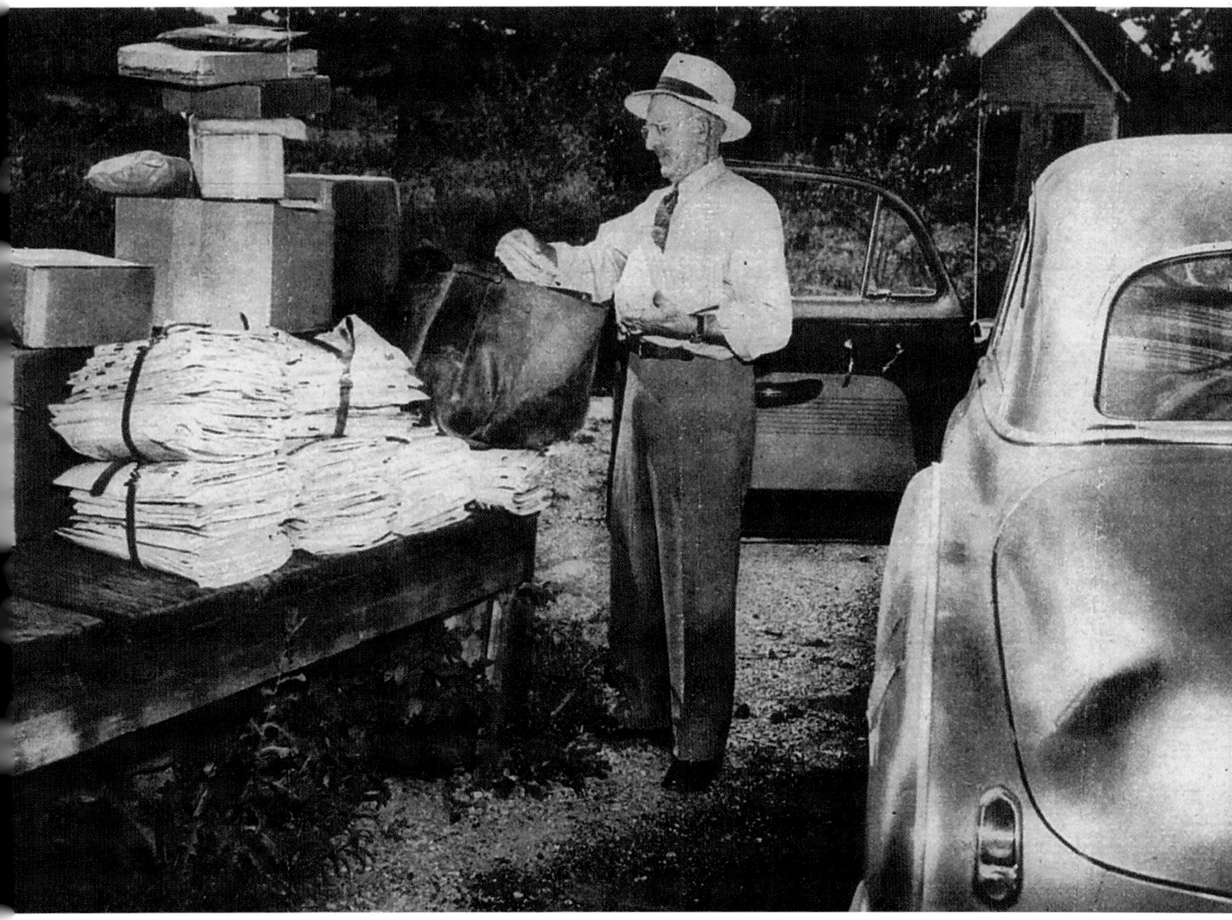

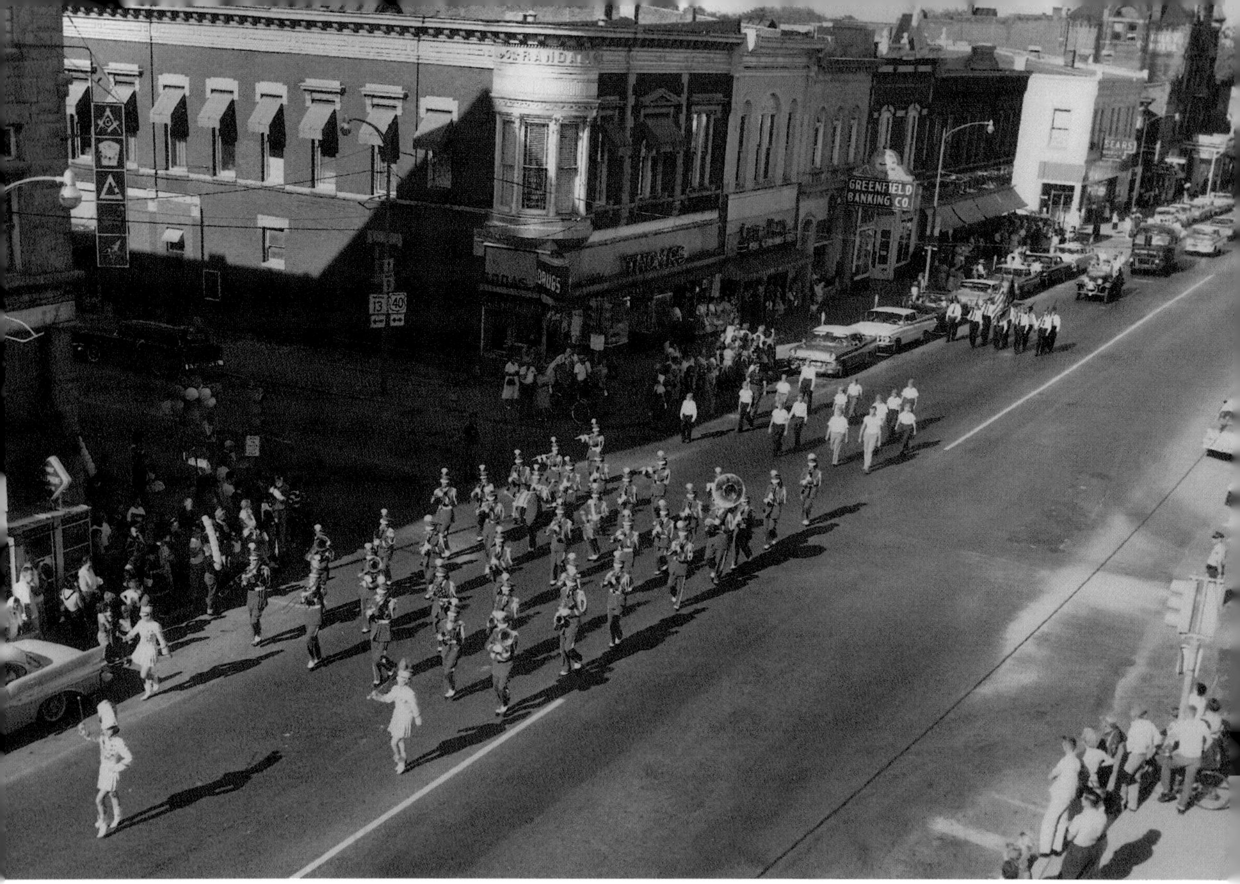

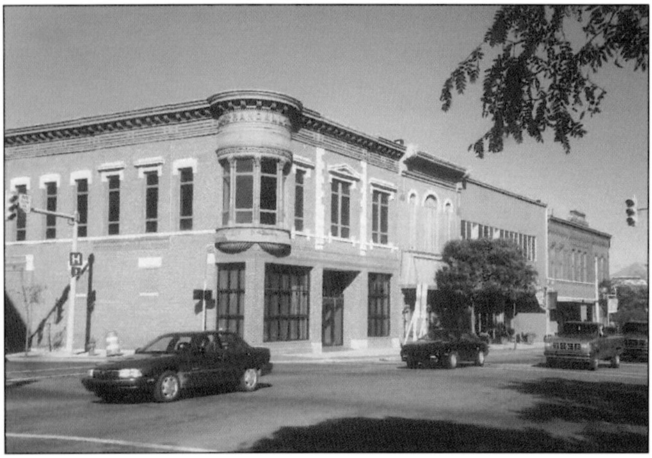

The parade and street scene are from *c.* 1960. Greenfield's downtown is the main retail area for the county at the time. The stores are, from left to right: P.N. Hirsh, Thomas Drugs (on the corner), Carr-Mac's Clothing, Greenfield Banking Co., Strickland's Grocery, Columbia Barber Shop, Danner's 5 & 10, Sears Roebuck, a restaurant, Lacey's Cigar Store, and the Riley Hotel. The years since the 1960s have brought a dramatic change to downtown. The major retailers have moved to the area on the edge of the city, and other businesses have taken over the buildings in the center of the city. The Randall Building is now occupied by offices of the Greenfield Banking Co., next is the Wolf Law Firm, then the Bank, Morris Inc.

The parking lot of the Christian Church, Hope House, and another parking lot complete the picture in 2001.

The members of the Greenfield Christian Church turn out for the turning of the first shovel full of earth for their new education building in 1954. In the background is the Regal Warehouse Market that occupied the I.O.O.F. building's first floor for many years. It is difficult to imagine the change that has taken place in the area of food markets in this period of time. In 1950, all food markets were located downtown except for the small neighborhood stores scattered throughout the residential area. Today the downtown locations of these former markets have been taken over by other operations, such as Morris Inc. lettering of T-shirts in this particular case. Today's large food stores are located in strip shopping centers on the outskirts of town.

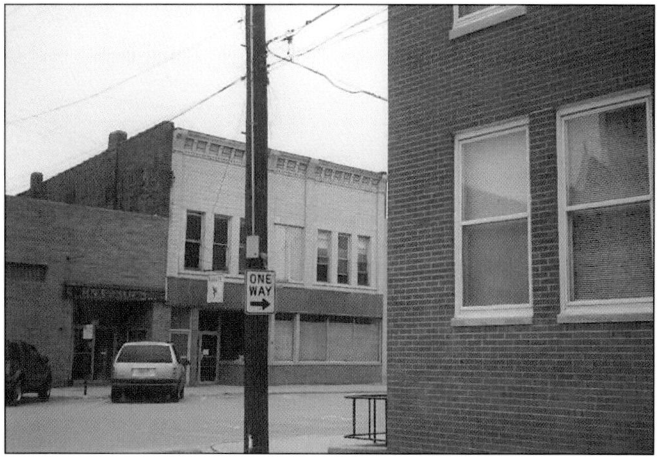

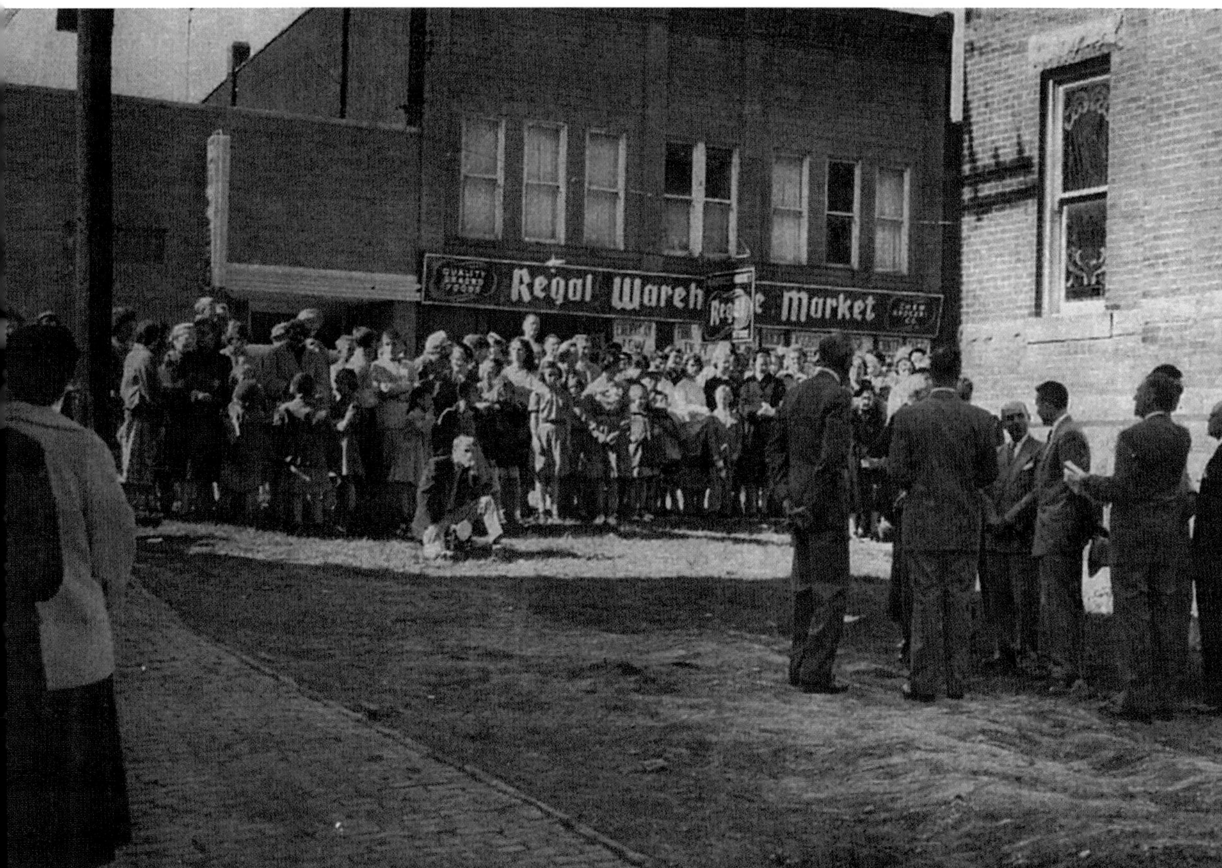

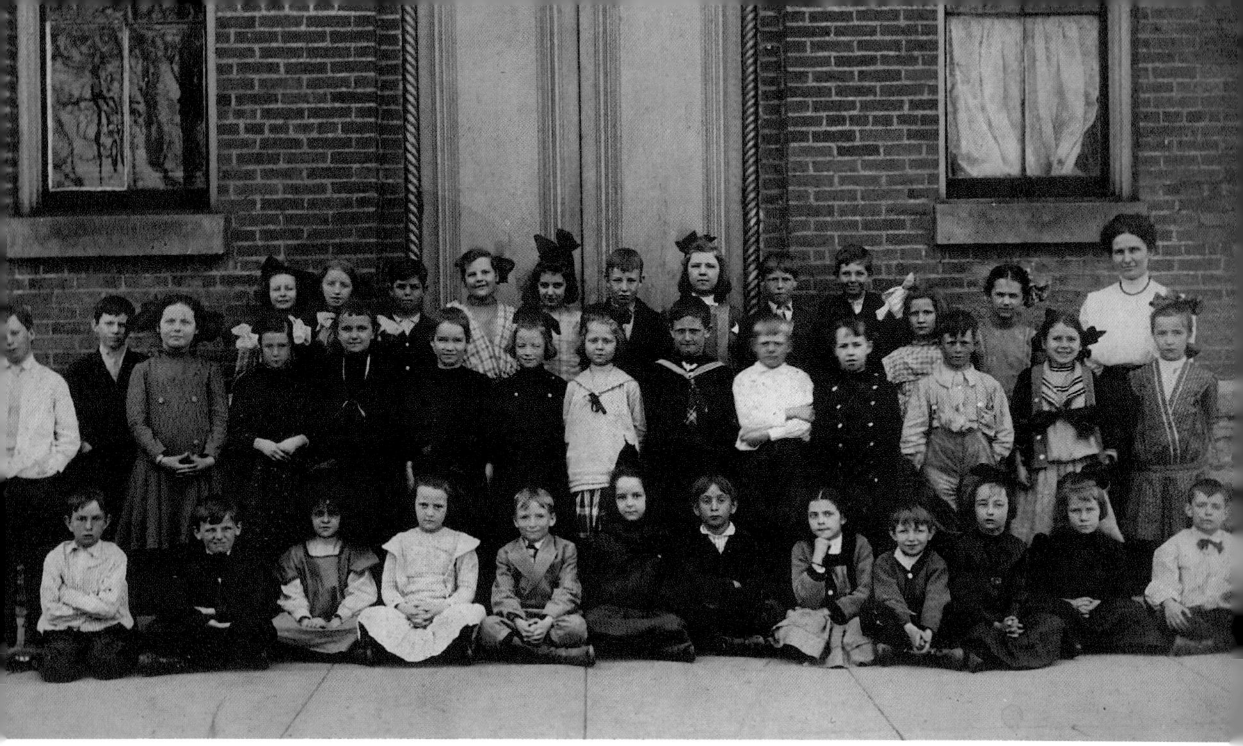

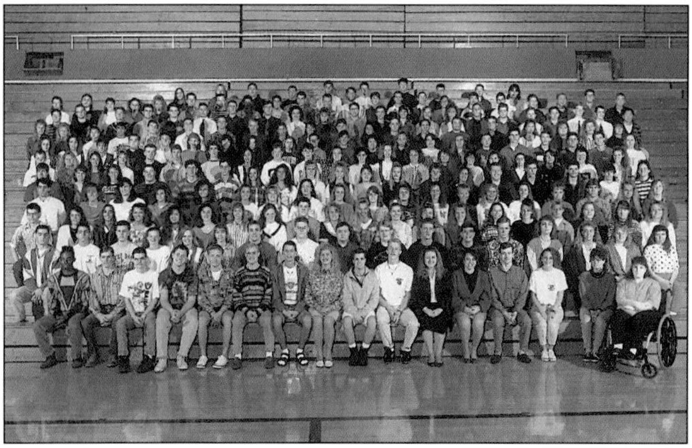

One of the earliest school buildings in Greenfield was located on N. State Street. Some private schools were held at various local sites. In the 1850s, school was taught in the old Masonic Hall on the southeast corner of W. Main and Pennsylvania. In 1861, Lee O. Harris taught a school in the Methodist Episcopal Church. A move toward the construction of a suitable large building was in progress around that period of time. Meetings continued to be held until the late 1860s when sites were put to a vote. The west site of Lincoln Park Elementary won out over the east site at Pratt and Main Street's northwest corner. High school as well as elementary classes held forth at that location until the construction of the Riley building for high school and junior high, located on the northeast corner of Pennsylvania and North Streets. The early photo shows elementary children in front of the old West (Washington) school around the turn of the 19th to the 20th century. The later picture is the class of 1993 at Greenfield Central High School, which combined in 1969 to serve Greenfield and the Hancock Central District. The Lincoln Park building was constructed in 1926 for high school and junior high.

The Philadelphia church is being moved to the east edge of the city of Greenfield. The old Philadelphia Methodist Church was built in 1856 on a site about a block south of the National Road. The building was moved to the site of the present church in 1906. When this move took place, they added a basement, a bell tower, two classrooms inside, and an auditorium style floor. The building was given to the Hancock County Historical Society, and they moved it to Riley Park in Greenfield under an agreement with the parks department in June of 1981. Many members donated time and money to make the move possible. The structure was placed on a new basement, and with considerable work, the project was largely completed in a little over two years. Today the "Chapel in the Park" serves as the headquarters and meeting site of the Hancock County Historical Society. There is now a county museum in the basement with some displays on the main floor. The Old Log Jail next door also holds numerous museum exhibits. The jail was moved to its site after the local gas company gave it to the society.

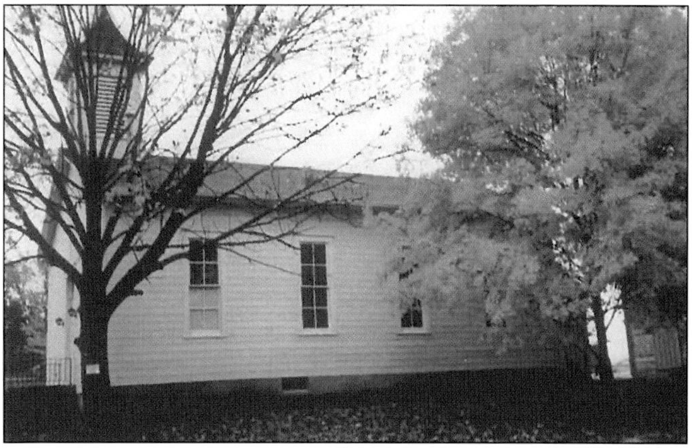

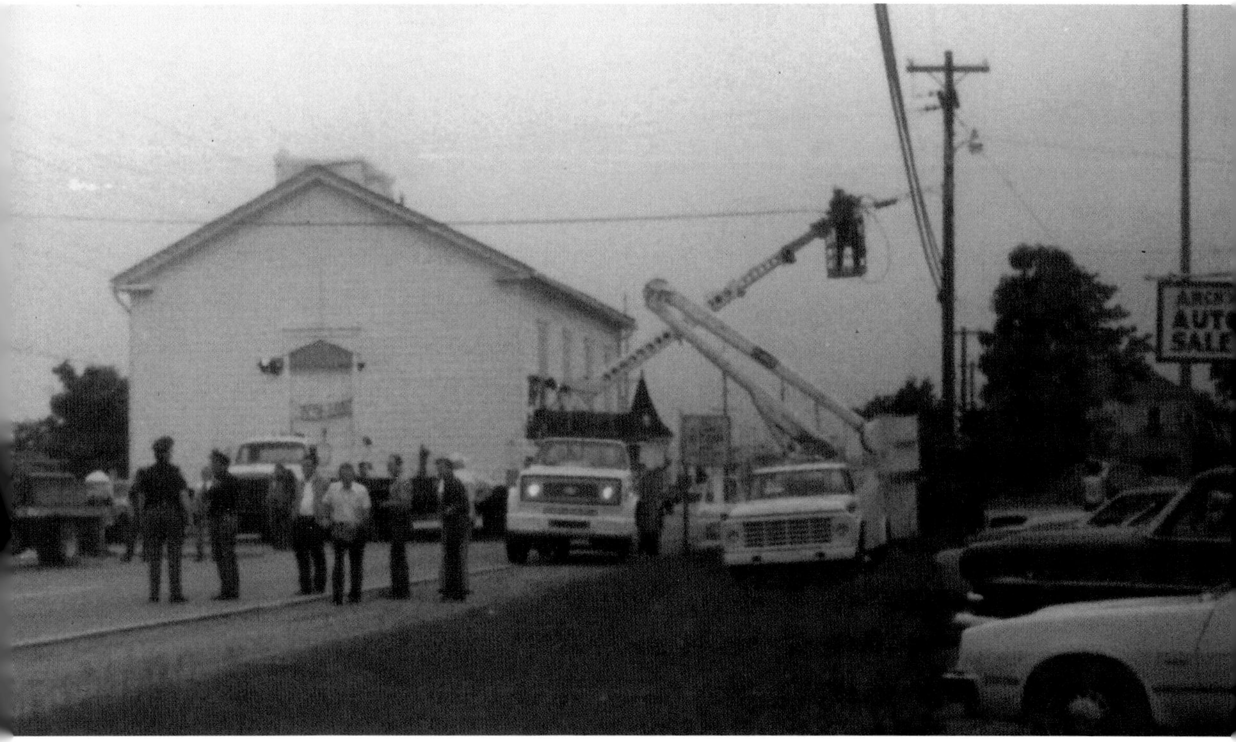

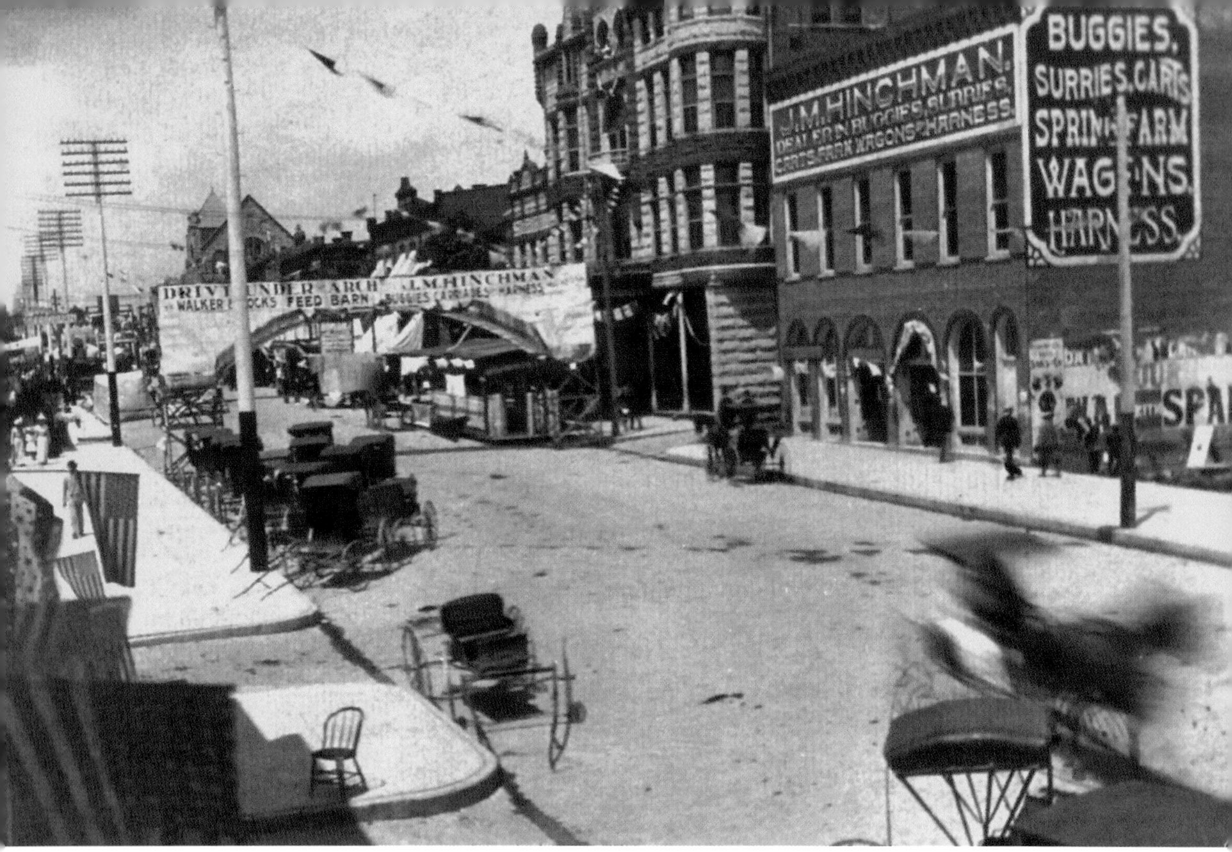

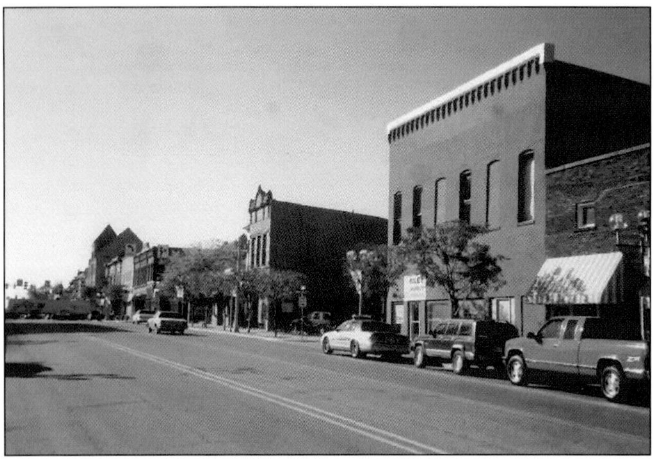

This picture was taken from the sidewalk in front of what is now the Main Street Hancock County Jail *c.* 1900. The horse and buggy would be the mode of travel, and the paving of the sidewalks looks fairly new. In the distance we can see the top of the Masonic Building and the Thayer, Star, and Gates buildings. Just west of Hinchman's we see the Columbia Hotel, which was later named the Riley.

The hotel had a lovely ballroom, beautiful restaurant, and a wonderful lobby with a grand staircase and a large ornate fireplace. The Hinchman building sported a second floor gymnasium where many early athletic contests were held. The Masonic, Thayer, Gates, and Hinchman buildings still stand. The vacant lot east of the Hinchman building is filled with a mid-1920s-style, one-story retail building. Morris Inc., the former Hope House, law offices, and other shops fill these spaces today that were once the retail center of Greenfield.

The Hughes Bank was a private institution established by John H. Hughes 1 July 1881. On 4 July 1884, it occupied 101 W. Main Street in Greenfield. Mr. Hughes remained with the bank until his death on 25 August 1885. Mr. William Hughes operated the bank until 1 January 1908, when the bank was closed with all depositors being paid in full. The Finance Center Credit Union on Greenfield's north side is an example of the new financial institutions and their facilities being located in the community today.

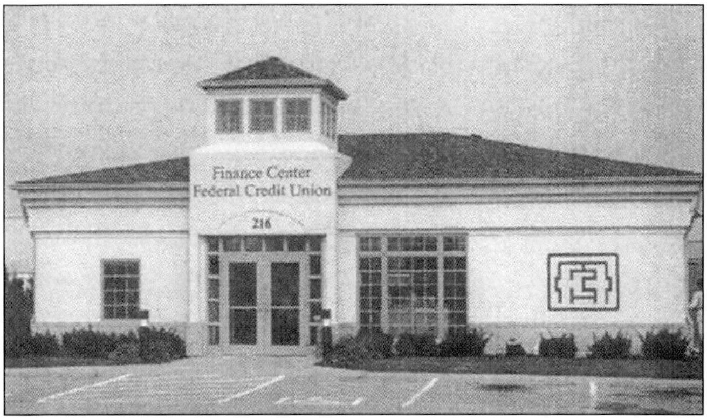

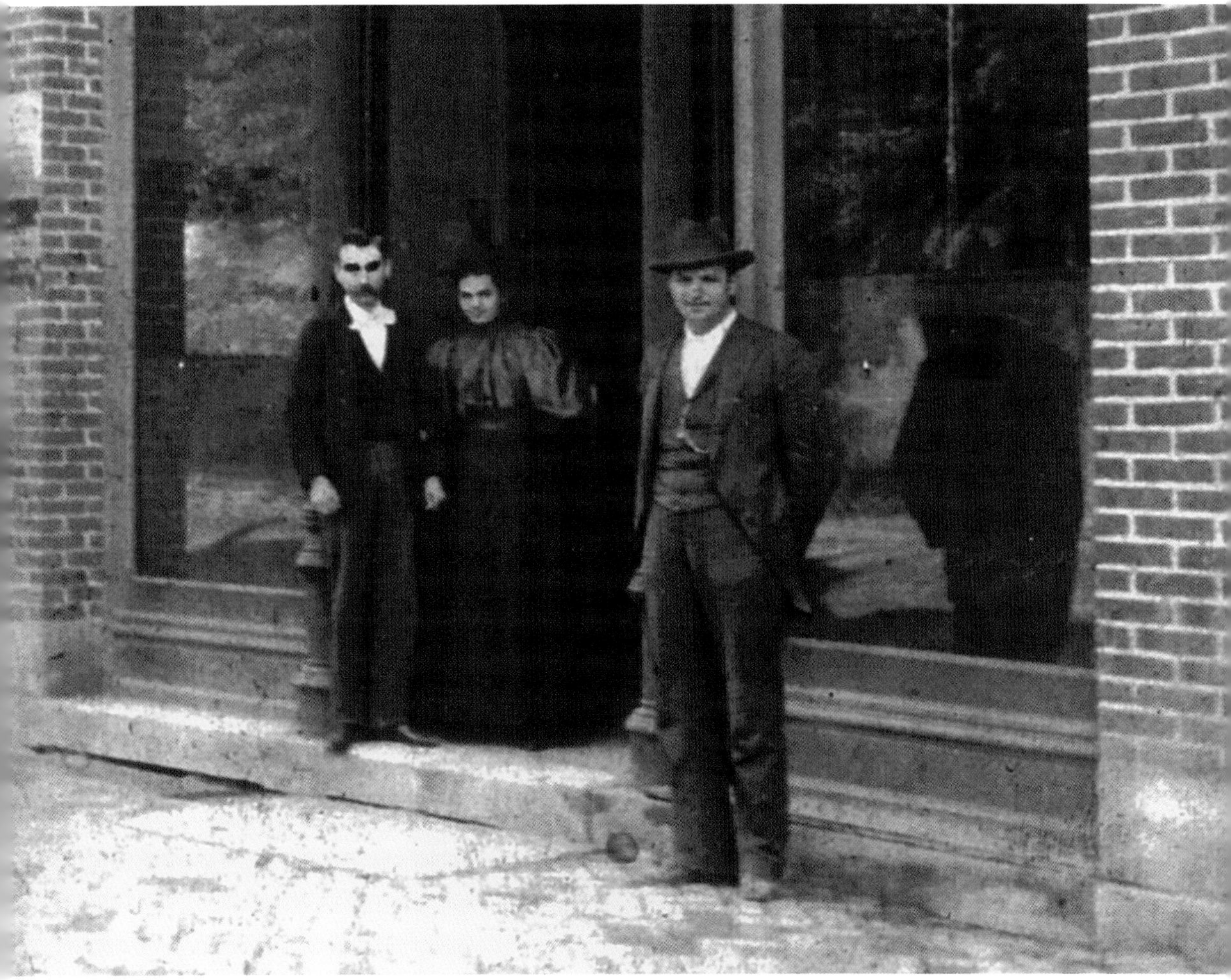

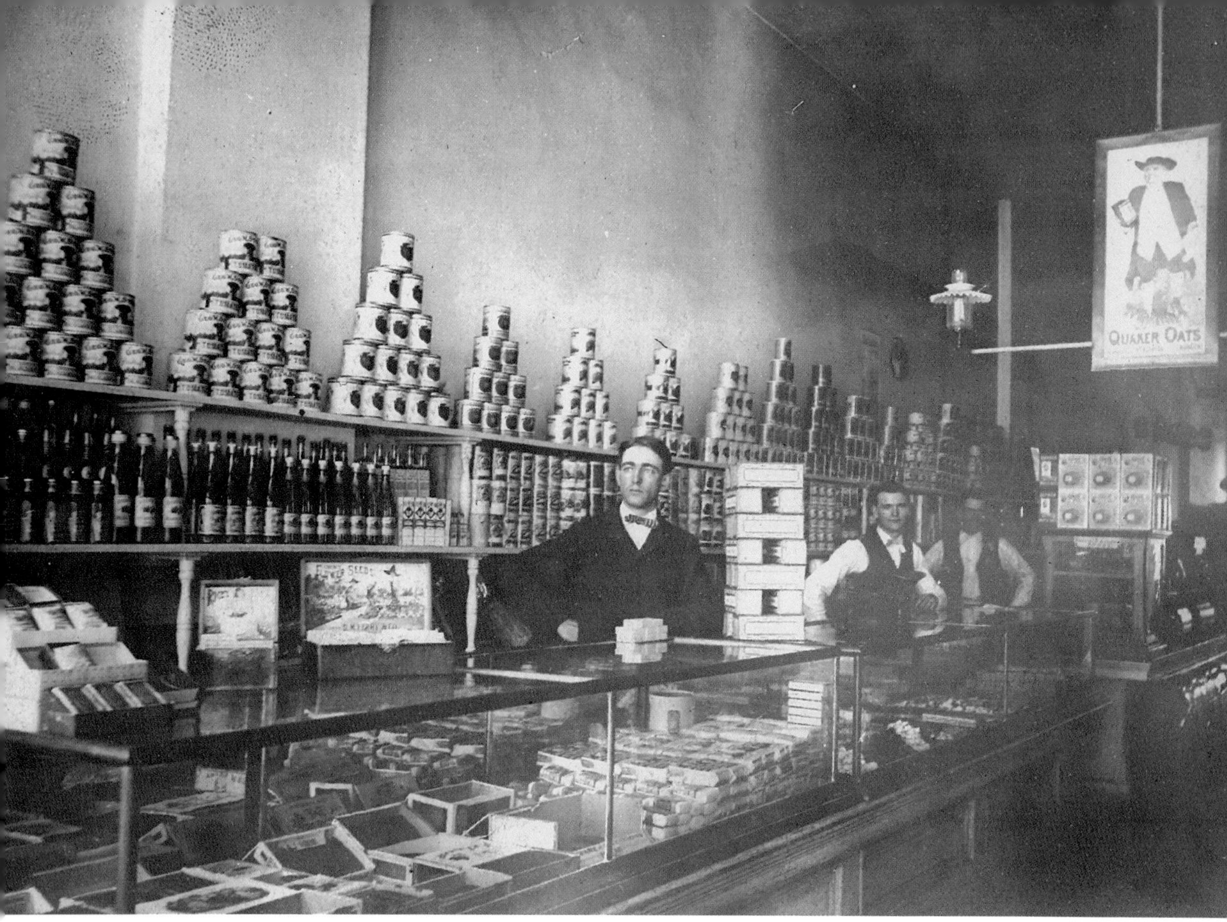

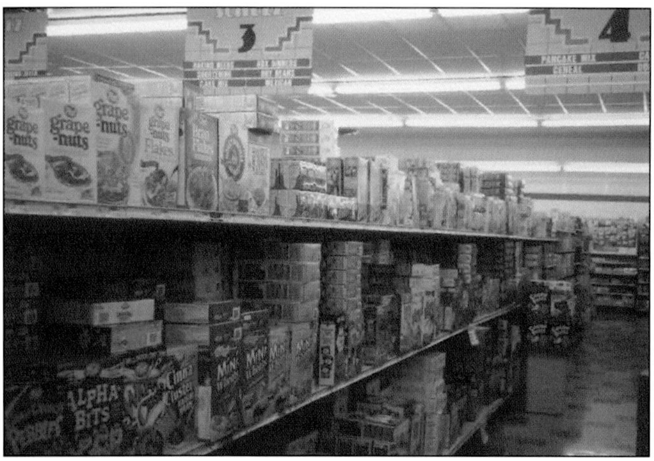

This early-1900s grocery belonged to E.P. Rock and Son of Greenfield. Note the light fixture and the advertisement for Quaker Oats in the background. The location of the store was on N. State Street. The photo is from the Tom Williams collection. The display of items for sale contrasts in an interesting manner with the display in the later picture. The shelving and display of the cereal aisle of the Schultz Market are more in line with the modern supermarket. That business is located in a shopping center originally built for A&P Stores on W. Main Street in Greenfield. Grocery stores before the 1930s usually did not handle a complete line of meat, canned goods, and related items. The stores of the period previous to that date tended to specialize.

Spangler's Dry Goods at Shirley *c.* 1920 was a well-known local business in the northeast corner of Hancock County. Their motto was "Where the Quality is Always Higher than Price." They were a member of Associated Stores and handled shoes, dry goods, groceries, and women's wear. The building just south housed a stationery store. The two brick structures still stand, although they have been greatly modified. Today their fronts are largely brick and there are no similar stores to replace them in this small town.

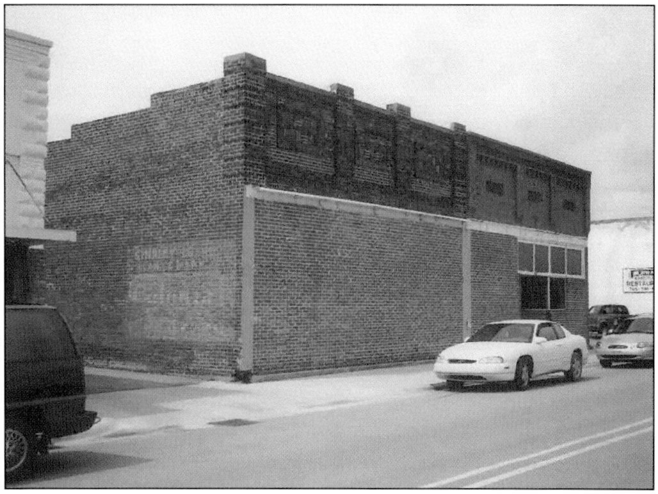

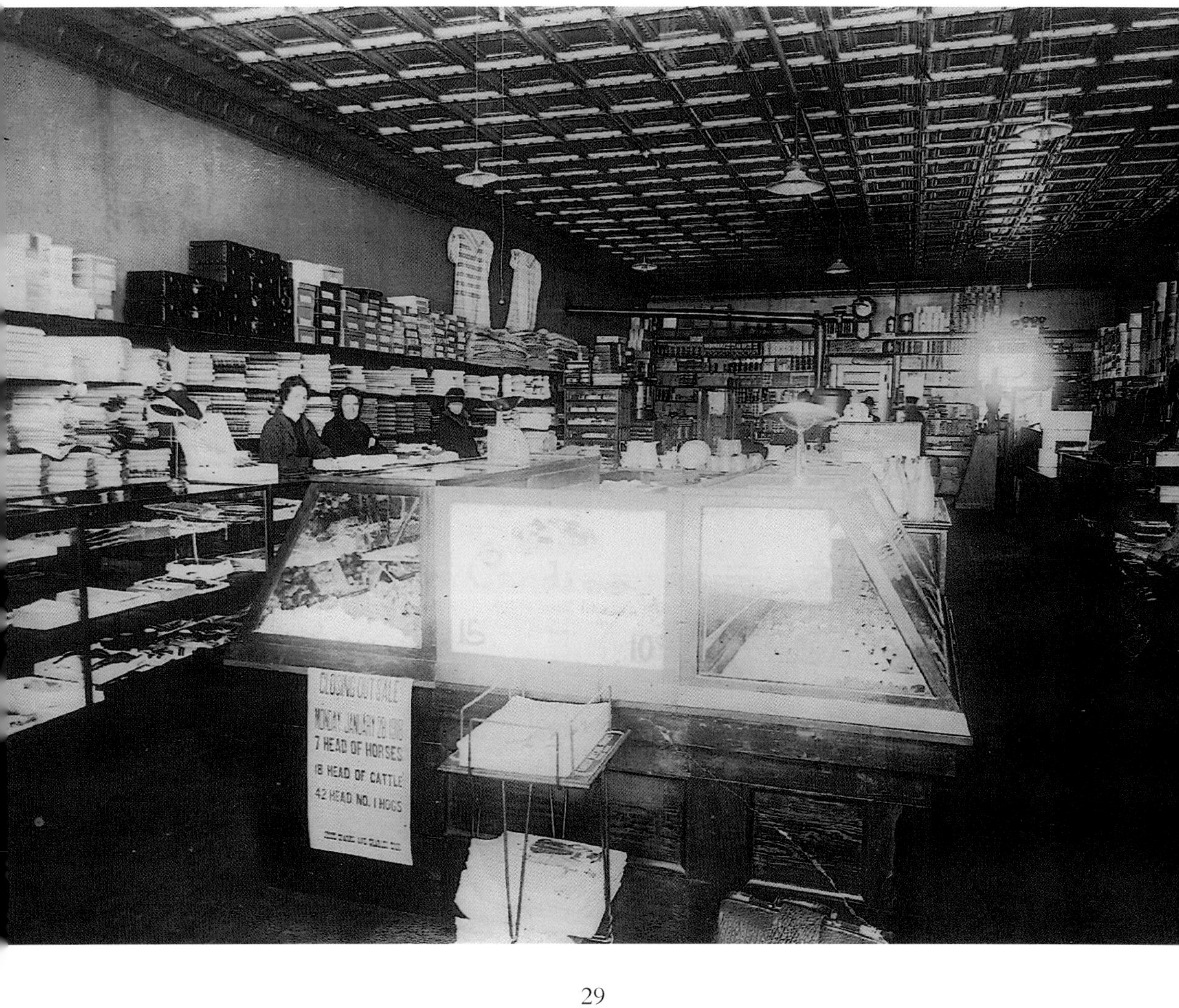

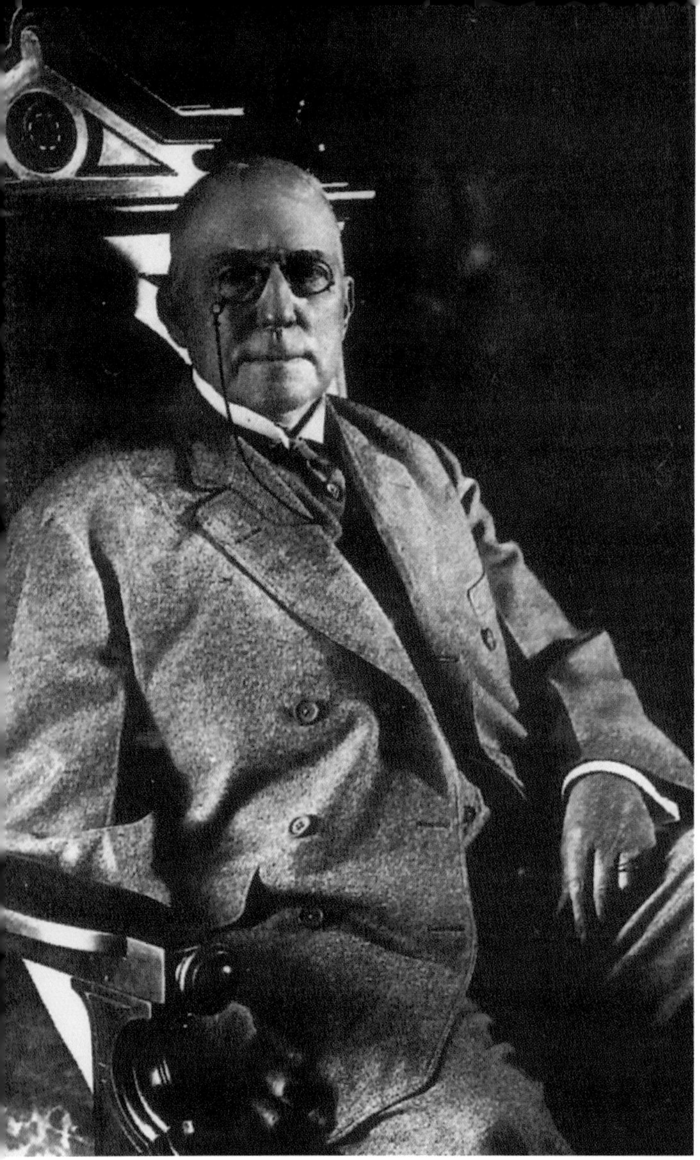

Children brought flowers to James Whitcomb Riley on his birthdays in 1912 and 1915. On 7 October 1949, during the centennial of his birth, a tower of flowers was erected at the courthouse. A smaller replica of the tower was erected for the celebration of his 150th birthday. The annual Riley Festival grew out of Riley celebrations and a merchant promotion, "Frontier Days." Also, the Riley Memorial Association of Indianapolis lays a wreath annually on the poet's grave in Crown Hill Cemetery. During the 150th birthday celebration on 7 October 1998, local historians Larry Fox and Joseph Skvarenina participated in the memorial observance. Mr. Fox is reading a Riley poem for the occasion. Mr. Riley's tomb occupies one of the highest points in Indianapolis. The view to the south from its steps includes the office towers of downtown seeming to rise out of a sea of trees. The view is even more impressive at sunrise.

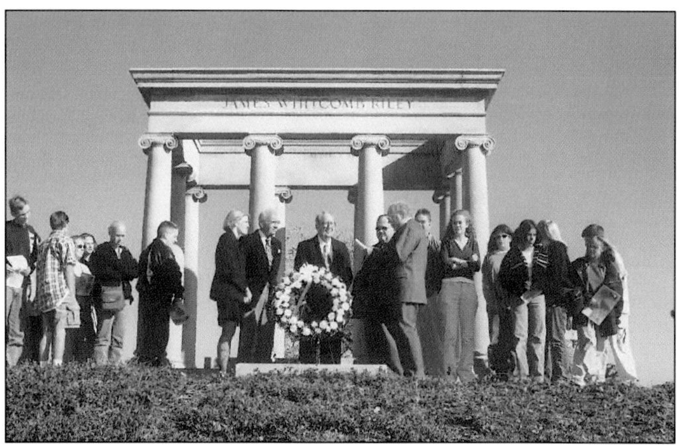

The Red Crown service station served E. Main Street for many years. This picture dates from the late 1920s, and it seems all trace of the Longfellow Elementary School, which sat behind the gas station from the 1880s until around 1920, is gone except for a stone wall that does not show. The contrasting building may not look the same, but inside is the structure of the Red Crown service station. For many years it was known as "Brads," and it now houses an auto repair shop. If you will notice on the hill behind the station is an apartment complex on the site of the Longfellow School.

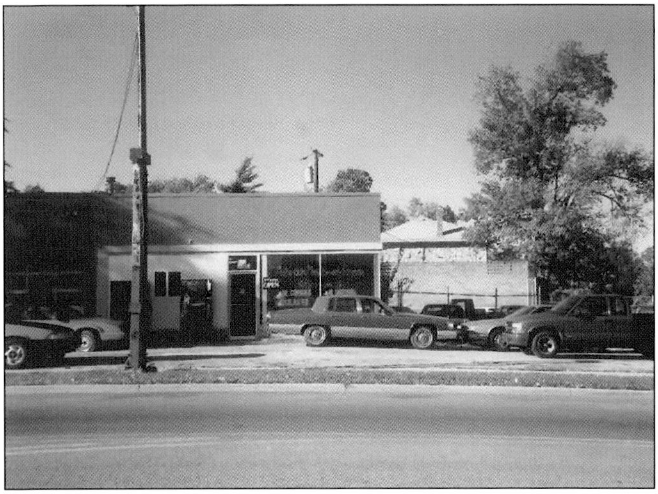

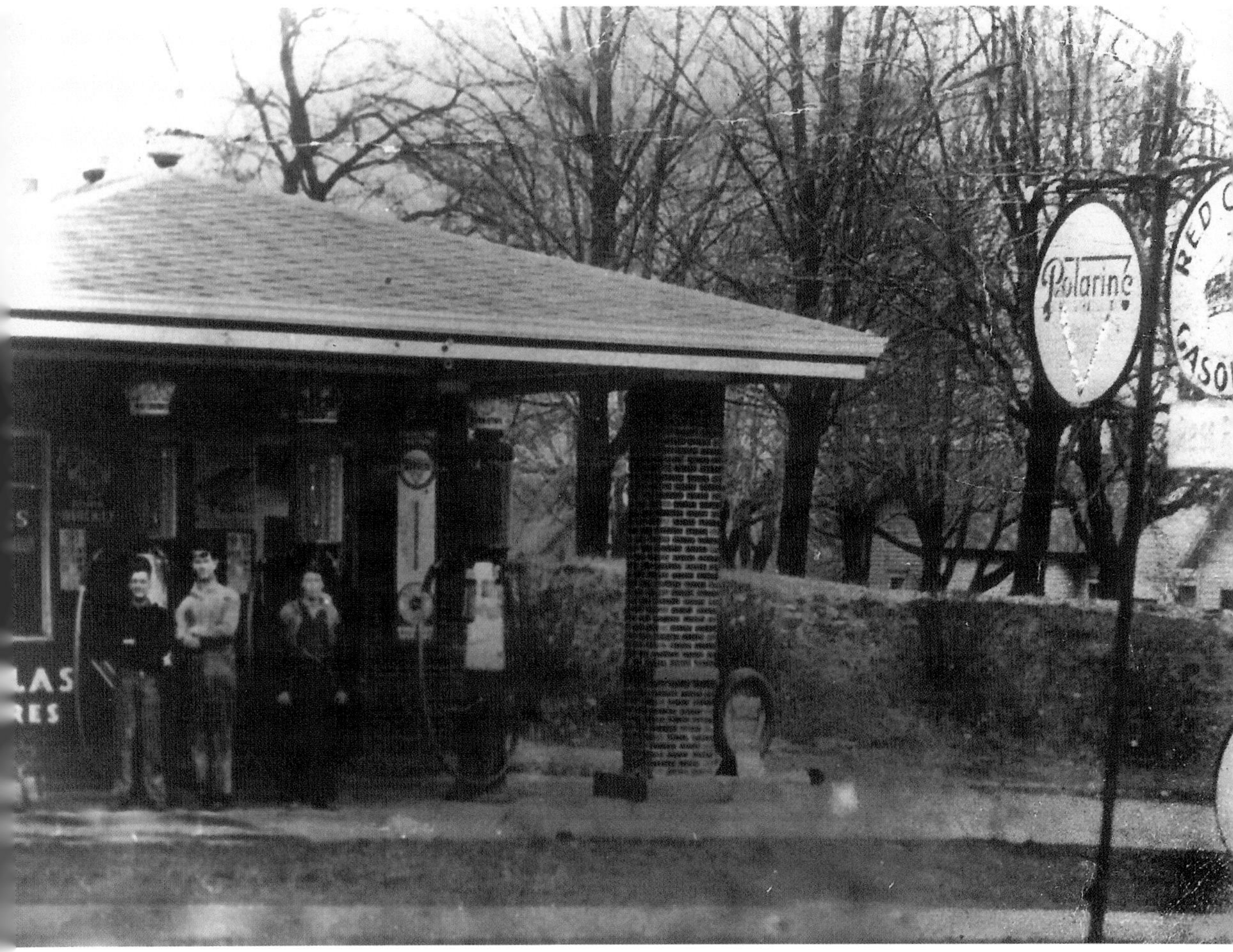

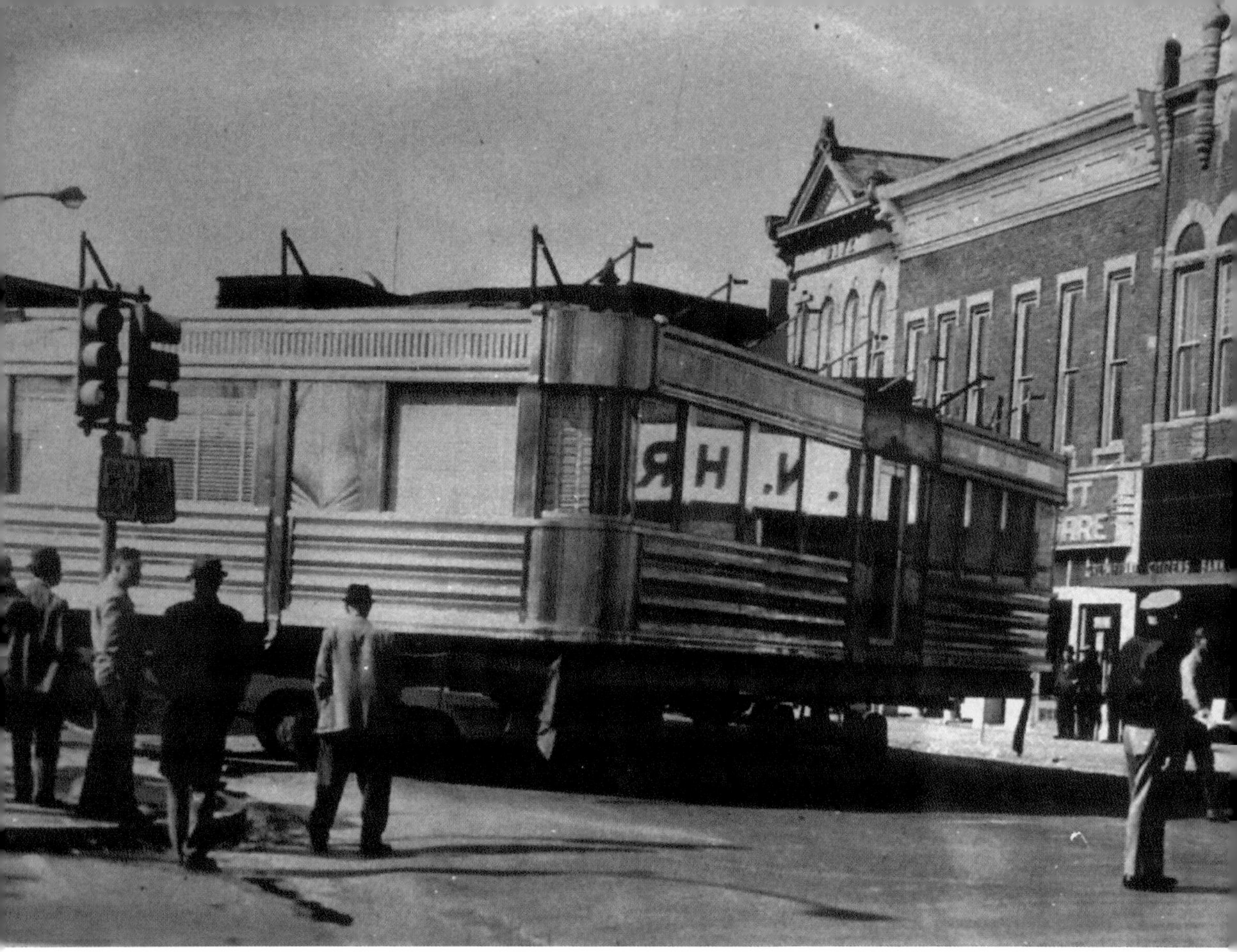

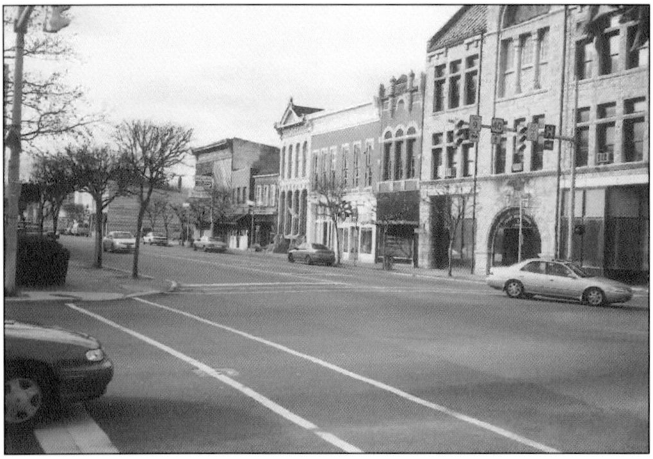

The Peter Pan Diner was located at the site of the National City Bank (now City Building) on the corner of Main and State Street across from the old Masonic Building. It was located in downtown from 1961 until March 1966. Prior to coming to Greenfield it was on State Road 67 and known as the Red Dragon. The Peter Pan was open seven days a week from 6:00 a.m. to 11:00 p.m. Eventually it was moved to 38th Street in Indianapolis. The Peter Pan Diner was the forerunner of the many fast food restaurants on Greenfield's N. State Street. A cup of coffee at the Peter Pan was a dime.

Chapter 2
GREENFIELD

The location is Main and State Streets in Greenfield. The site was the location of the National City Bank Building or Gooding Corner. A service station was located at the site for many years along with the sign advertising the Weston Motel, which was the Howard Hughes and is now the Budget Motel. A committee of the Indiana Legislature selected Greenfield as the county seat of Hancock County on 11 April 1828. The original site included 60 acres donated by Cornwell Meek, Benjamin Spillman, and John Wingfield. Jared Chapman was appointed county agent to sell lots and account for funds as well as expenditures.

The first road running east and west was the old Centerville Road that ran south of the National Road. Around 1834 to 1835, the National Road was built through Greenfield. Greenfield was incorporated in 1850, and became a city in 1876. In 1887, natural gas was discovered in the Greenfield area. Over the next 20 years, the city became a boomtown with manufacturing plants and other industries being established.

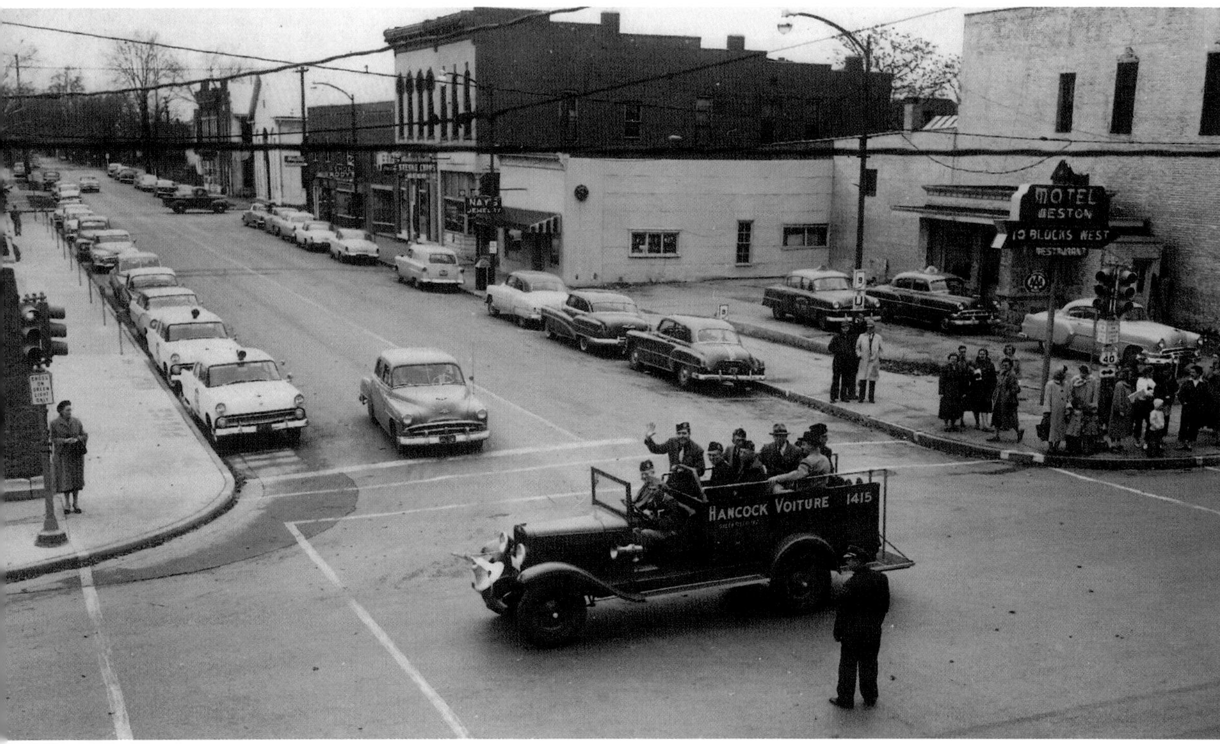

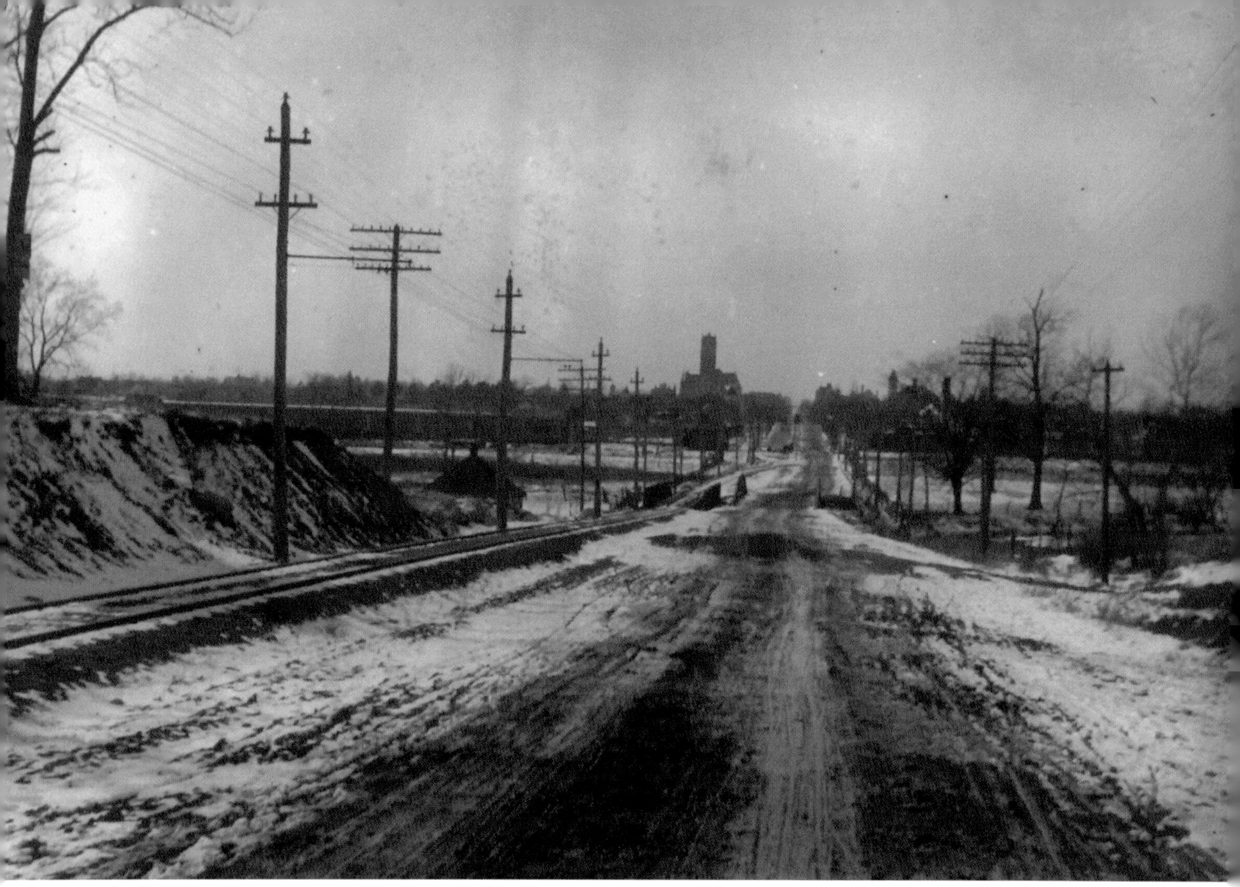

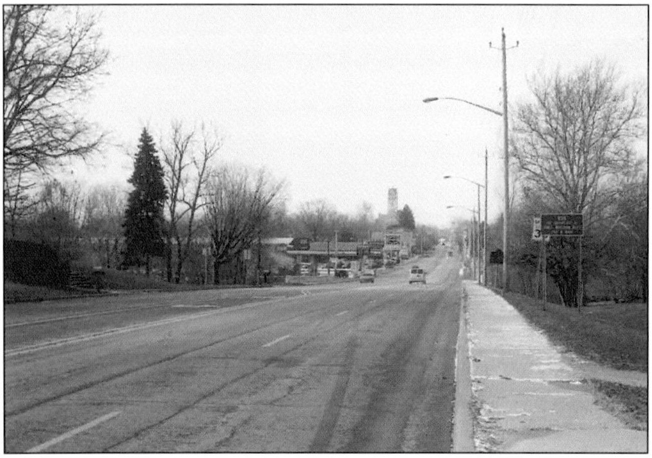

This is Greenfield's Main Street, the National Road, looking west. The tower of the courthouse on the left, and Riley School on the right can be seen on the horizon. This was before the National Road was paved. It was taken at the intersection of Apple and Main Streets. Interurban tracks can be seen on the left, and the old Riley Park Tire Building can also be seen on the left. It served as the Interurban Barn when this picture was taken. The Interurban line began carrying regular passengers on 17 June 1900. Service came to a halt 15 Jan. 1931 when Carl Knox piloted the last car over the line at 4 a.m. The photo is from the Ora Myers collection. You can see how the area has changed in the last 90 years with the road's widening, removal of the tracks, establishment of Riley Park on the north, commercial development, and residential development on the south.

This is the Jeffries and Son Livery Stable at the southeast corner of North and State Streets *c.* 1900.

This was the location of the old Ashley's Carpet Building until 2001. Level Jeffries, who is standing, and Ray Jeffries are getting ready to go to a funeral. The Jeffries were related to the current owners of Ashley Carpet. There was also a livery barn at this site that was owned by W. Huston Jr. who lived on S. Pennsylvania in Greenfield. Dr. Noble Elsbury, a veterinarian, was also at this location. Cooper Brothers ran a livery and feed stable at one time on this site. In later years Johnson's Hardware, an implement dealership, and Ashley's Carpet were located here. In the spring of 2001, this building and the old Eagle's Lodge to the south were torn down to make room for a parking lot. (Photo courtesy of Minnie Jeffries Walls.)

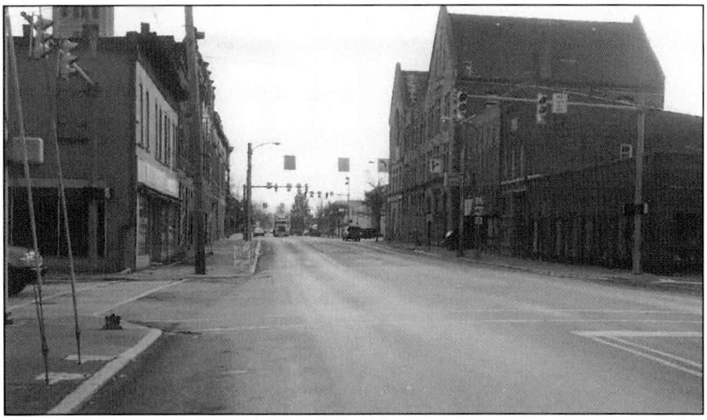

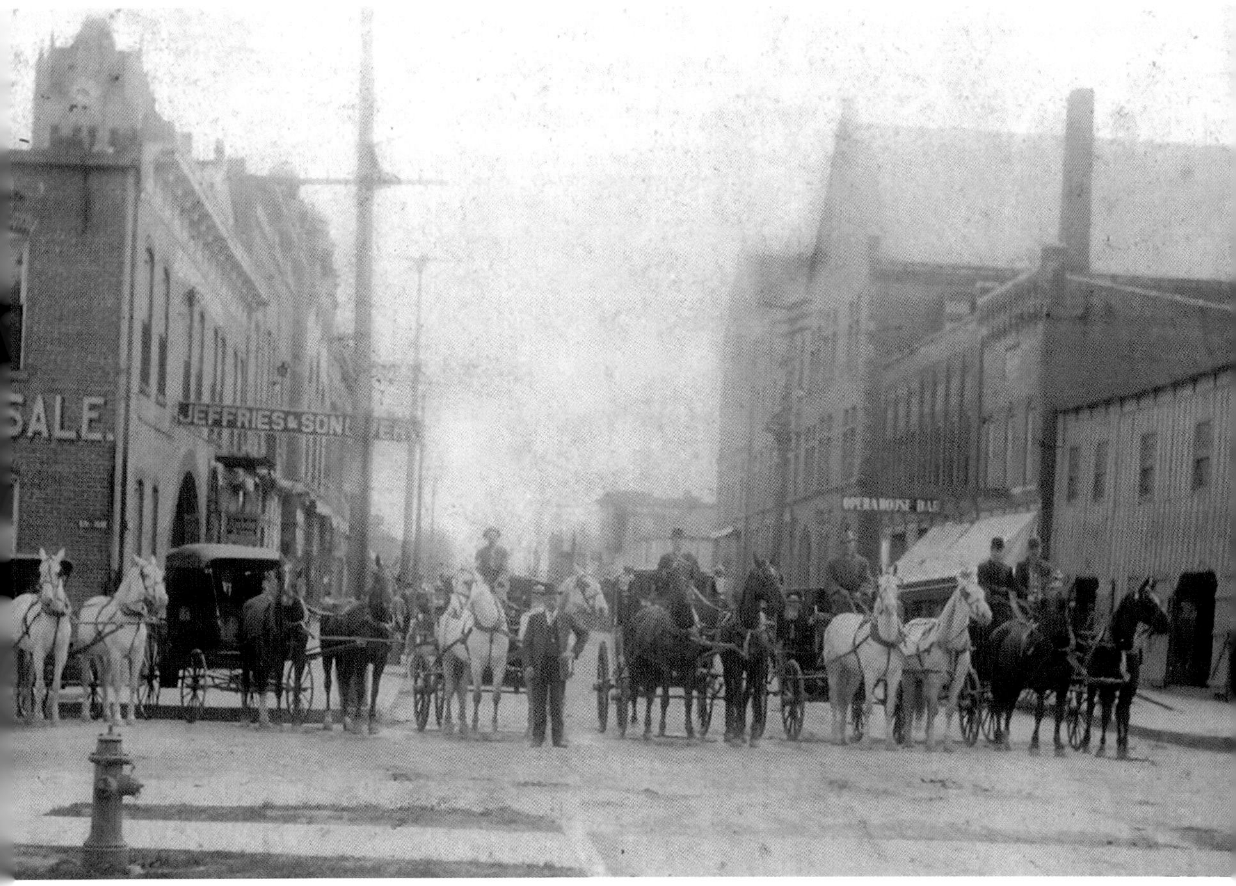

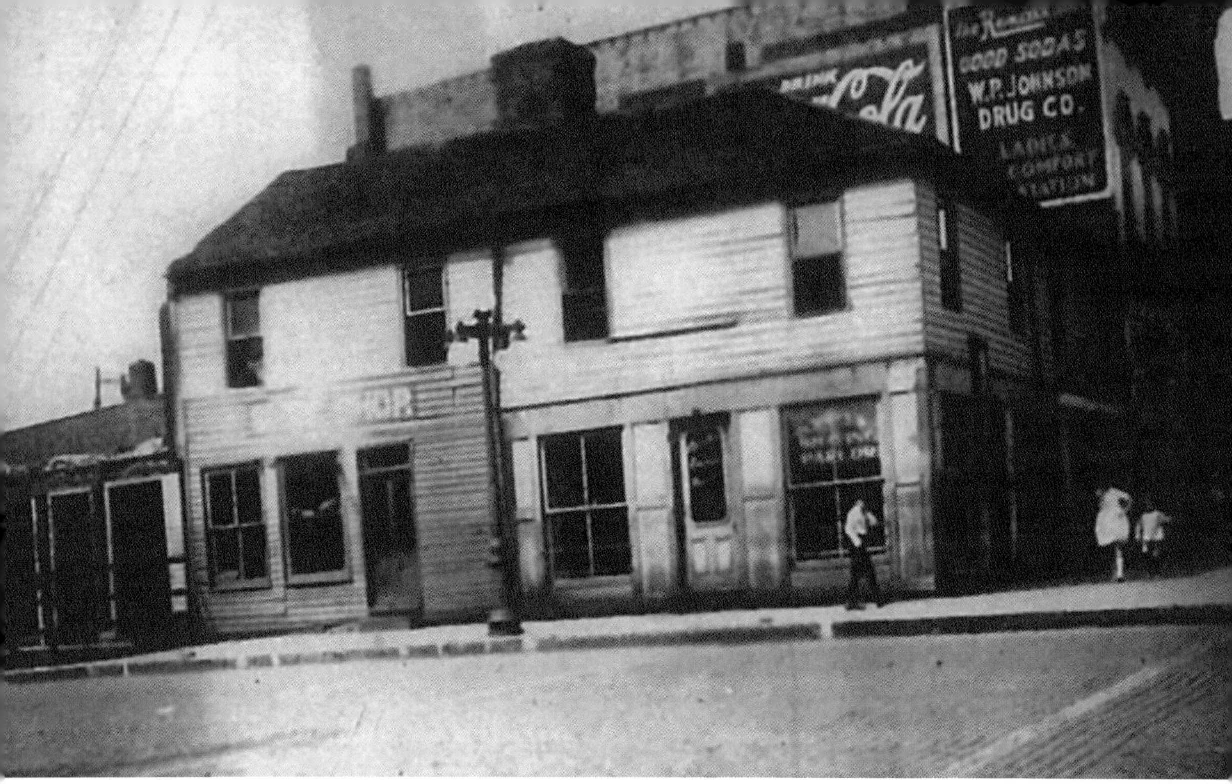

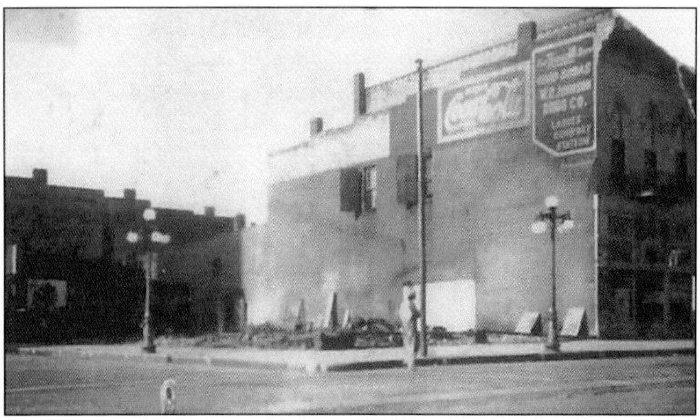

The Gooding Tavern was located at the corner of State and Main Streets. In the 1920s it was demolished. Gooding Tavern had many famous visitors, including former President Martin Van Buren and Henry Clay. Joseph Chapman began the structure in 1832, with later additions being added by Asa Gooding. For many years Gooding's wife Matilda ran the early hotel. To the right of the tavern was a depot for the Indianapolis, Greenfield, and Richmond Traction Line. Other famous Goodings include David S. Gooding who was appointed as the United States Marshall for the District of Columbia from 1866 to 1869. He was wounded in Morgan's Raid. Another family member was Civil War Gen. Paul Gooding who distinguished himself in the 1864 Red River Campaign. It is also interesting to note that George L. Knox, a leader of Greenfield's African American Community, had a barbershop in the Gooding Corner. Knox later had a barbershop in the Indianapolis Bates Hotel and published an early Civil Rights newspaper called the "Freeman." The Bates Hotel was located at the site of present day Embassy Suites in downtown Indianapolis.

A.A. Gappen Sporting Goods in Greenfield *c.* 1920s specialized in bicycles before they sold Harley-Davidson motorcycles. The method of display included a line up out front, which is very similar to the common appearance of car lots in the year 2001. Most transportation sales today take place on the west edge of Greenfield at locations like Inskeep Ford. The big automobile dealerships on US-40 west of Greenfield capitalize on the large number of local people that use that route to go to work on the east side of Indianapolis. (Old photo courtesy of Kenneth Jackson.)

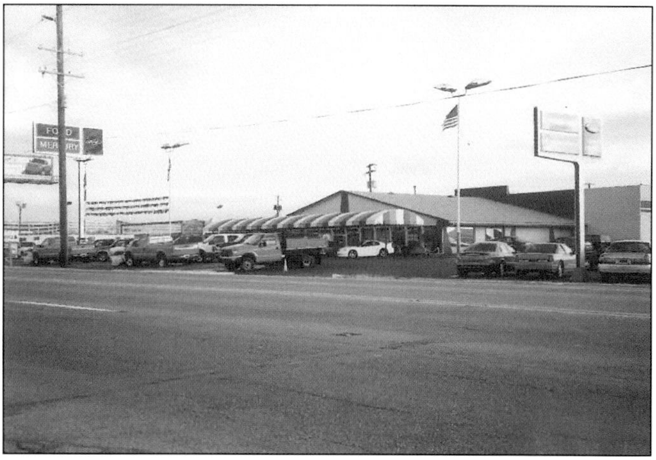

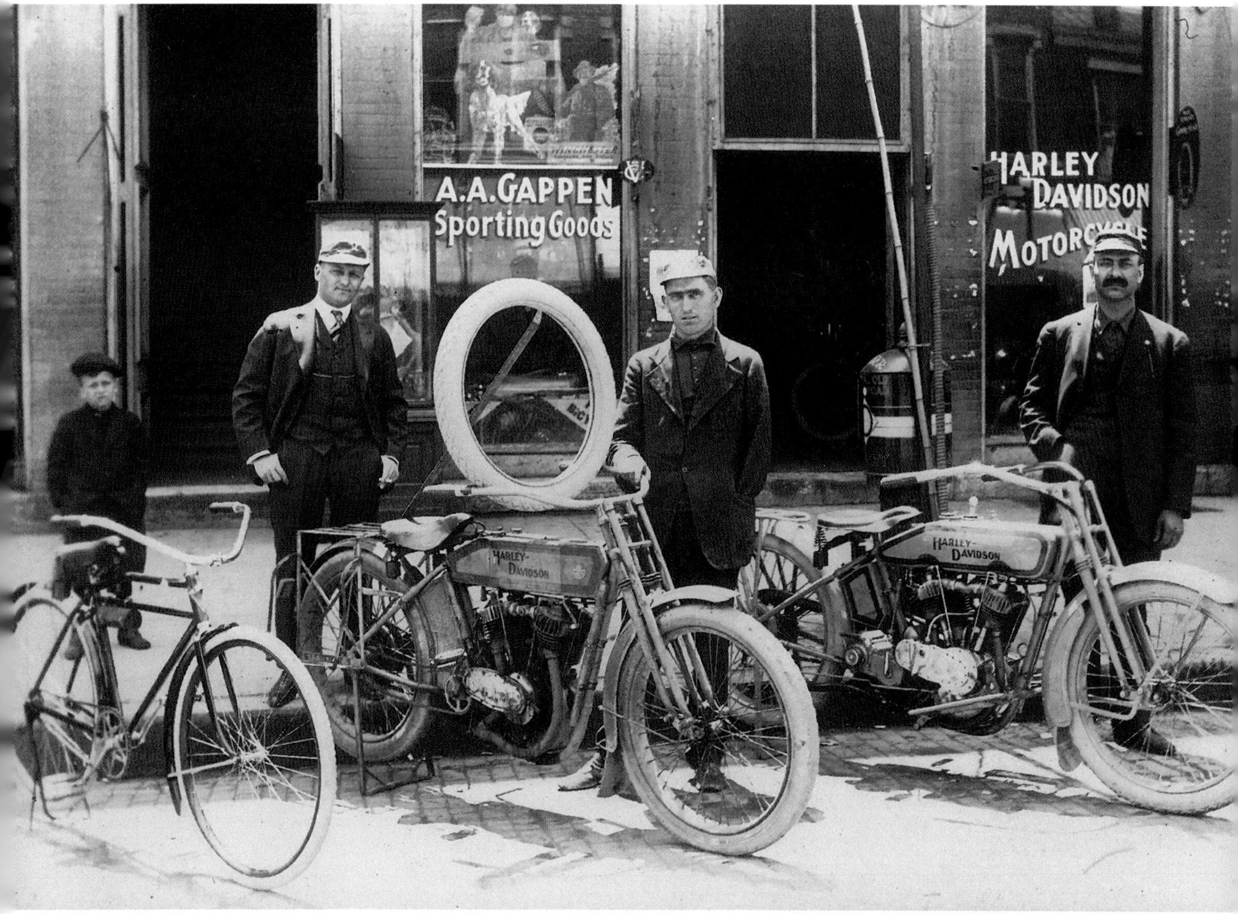

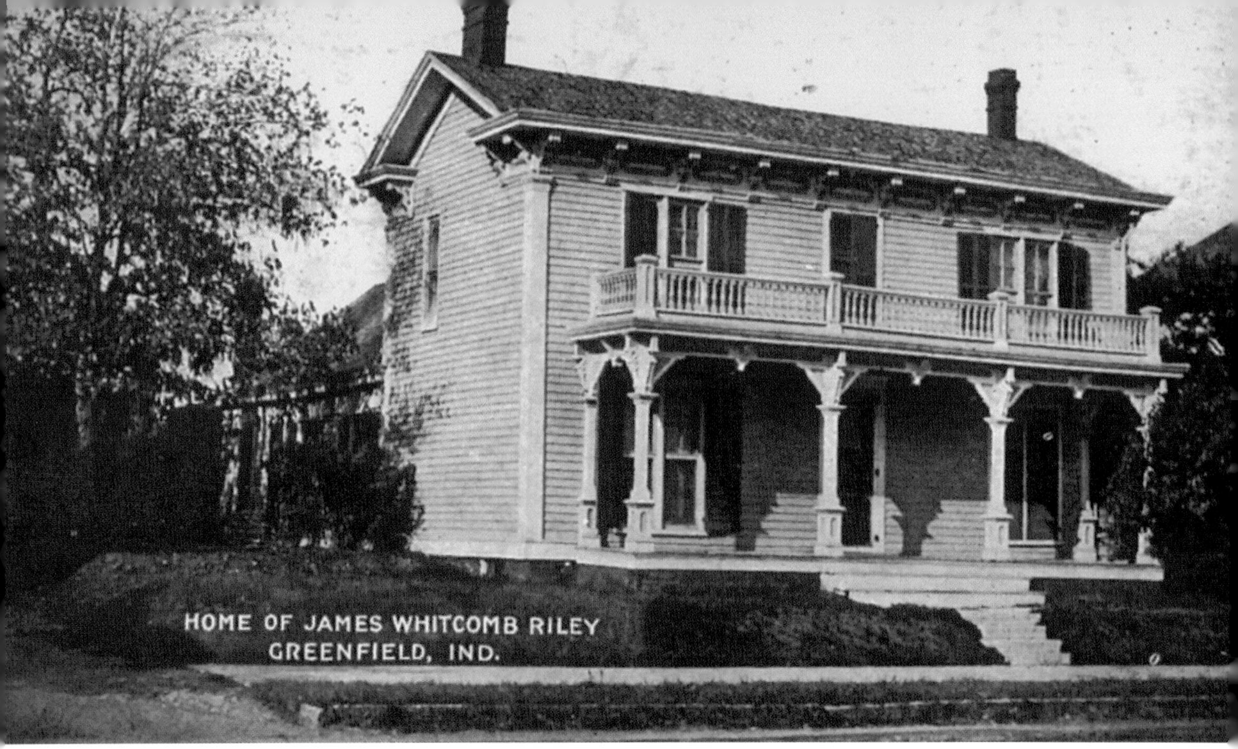

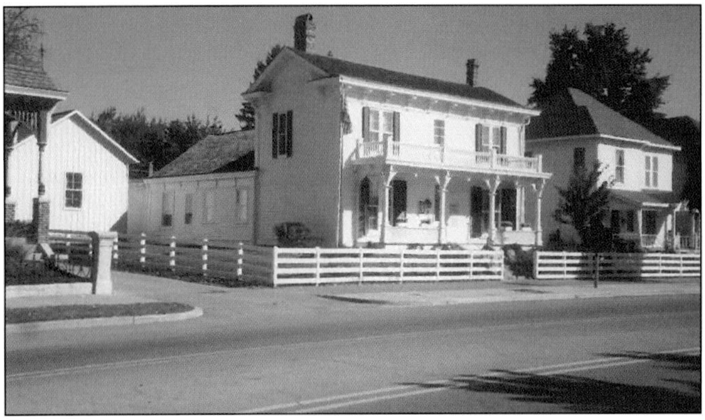

James Whitcomb Riley's father built this home in 1853. By the turn of the century it had lost an inset porch in the middle of the first and second floor and gained the 1870s-style porch, which runs nearly the length of the front of the house. The color was probably yellow with white trim and green shutters.

When Mr. Riley became famous and rather wealthy in 1893, he repurchased this home, which his father had lost after the Civil War. He later furnished the house and asked his sister-in-law Julia to take care of it. She continued to live there after his death in 1916, and finally left to join family in California in the early 1930s. The city purchased the house when the Riley Old Home Society was unable to raise the money to make the purchase. The society did pay for and/or do the work necessary to repair, clean, and open the home in 1937. When Julia died, her ashes were returned to Greenfield, and they rest in the Riley family plot in Park Cemetery. Many of the Riley home's furnishings were purchased by the society, while others were donated over the years. Today the society owns or holds title through donations and/or loans to the contents of the Riley home, as well as the displays in the museum next door.

The Masonic Building in Greenfield was built in 1895. Its style of architecture and cut of stone were quite popular in the Greenfield at the time. The early photo was taken around the turn of the century when the J. Ward Walker Co. occupied the first floor. The second floor was rented as office space, and the third floor included meeting hall, game room, and lounge facilities. An elevator gave easy access to the upper floors from a side entrance. Some years ago, the county purchased the building from the Masons and reworked the front to look much as it did in the early photo. A copper raised seam roof was added, and governmental offices have been located in the building since that time. The county has been unwilling to spend the money for a full upgrade, so the structure has not seen full use. The dormers and stone ornaments on the roof were removed many years ago. Left of the Masonic Building is the Davis Building, which housed the Citizens Bank for many years, and the next is the long time home of Pickett Hardware.

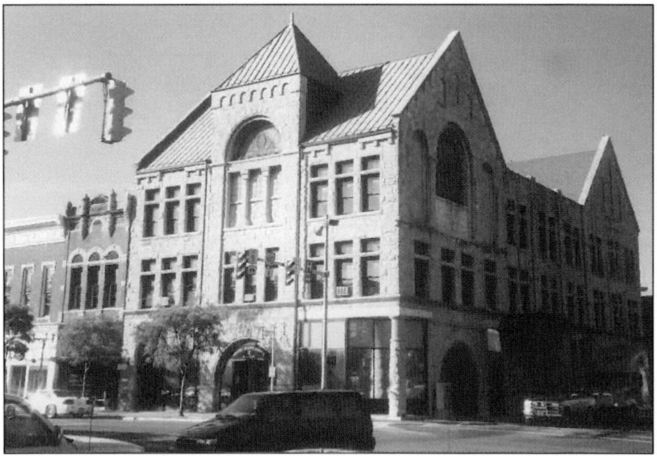

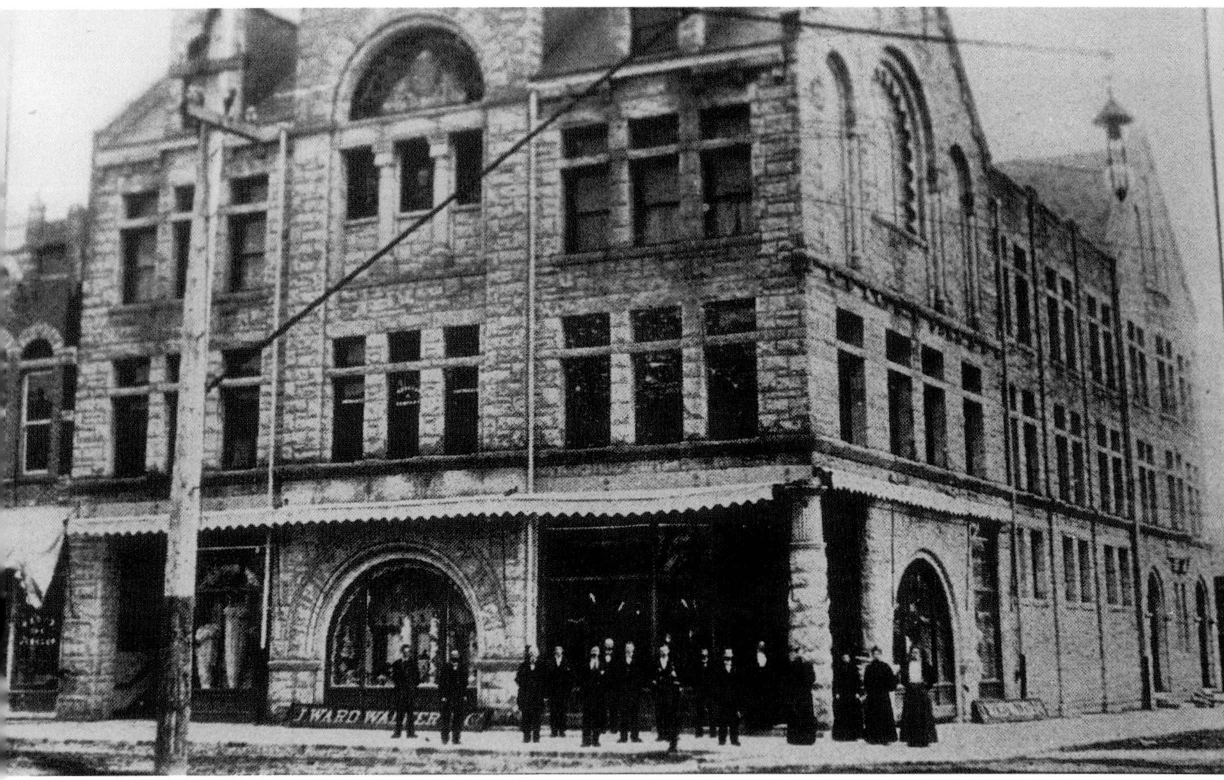

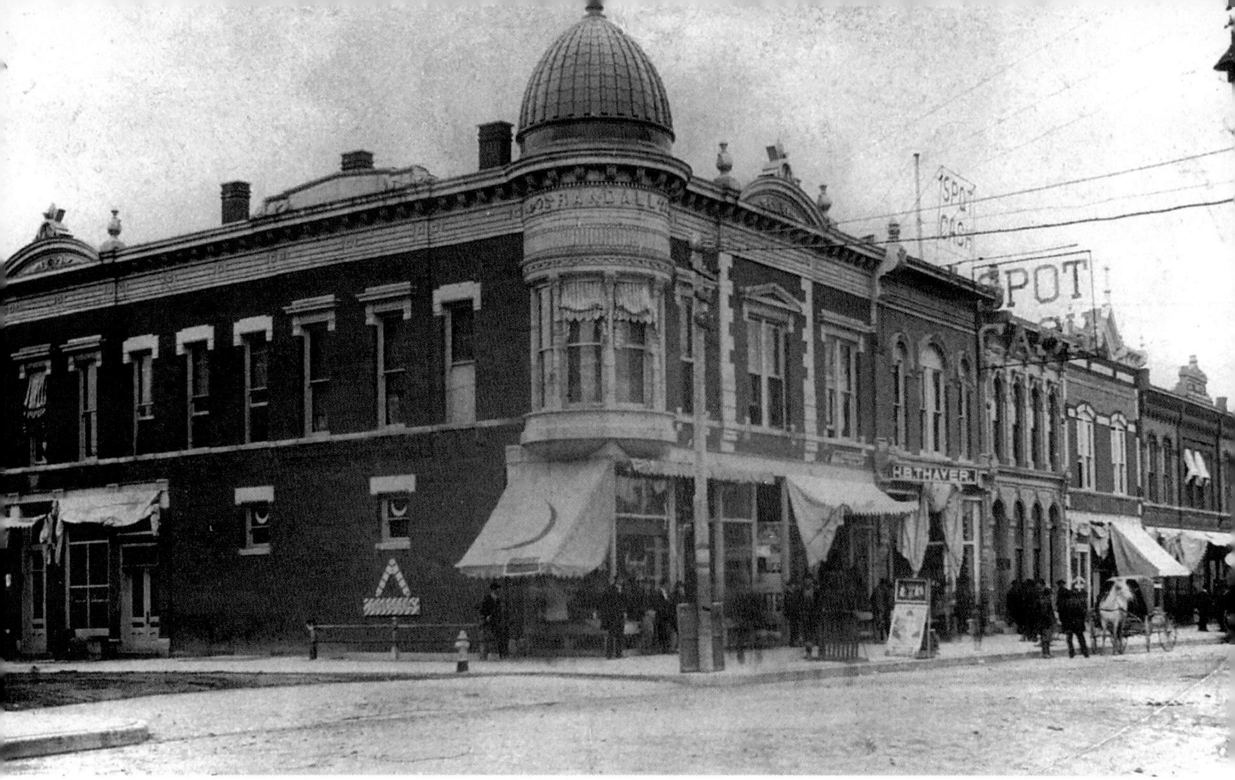

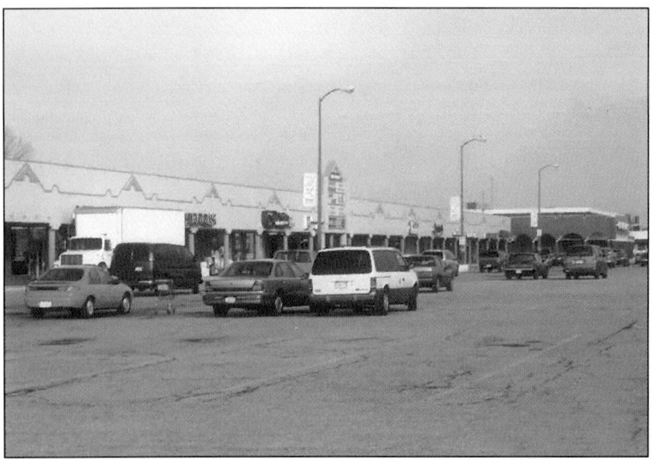

This is E. Main Street, the first block east of State Highway 9, probably *c.* 1915. The second building and some others in the picture were home at the time to one of the earliest department stores in this part of the country, known as Spot Cash. This was one of the major business blocks during the period. The back of the block (not shown) housed a livery stable, and in that sense indoor "parking" and shopping was provided in close proximity. Today, the major shops are on the north side of town in several retail strip malls. This is Green Meadows Shopping Center. Green Meadows is one of the older centers on the north side of Greenfield. The exterior facade of the center received a major face-lift in the 1990s that improved its appearance dramatically. The large parking lot attests to the importance of parking to modern retail from 1970s to the present.

One of the earliest buildings in Hancock County was the Gooding Tavern. Much of the early life of the local community revolved around this location. The travelers moving through often stopped here for food and drink. Horses were watered in a pond that covered the northeast corner of the courthouse square. The two story brick building next door housed a number of businesses including Gambles Hardware in the 1940s and 50s. The three story brick building next door housed James Whitcomb Riley's sign shop on an upper floor. The time period of the picture is around 1900. The same site was cleared for a Standard Station in the 1920s, and then again for a diner in the 1960s. Hancock Bank and Trust cleared the area including the first of the brick buildings in the late 1970s. The three-story brick and the first store front of the next building which once housed Goff's Meat Market in the 1940s and 50s was cleared in the late 1980s for another addition to the bank building. It was purchased by the City of Greenfield for use as a city hall in 2001.

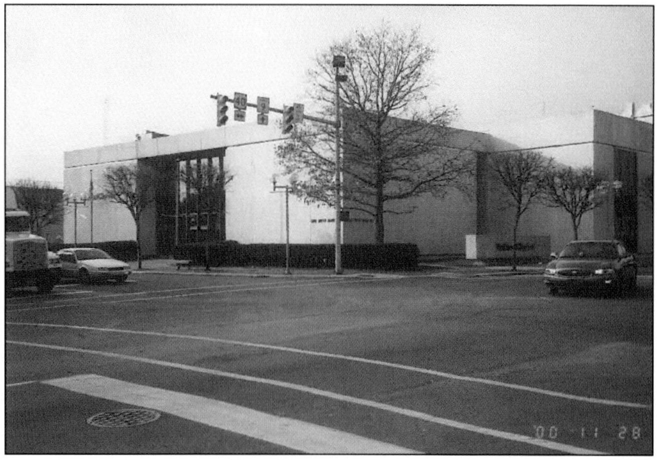

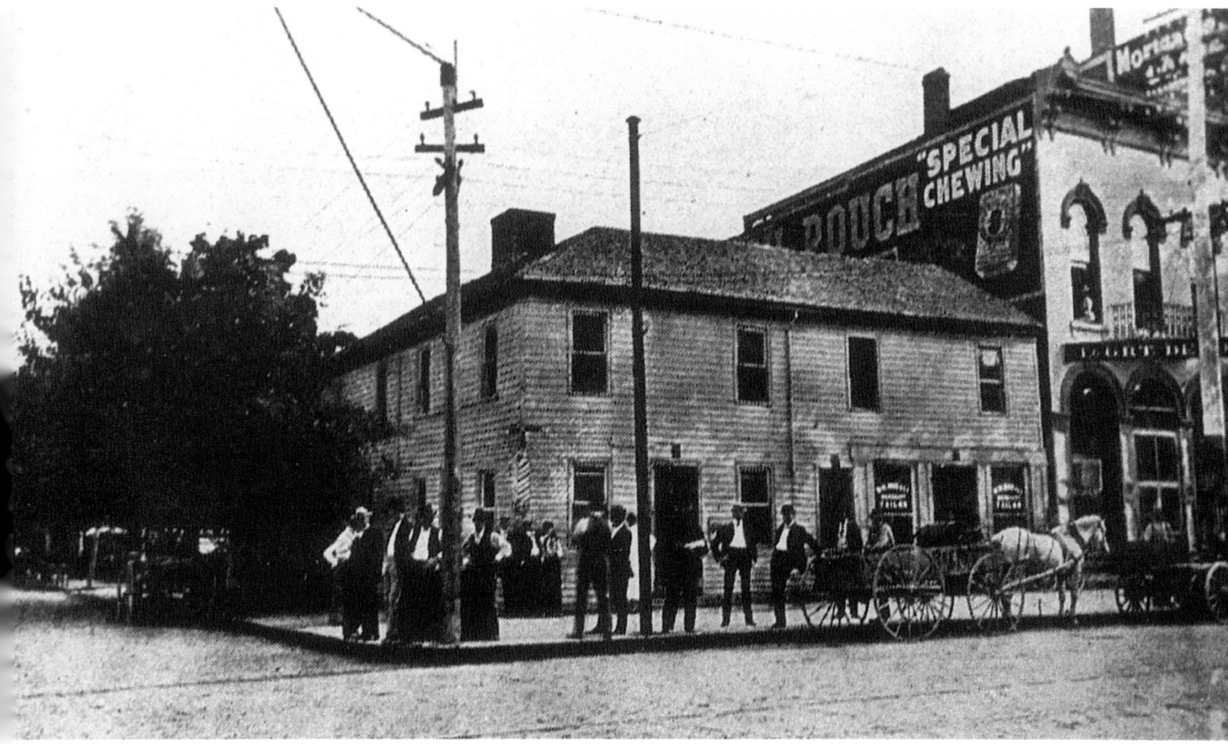

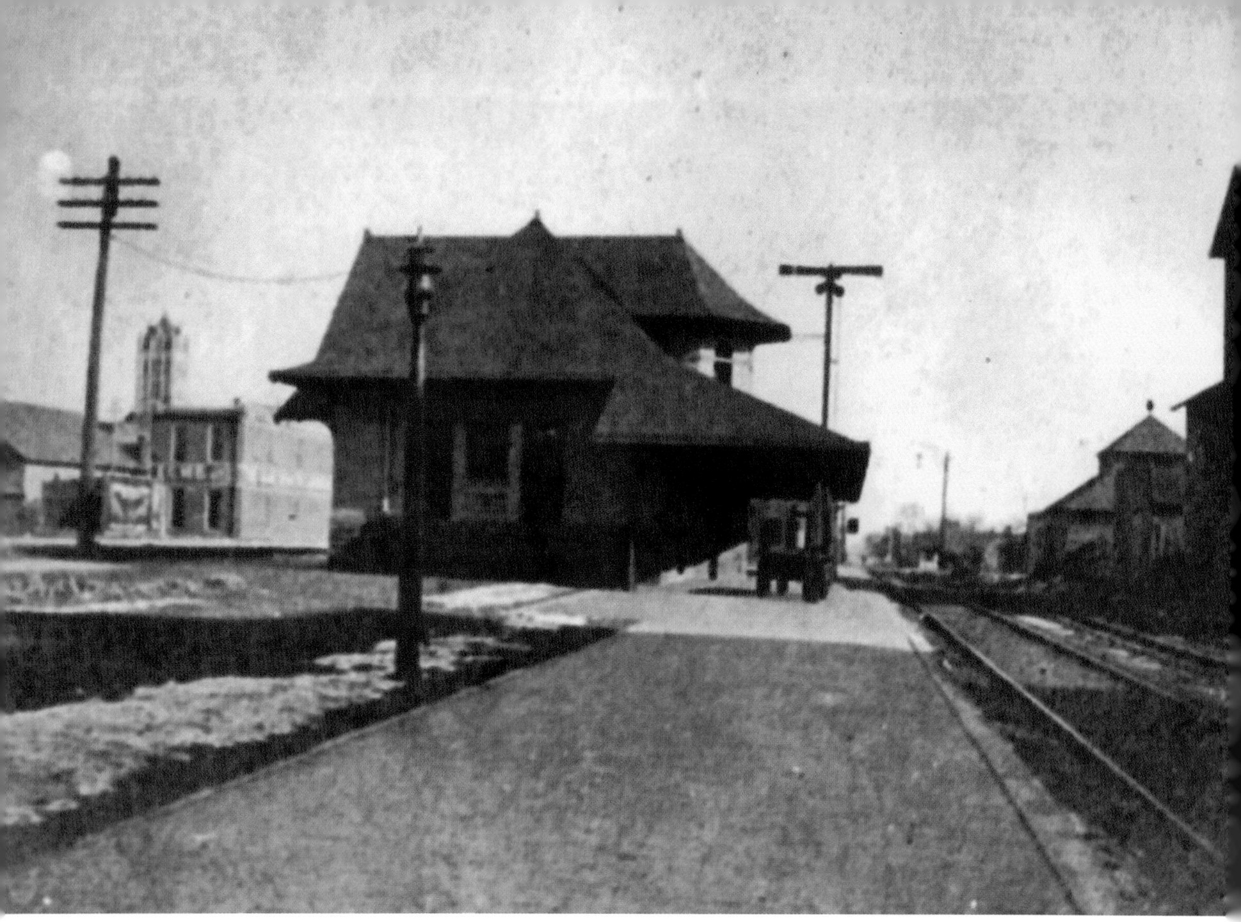

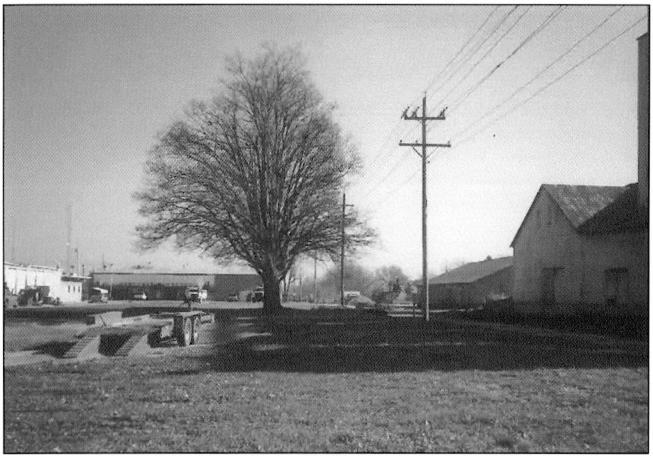

Greenfield's picturesque train station is no longer in existence. In 1943, a train wreck tore away both ends of the building, scattering freight and wreckage for almost three blocks and halting rail traffic for 12 hours. Rails were twisted and torn from ties for approximately three blocks. The mishap occurred shortly before 8 p.m. Saturday evening. The train was a westbound freight of approximately 80 cars. It took 100 men to restore the tracks for rail traffic. The time required getting the trains going again would be of importance to the World War II war effort. The location is along the current hiking trail, perhaps at the location of the small park like area on Depot Street.

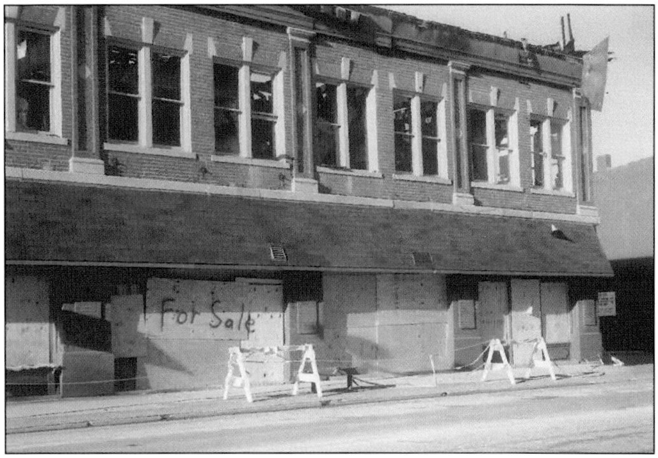

This sizable frame structure probably dated from the 1840s or 50s. The building was home to the Guyman-New Hotel on the north side of Greenfield's W. Main Street. Many Hancock County political events of the Civil War era took place in this and other similar hotels in town. Many of the meetings of local political parties took place in its rooms and halls. The Dunbar House at the corner of State and Main was the scene of a knifing over a Civil War era political argument. The second story balcony of the Guyman-New Hotel was an excellent location for political speakers to address a crowd of local people. The photo dates after 1895 because local streets were bricked about that year. In the spring of 2000, the building that replaced the Guyman-New Hotel in the early 1900s was destroyed by fire. The blaze resulted in the death of an older gentleman who was trapped in one of its rented rooms. Sadly his death was the result of an arsonist. This structure was a hotel and represented some of the best of its day in facilities. The community enjoyed meals and events at its roof garden for many years.

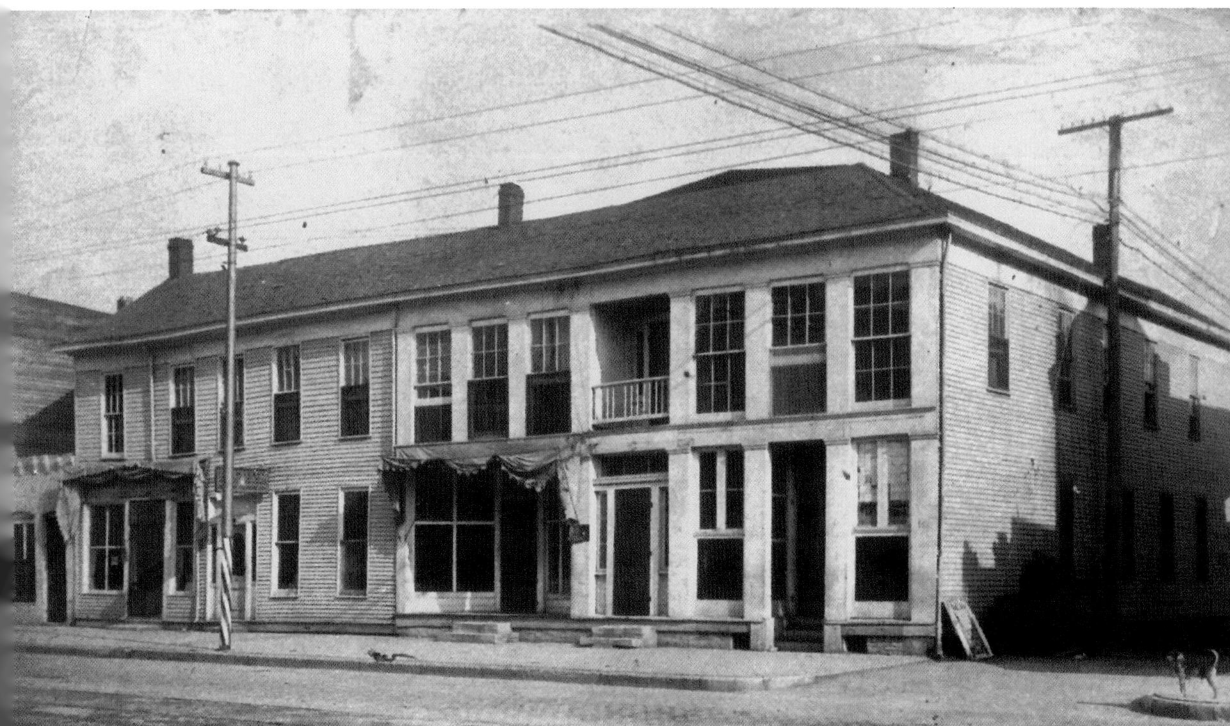

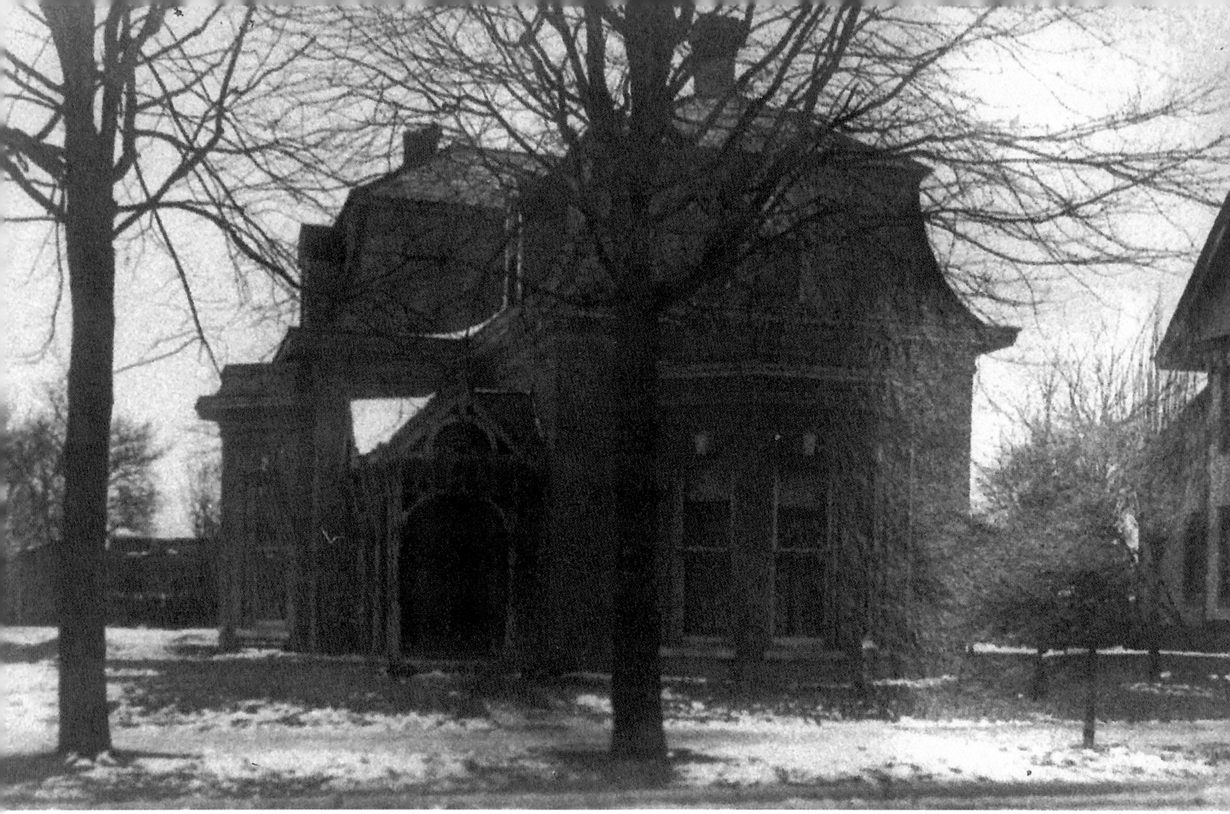

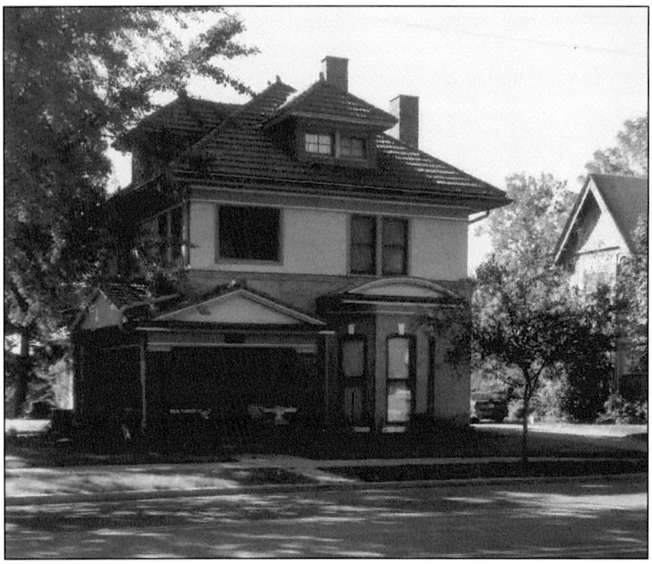

This photo of a home on W. Main Street in Greenfield was taken around 1912. The house enjoyed a wonderful "bay" window and a mansard roof, which may date from the 1870s. The house was a substantial brick with interesting lines. One might consider the original to be a variation of Second Empire in regard to architecture. The second photo presented is the same house at the same address after the addition of a full second story with a third story tucked under the eves. In case you doubt the history and change of the house take a good look at the front windows and the details of the lower story. The lower floor was changed little in this addition except for the redesign of the porch. Perhaps due to foundation limitations the second floor was done in stucco instead of brick. The end result might be considered related to the "Prairie School" and or the American Four Square design.

Until 1945–46, this large brick home often called the Thayer house (named for the family who lived there many years) occupied the northeast corner of Main and Pennsylvania in Greenfield. Many local social events took place here and its prominent family was greatly involved in Greenfield and Hancock County. The house was wrecked to make way for a new retail endeavor. The building, which replaced the Thayer house, was this former gas station. By the 1990s it became a muffler shop and no longer sold gasoline. The building is not totally out of its element because it anchors the end of the downtown business district.

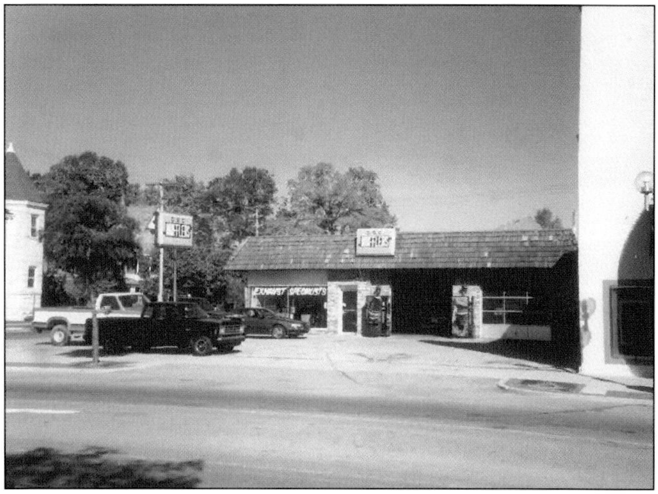

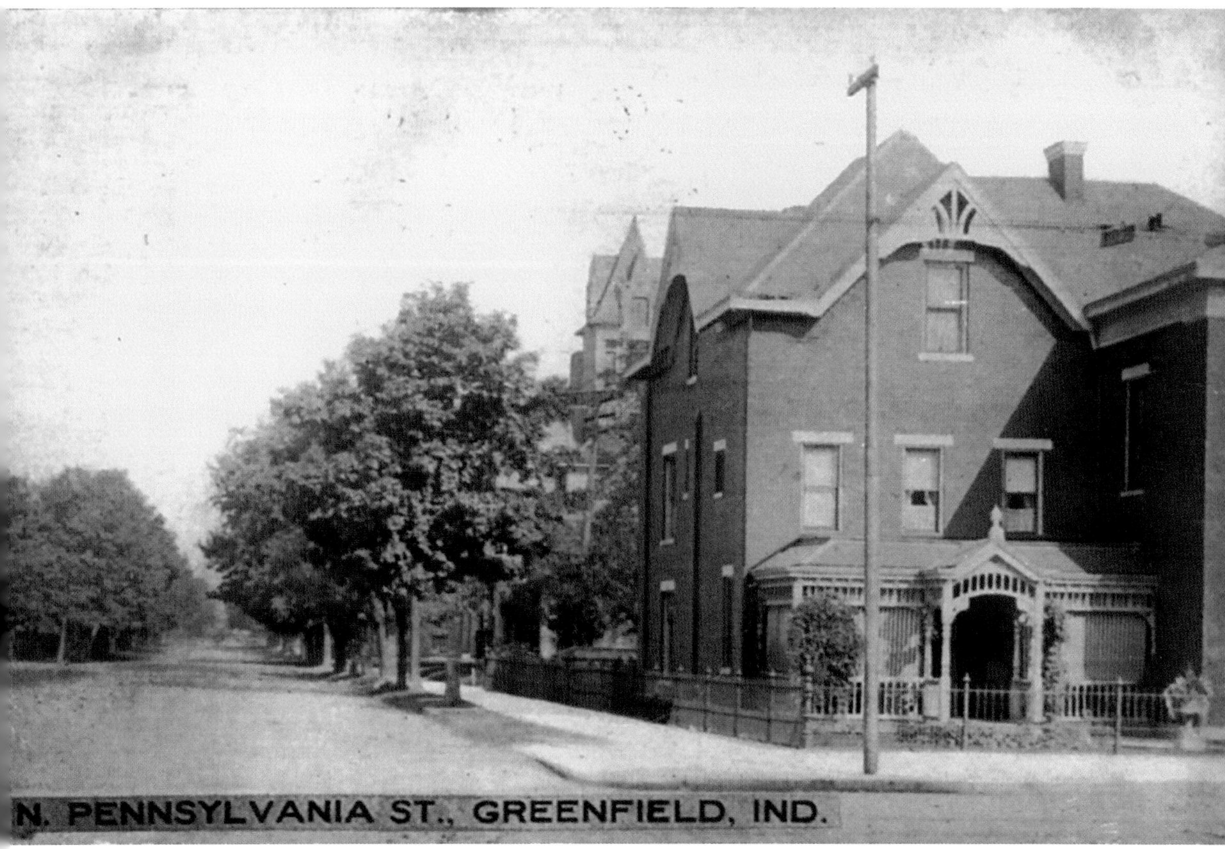

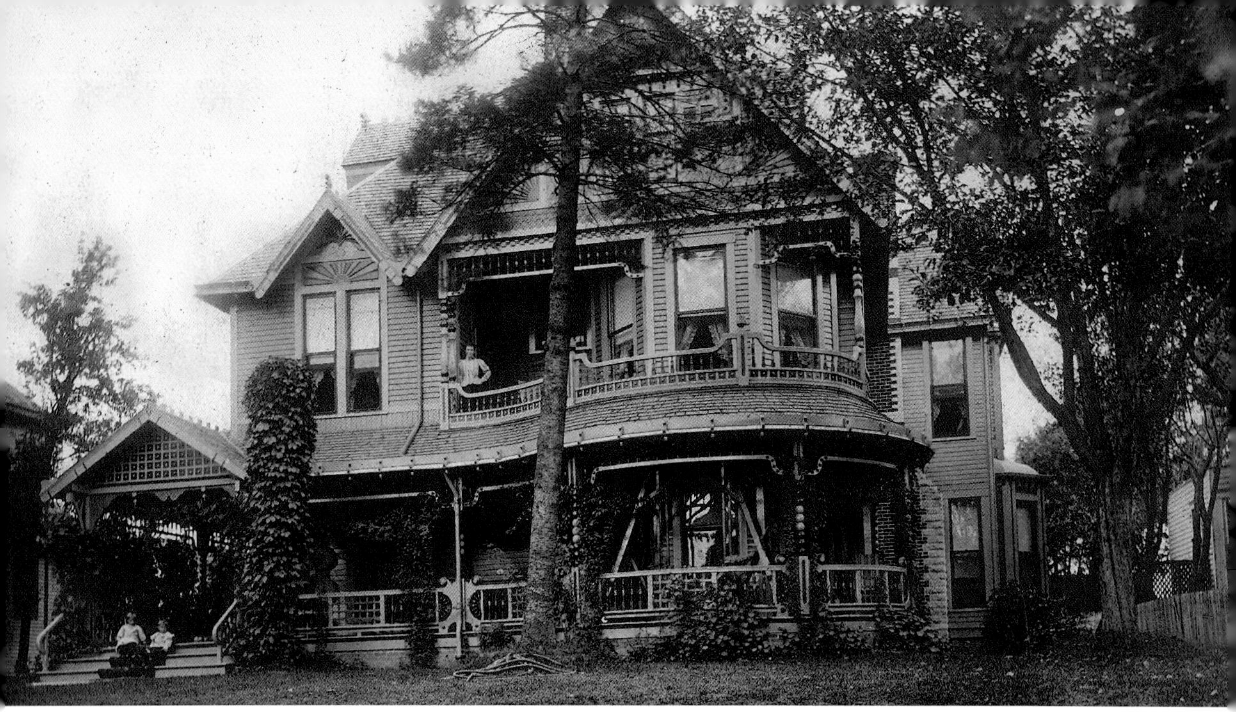

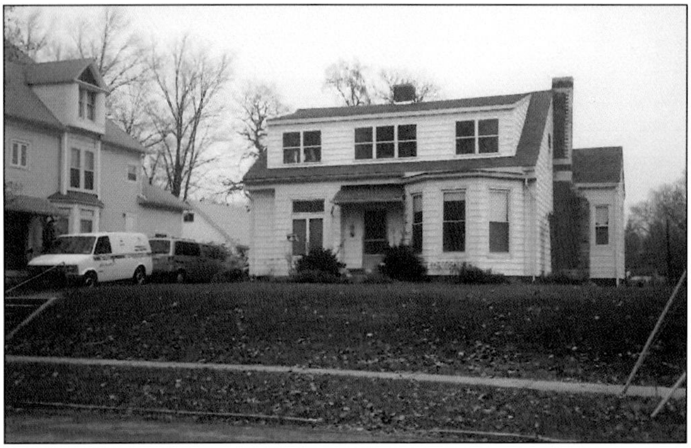

This Victorian home was built around 1895 on the north side of Walnut Street in the first block west of State Street. The design was by John Felt, a gentleman from Greenfield who became a noted architect after moving to Missouri. Mr. Felt designed a number of Greenfield buildings for residential, commercial, and religious purposes. Felt designed homes similar to this with sweeping verandas, steep roof lines, and the interiors were light with lovely woodwork including spindles, elaborate stairways, and high ceilings. The local gas boom brought wealth to many Hancock County residents in the 1890s. The inexpensive fuel attracted new industry and construction. People thought there would be no end to the fuel or the growth.

This particular house has undergone major change in the 100 years since its construction. One might even think this is not the same home. The truth is the house and location are the same, and if you will notice the chimney in both pictures along with the basic outline of the main floor you will come to the same conclusion. There are other buildings designed by Felt that have suffered similar fates. In some cases fire was the culprit, and in others remodeling has taken its toll. A few of Felt's buildings in Greenfield have been torn down for parking lots.

Two children play on the sidewalk on N. East Street in the late 1890s or early 1900s. The Victorian homes show some change in porches and gingerbread. The location today retains much of its flavor in spite of the intervening years. The owner's have maintained their properties well. The 100-year-old neighborhood remains a popular place to live located between Greenfield's original downtown and Hancock Memorial Hospital.

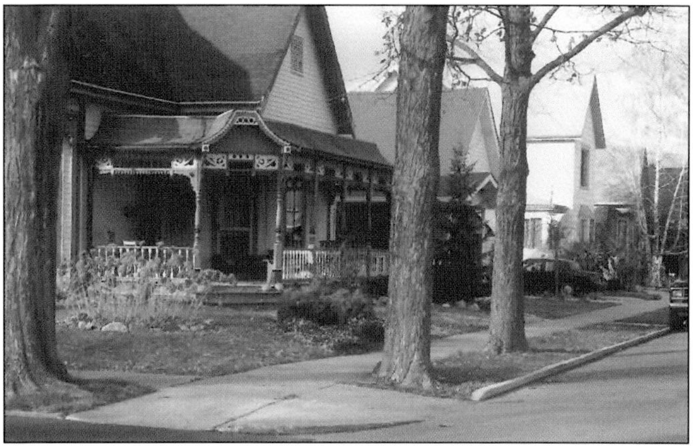

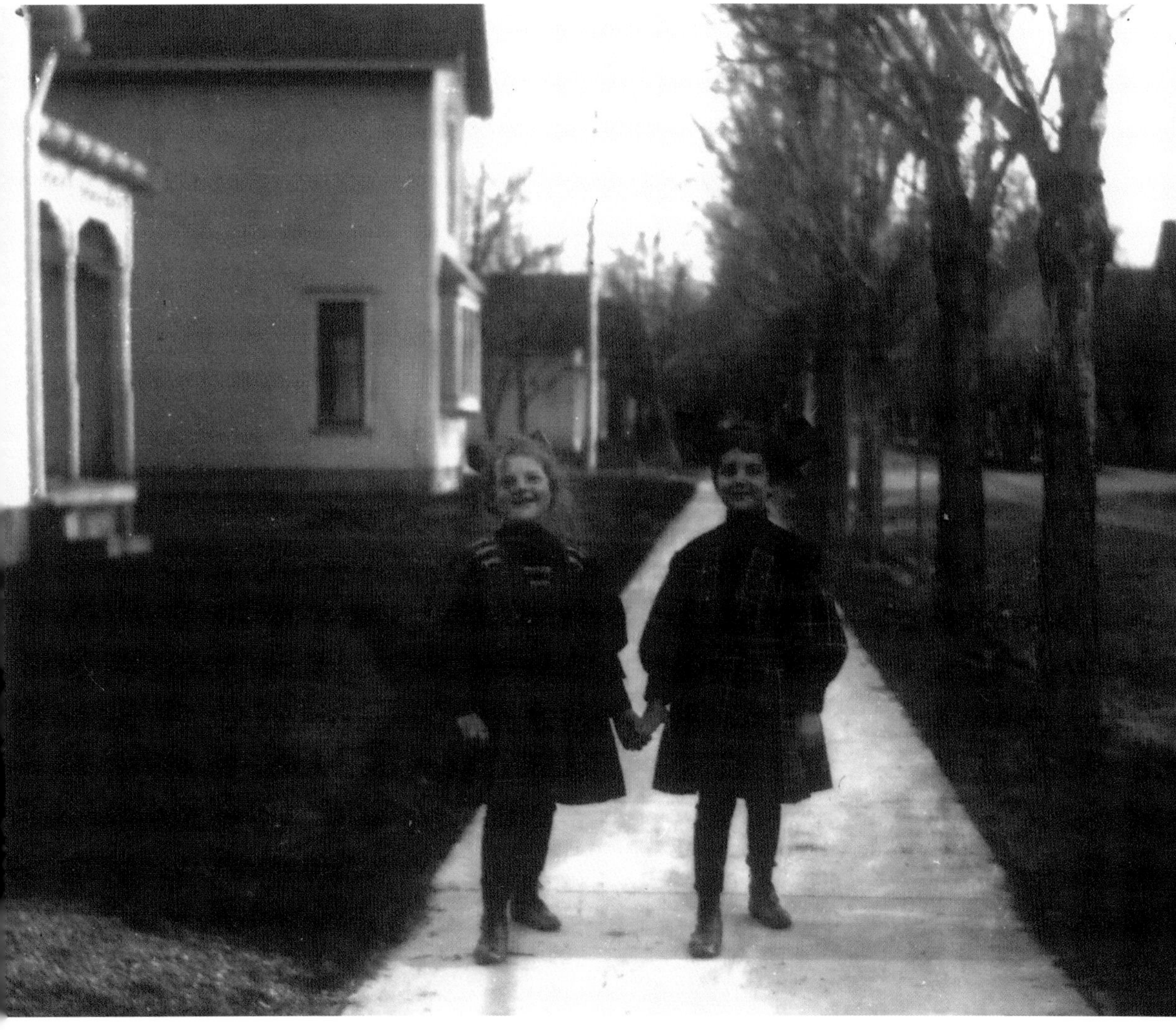

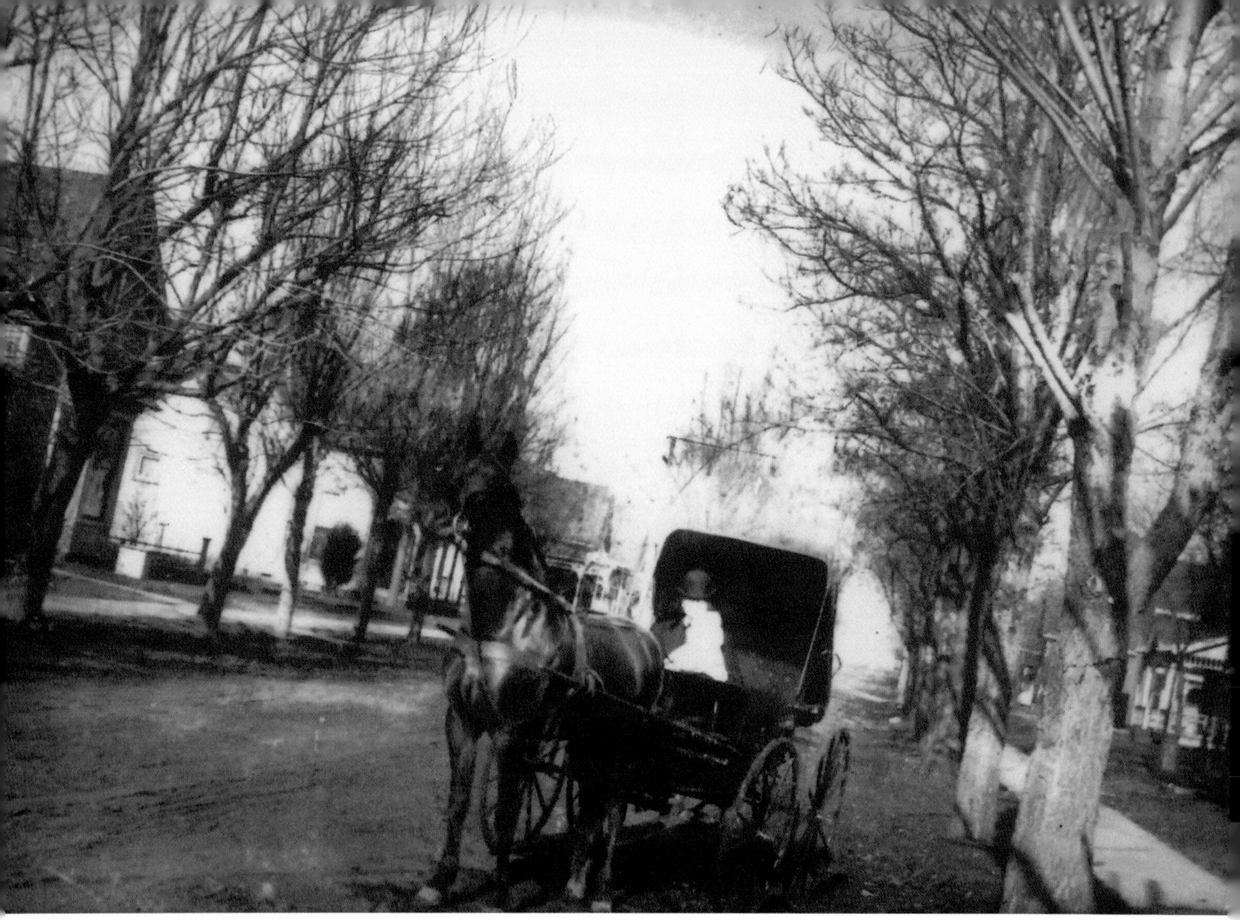

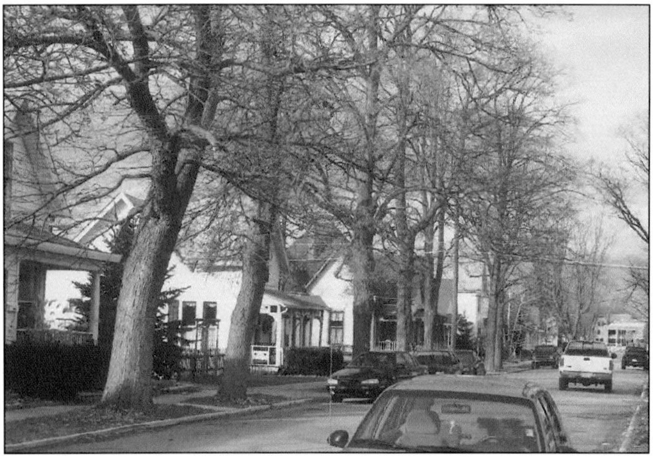

N. East Street in Greenfield in the 1890s and as seen today. The trees have grown and the homes show some change. The method of transportation is the most startling change. In the early years almost every home had a small barn on the back of the property for the horse and buggy. You might hitch up to go across town or for a Sunday ride out to "Old Aunt Mary's." If James Whitcomb Riley was in town for a visit you might want to pick him up for a ride out to Brandywine Creek. The nearly 100 years have seen the automobile and the garage replace the horse, buggy, and barn. The building at the far north end of the Street is Hancock Memorial Hospital.

This local home became the Pasco Funeral Home many years ago. Pasco's was established in 1912, and this structure housed the business until the year 2000 when Pasco's moved to new quarters on W. Main Street. Additions had been added to the original building in the late 1940s or early 1950s, and other additions came later until the style of the building was changed to incorporate the new facilities. Today the Hancock County Foundation occupies the structure after the interior was remodeled.

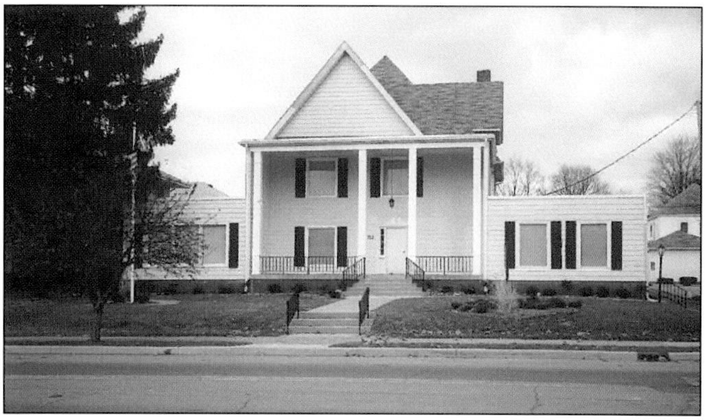

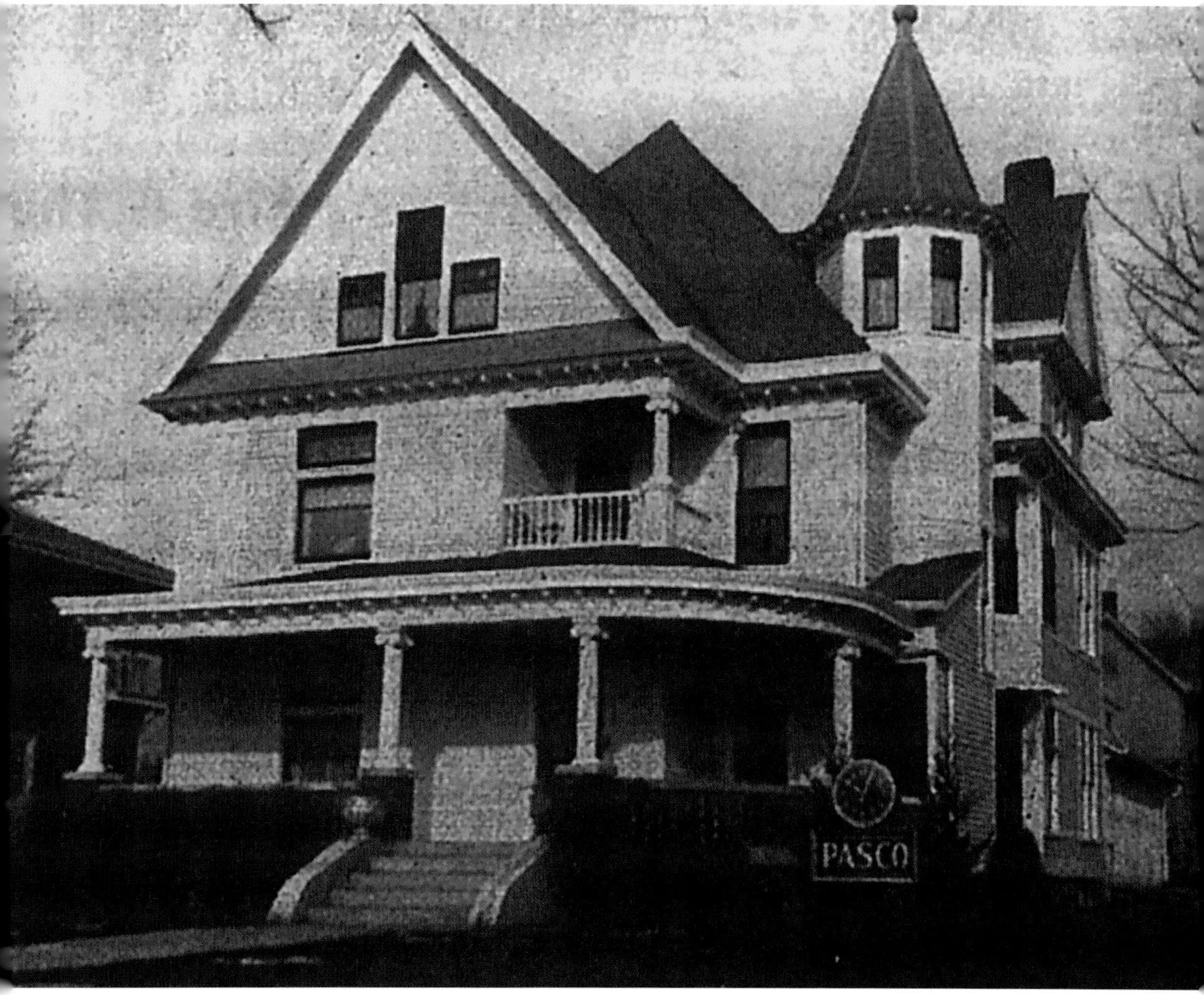

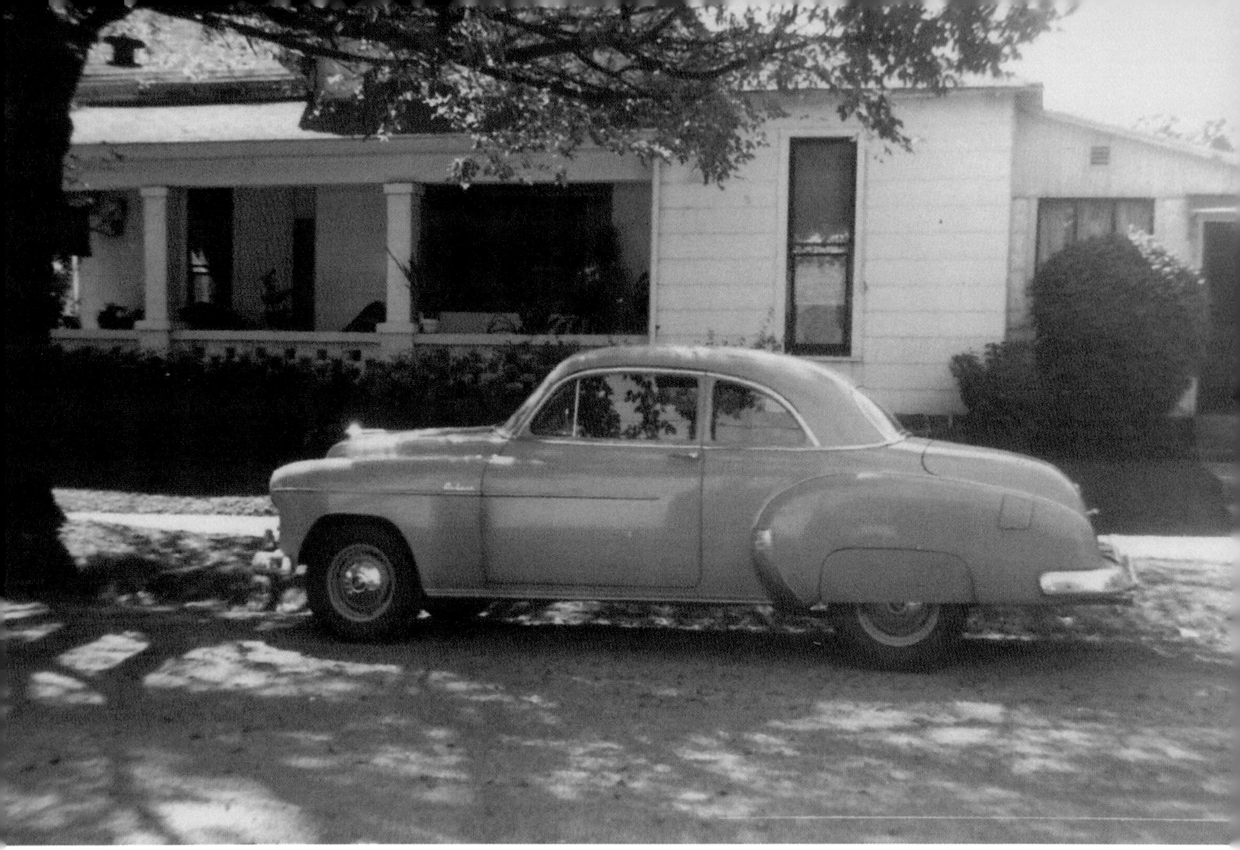

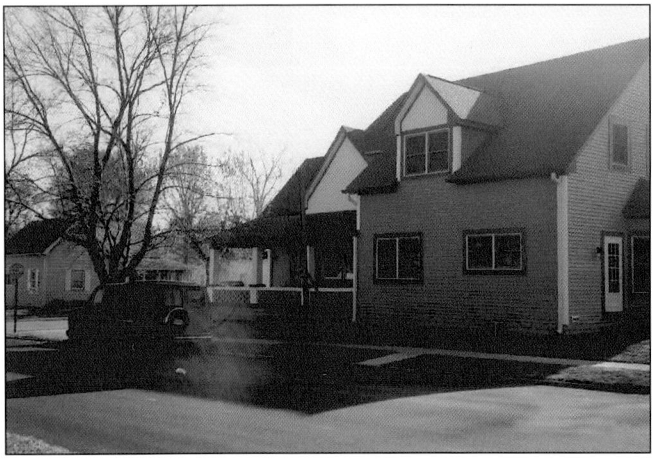

The location is 214 Baldwin when it was the home of "Skeet" Varner. The year was about 1952, based on the automobile sitting beside the house. Mr. Varner and his wife were well known residents of Greenfield.

Their home was located on the southwest corner of Grant Street and Baldwin. In the years since the early photo the house has gone through a major remodeling that was not complete in the fall of 2000. The front of the house and the porch still retain much of the character apparent in the early 1950s. The home was probably built before 1900.

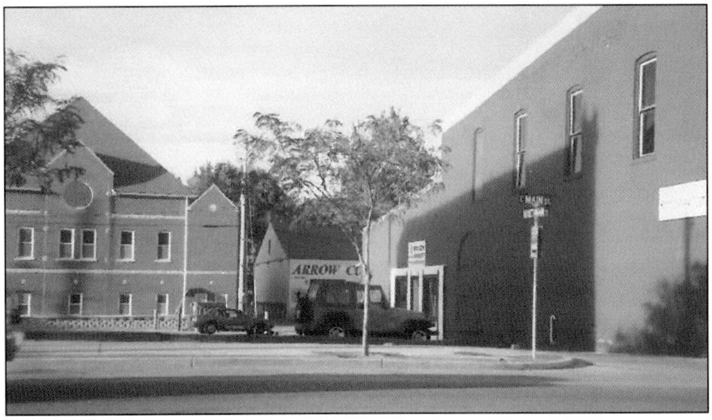

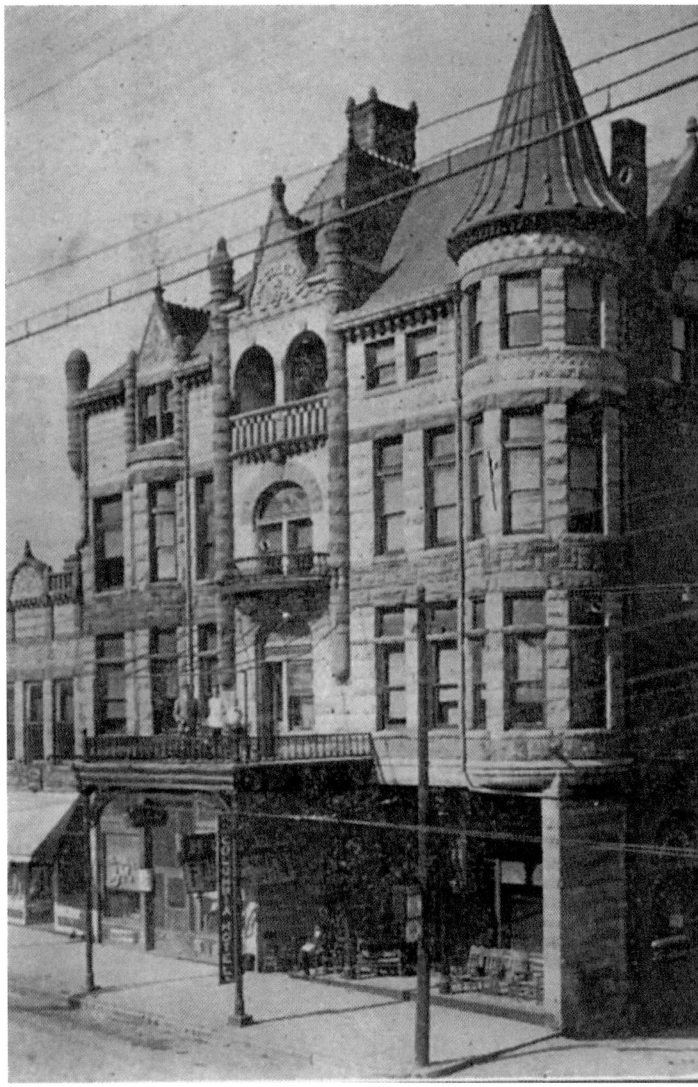

The Columbia Hotel was constructed in the 1890s with turret, balconies, and a third floor ballroom. The lobby was large with a big fireplace, and the walls were decorated in fine style of the period. The restaurant was famous for its fried chicken, and could seat a large group for dinner. The main staircase was open and impressive in the lobby. This landmark dominated Greenfield's East Main Street for half a century.

In the 1950s the hotel struggled for survival and its managers, needing someplace to dump the ashes from the large coal furnace, filled the basement with the remains. In the end no one seemed to know what to do with the building or the ashes, so the wrecking ball ended the saga of this wonderful landmark. In its place, as is so often the case in Greenfield, we have a parking lot, which is backed by a reasonably sympathetic addition to Greenfield Christian Church. Arrow Collision occupies the former Sears Auto Store building directly east of the church on North Street.

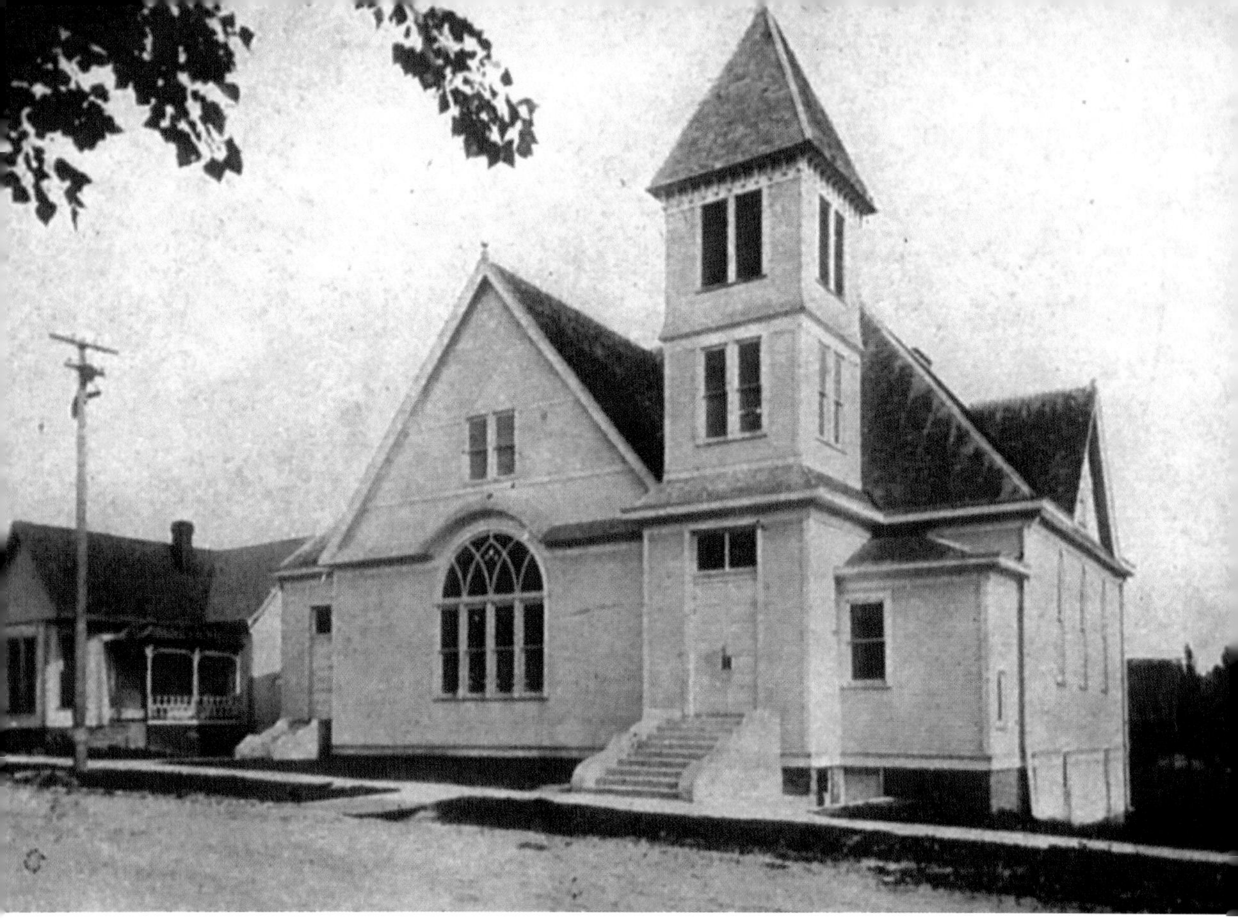

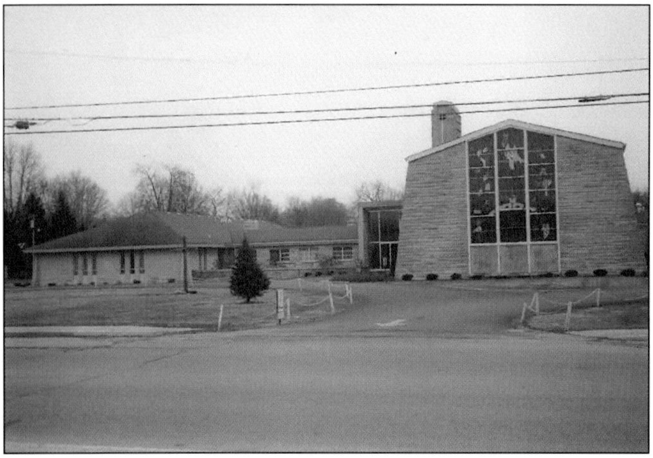

The South Street Methodist Church was organized in 1885 at the Presbyterian Church in Greenfield. This building stood on the north side of South Street where the present Hancock County Jail is located. The Sunday school was organized in 1885, and Lawrence Wood was elected its superintendent in 1898. Years later, the church saw a need for change that led them to search for a new site. The Park Avenue area had developed nicely after the construction of the Greenfield Junior High in 1952, and other buildings in the area including the Nazarene Church and the Friends Church. The location seemed like a natural choice and land was available. South Street Methodist was renamed Trinity Park Methodist when the move took place.

Bradley Methodist Church was built in 1907, and is in similar style shared by the 1895 former Masonic Hall and the Hancock County Court House. The style is a variation of Richardson Romanesque. The church is a massive structure with interior fittings that are largely still in place. The stained glass windows are a wonderful works of art especially the large windows, which carry a panel that pictures Jesus, being truly outstanding. Bradley Methodist Church still looks much as it did when constructed, with the exception being the bell tower. Some say that the original was removed because it was exerting too much pressure on the building below and causing structural problems. The building is still very pleasing to the eye.

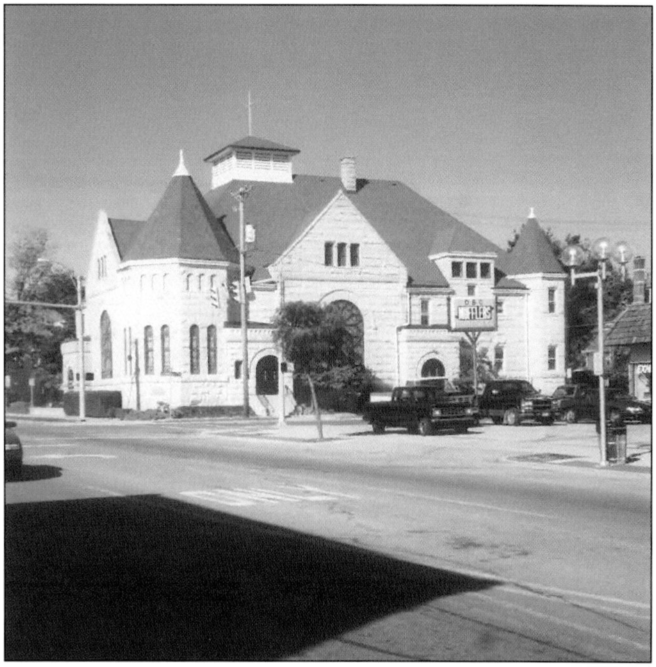

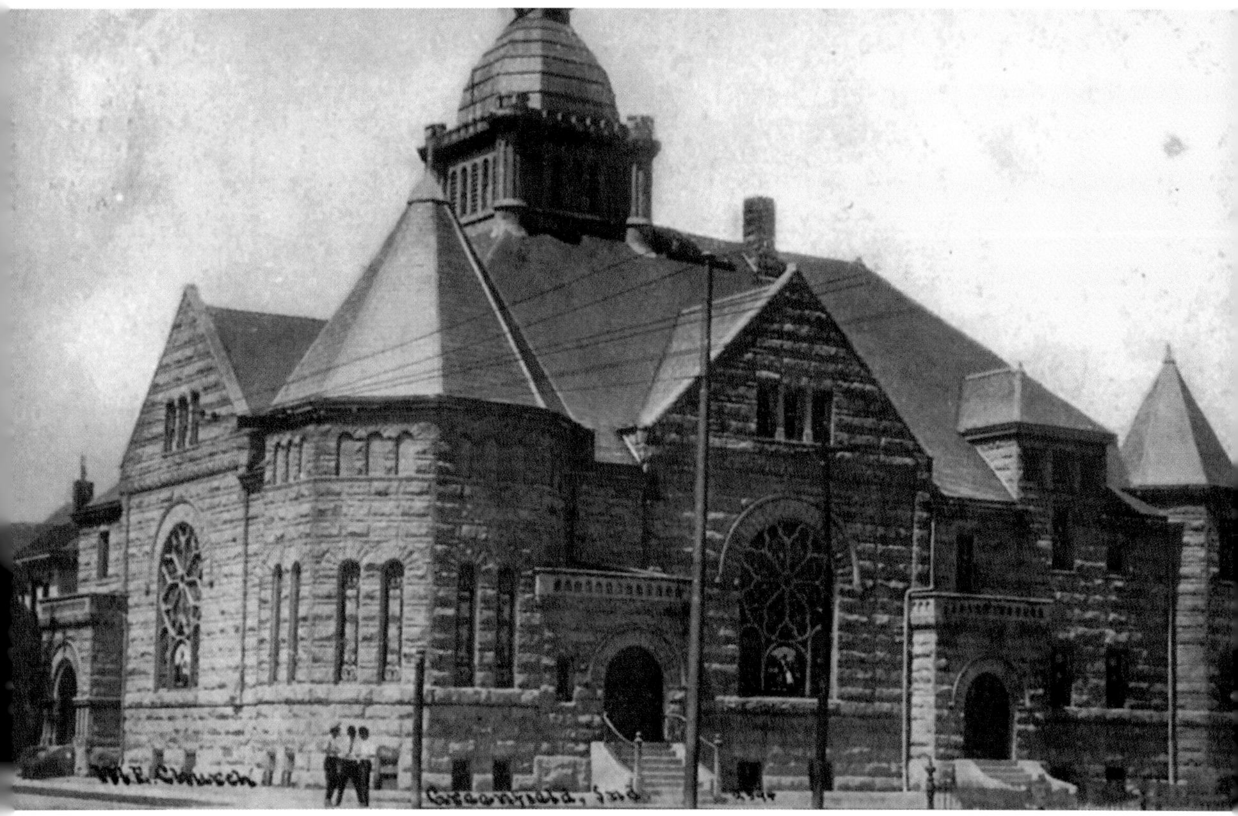

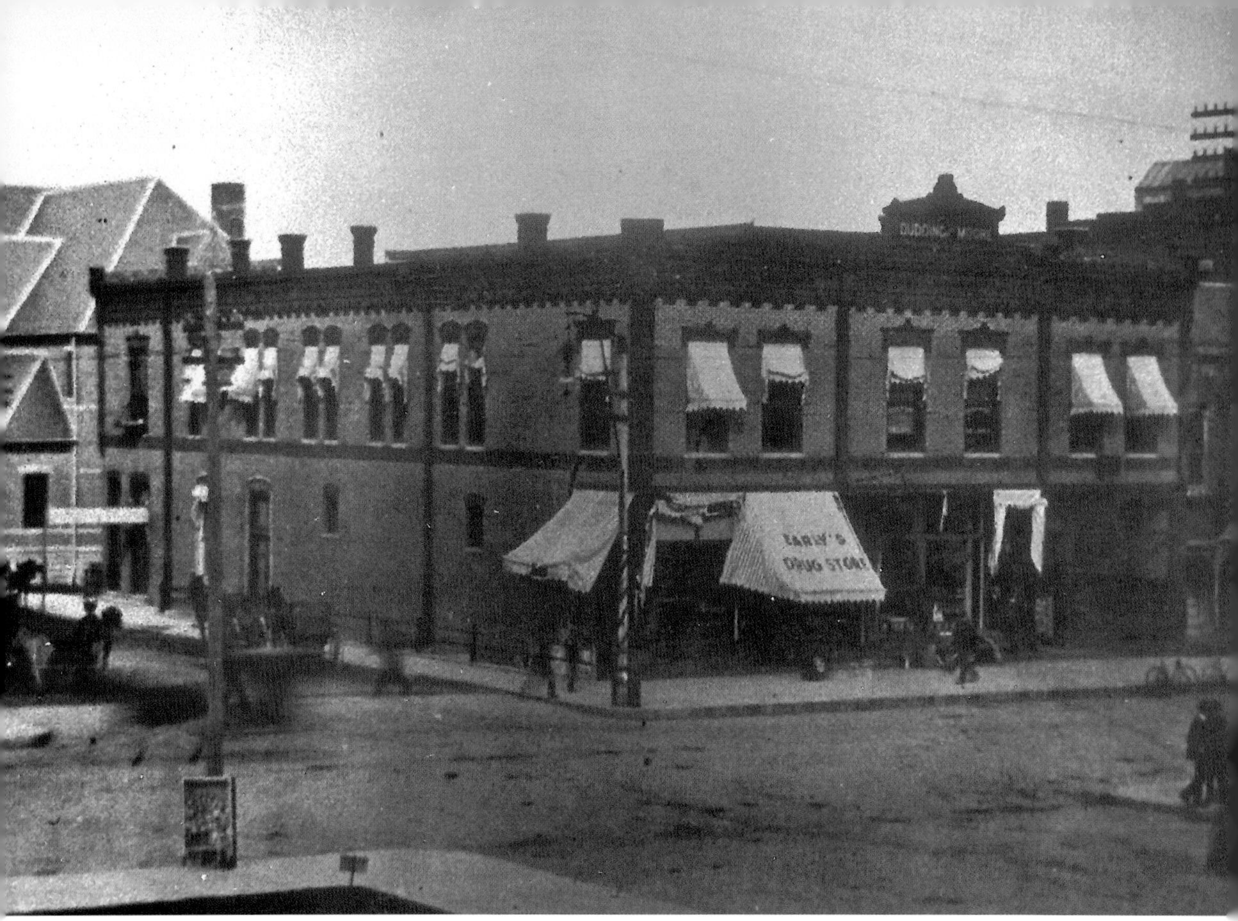

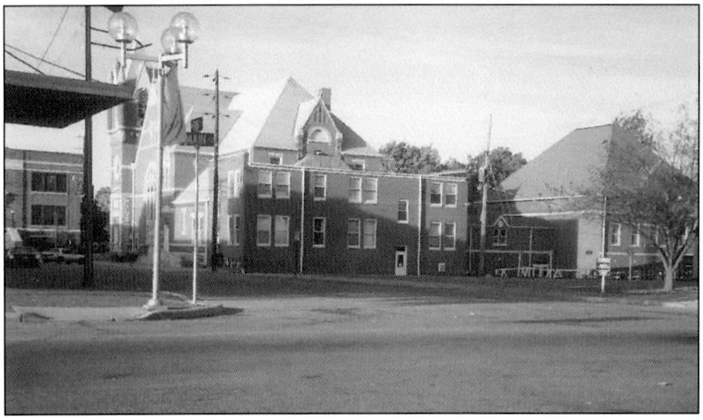

This building stood at the northeast corner of American Legion Place and E. Main Street in Greenfield.

The structure was built in the 1890s and housed a number of businesses over the years. When this picture was taken in the early-20th century, Early drugs was located here. Later, the local Sears Roebuck occupied the building during the 1940s to 1960s. Jay Wilfong operated a music shop here for several years after Sears vacated the building. The building was purchased by the Christian Church and torn down for parking in the late 1960s or early 70s. The church paved the lot and then planted a tree in an attempt to improve the corner. The rear of the church can be seen in the photo and an addition to the original building is in the area to the back of the lot. This addition was added to the church in the 1940s. A much later addition can be seen to the right of the picture.

The cornerstone laying for Bradley Methodist Church took place 22 May 1902. In the background can be seen the Banks House, the old St. Michael's Roman Catholic with an early bell tower and barns that no longer stand. The earlier church stood on the southeast corner of State Street and South Street. That building became a part of Mitchell Printing Co. in the years that followed. There was considerable activity in church building around 1894 to 1910 in Hancock County. Just one block south of Bradley Methodist, the Presbyterians built a new church to replace an earlier structure on their site. The United Brethren constructed a church at the southwest corner of Lincoln and Swope Streets in 1898. There is much church construction in the area to this day, and many churches have been founded in the last 20 years. Park Chapel Christian Church is an excellent example, and its addition started in 2000 is shown in is advanced stage in the other photograph.

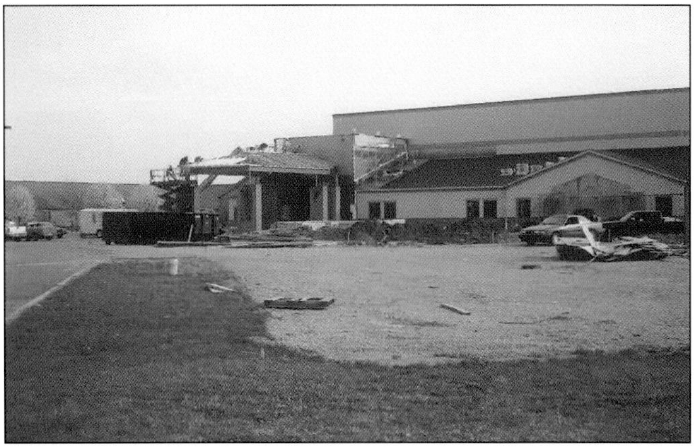

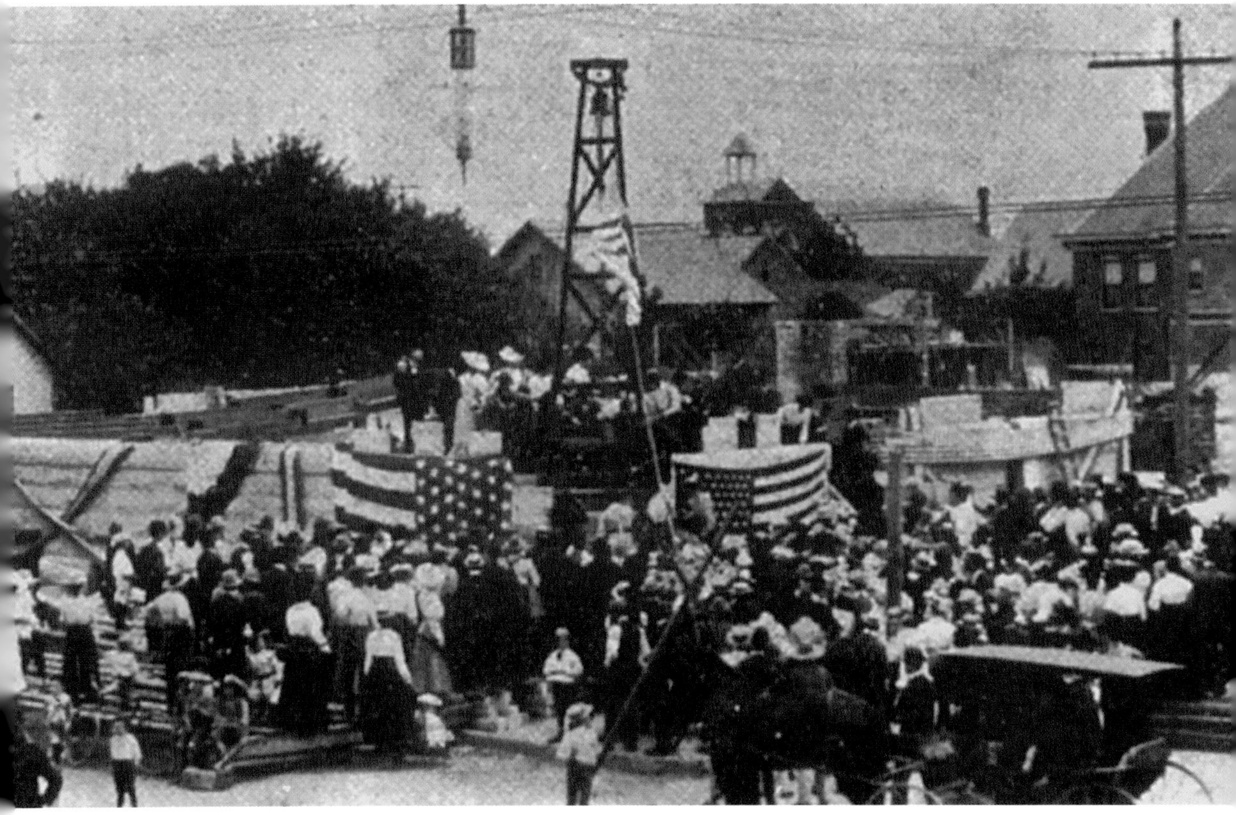

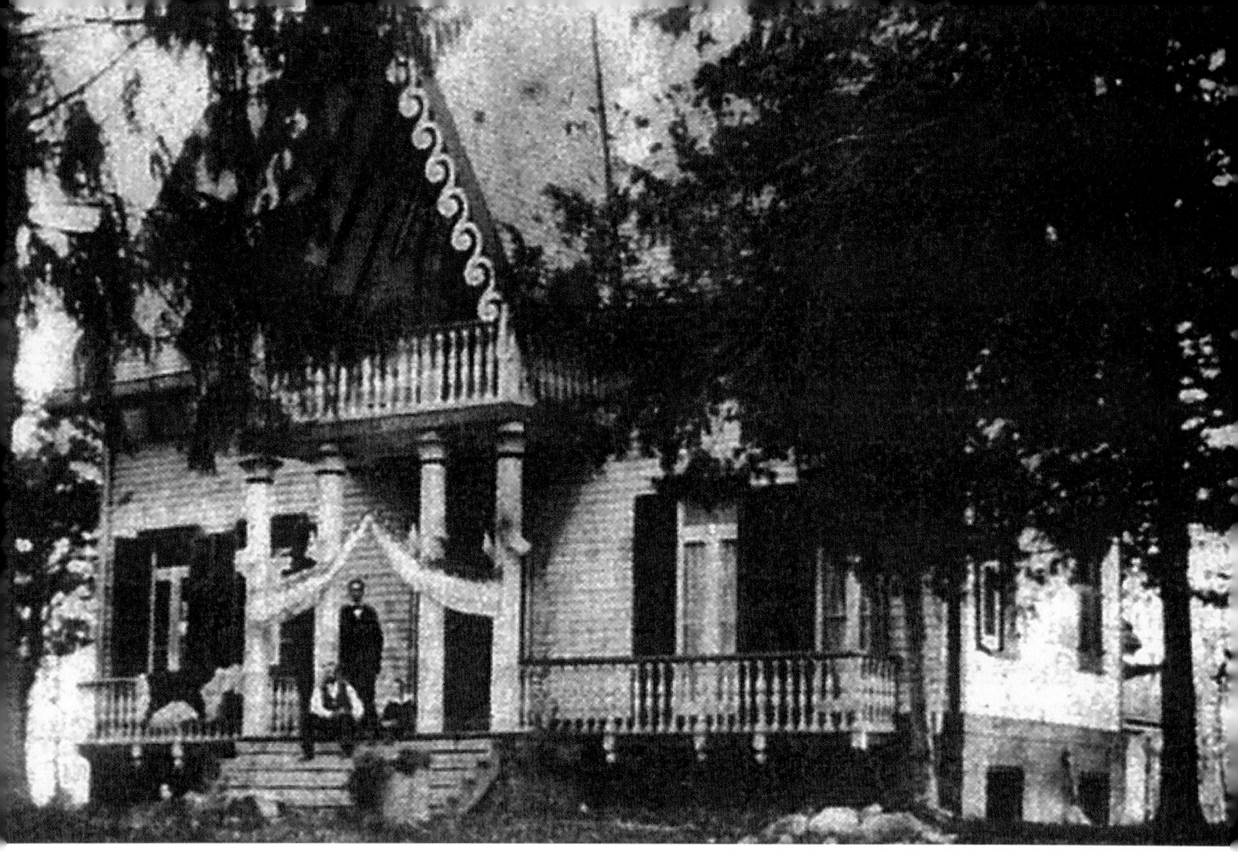

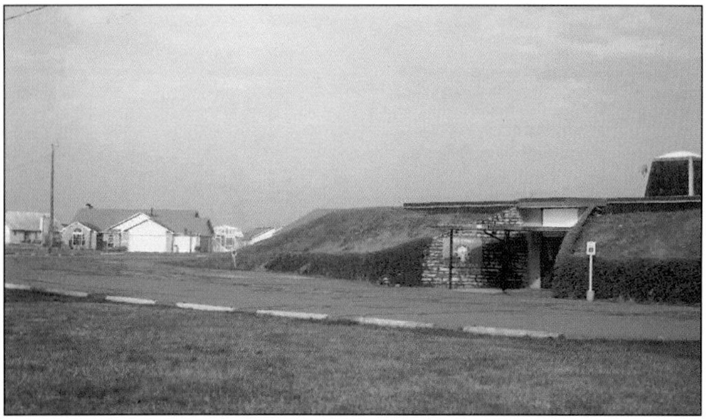

This early home sat back off the road on State Highway 9 just south of Greenfield. The structure likely dated as early as the 1845 to 1855 period, and certainly was constructed before the Civil War. The basic lines of the house and the unusual treatment of the second story of the front porch give the house an almost modern flair if it were not for the "gingerbread" designs that outline those areas. The home sat empty for years, and many talked of it being haunted. The reason that people singled it out may in part relate to the unusual design. For years a business operated out of a block building that was located in front of the site of the old house. The Elks Lodge had been located in the middle of the block in back of the courthouse and room did not seem available for its expansion, so the Elks thought moving to the edge of town was a good idea. They purchased land for a new hall and located their new structure just in front of the block structure already on the site. The design leads many to refer to it as a bomb shelter.

Riley Park Swimming Pool opened to children and adults in the early 1930s. The facility was considered "state of the art" at the time. Year after year the pool served the community with a safe place to swim. It was situated in the low area directly south of the Shelter House. The pool was raised above ground, and the dressing rooms and other facilities were under the pool deck. By the 1970s, the maintenance of the building and the pool became more difficult, and finally closing the pool seemed the only answer.

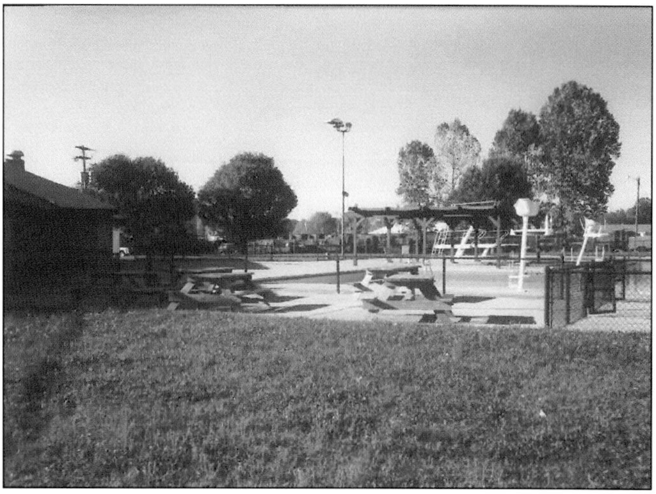

Plans for a new pool were developed and it was planned for the area northeast of the Shelter House. This pool would set in the ground with dressing rooms and other facilities placed in a brick structure to one side of the pool. The result of the construction has pleased many people since the day it was opened in 1981.

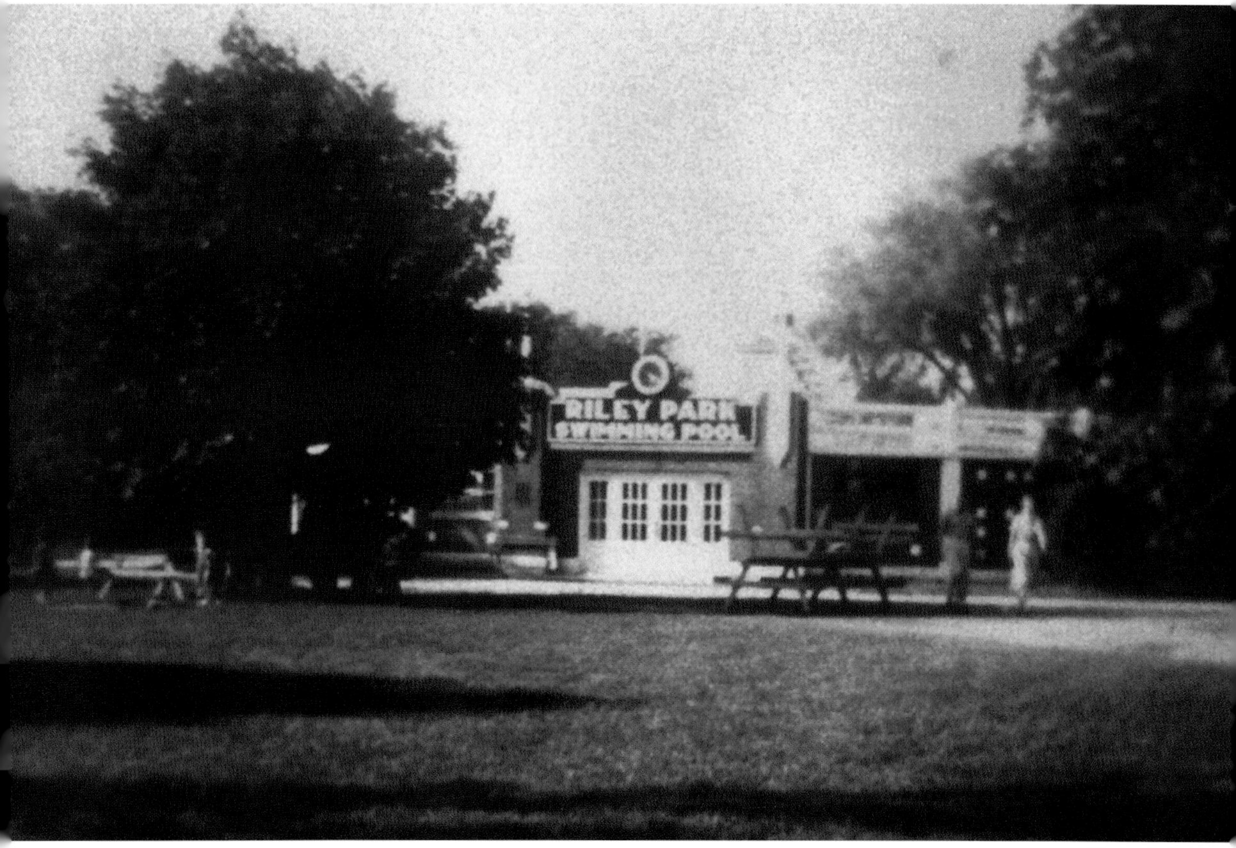

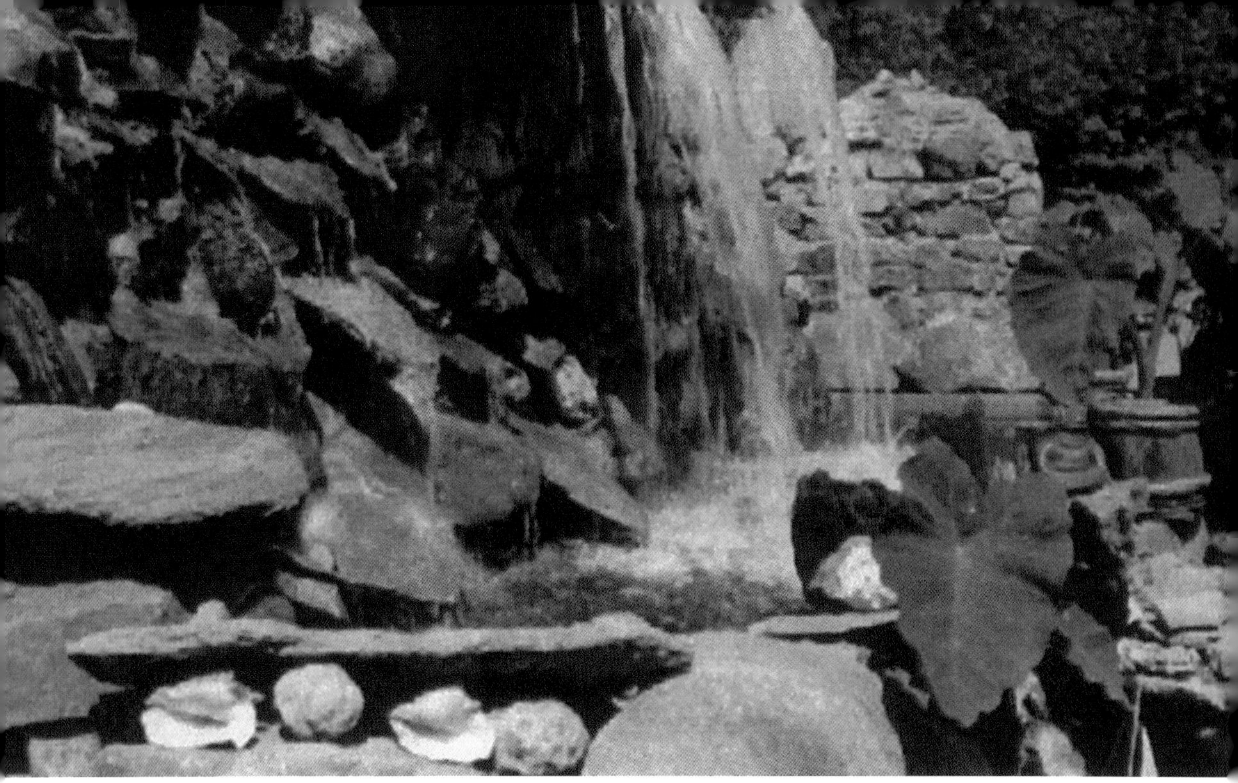

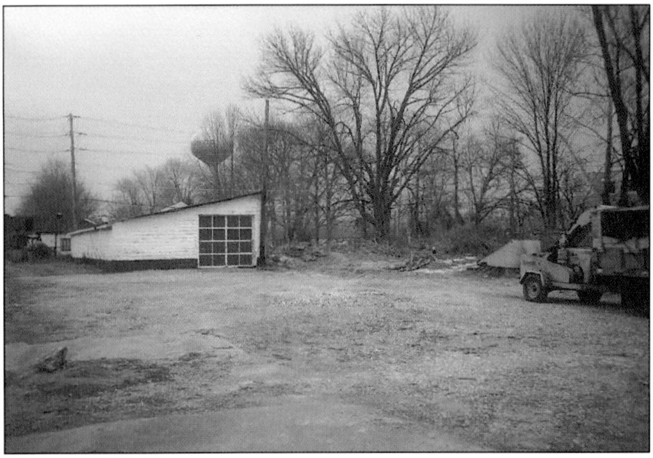

On the north edge of Greenfield a local couple built a fantastic rock garden with waterfalls and exotic plant life for their enjoyment. L.E. Harker began building the Rock Garden in the 1920s. He also raised peonies to the north of his home on N. State Street in a field that covered most of the area between his house and McKenzie Road. The flowers also covered much of present day Holiday Park. In the spring of 2001, the new owner preferred parking instead of the Rock Garden so earth-moving equipment was used to clear the area. The Harker home was to be the new location of the Head Shop (barber and beauty shop).

Greenfield Ice Cream was sold from this building on S. Pennsylvania for many years. The picture is *c.* 1958 or slightly later. When people came to town from far and wide they often talked of stopping for some delicious ice cream. The building is now long gone and in its place is Mad Dog's Pizza, and the location is just across the street from Newcomer's Lumber. Mad Dog has good pizza, but the structure does not have the class of the earlier structure.

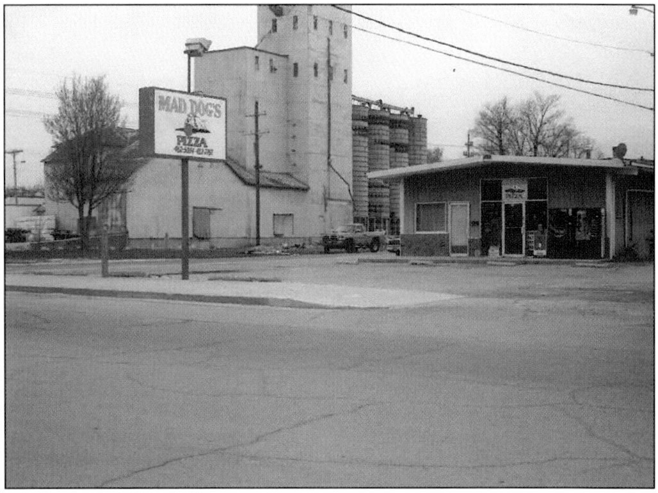

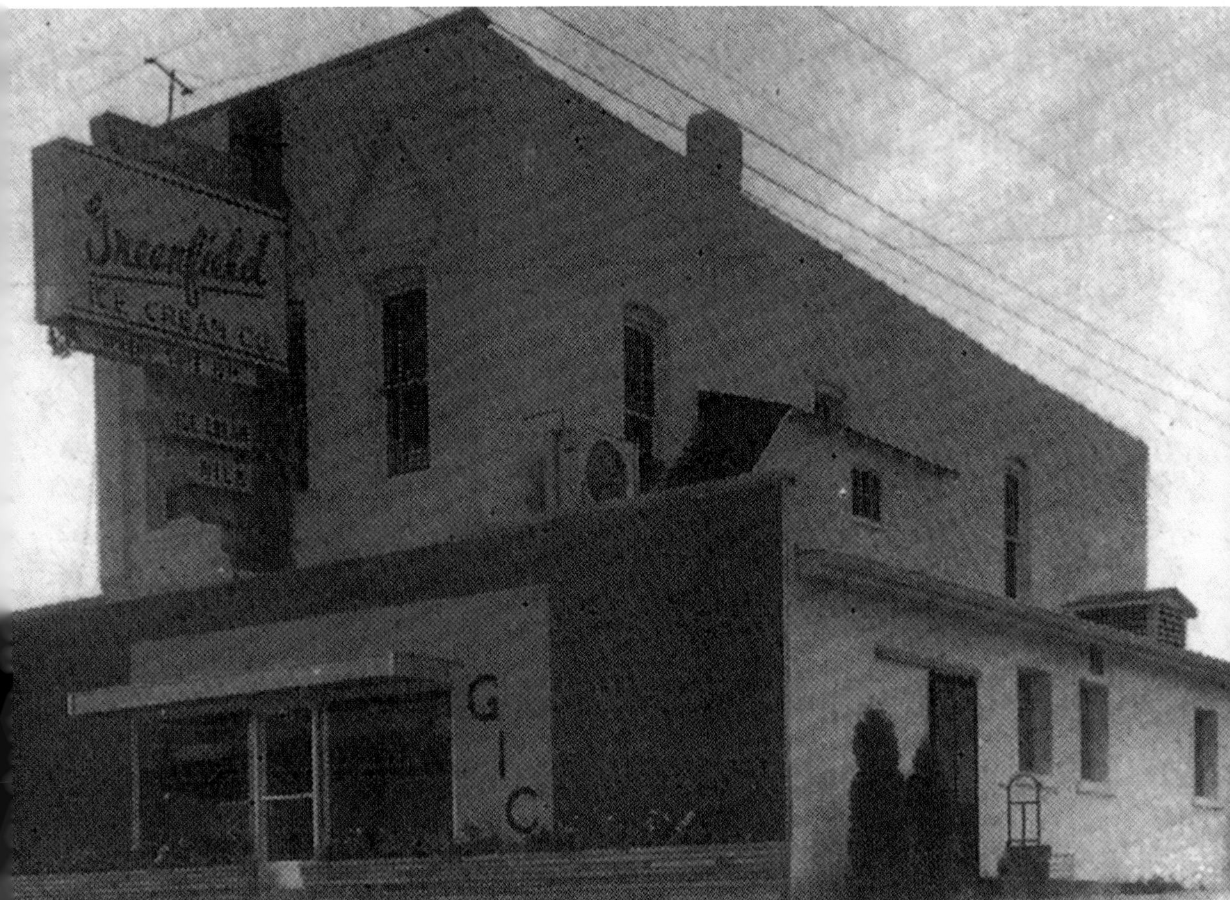

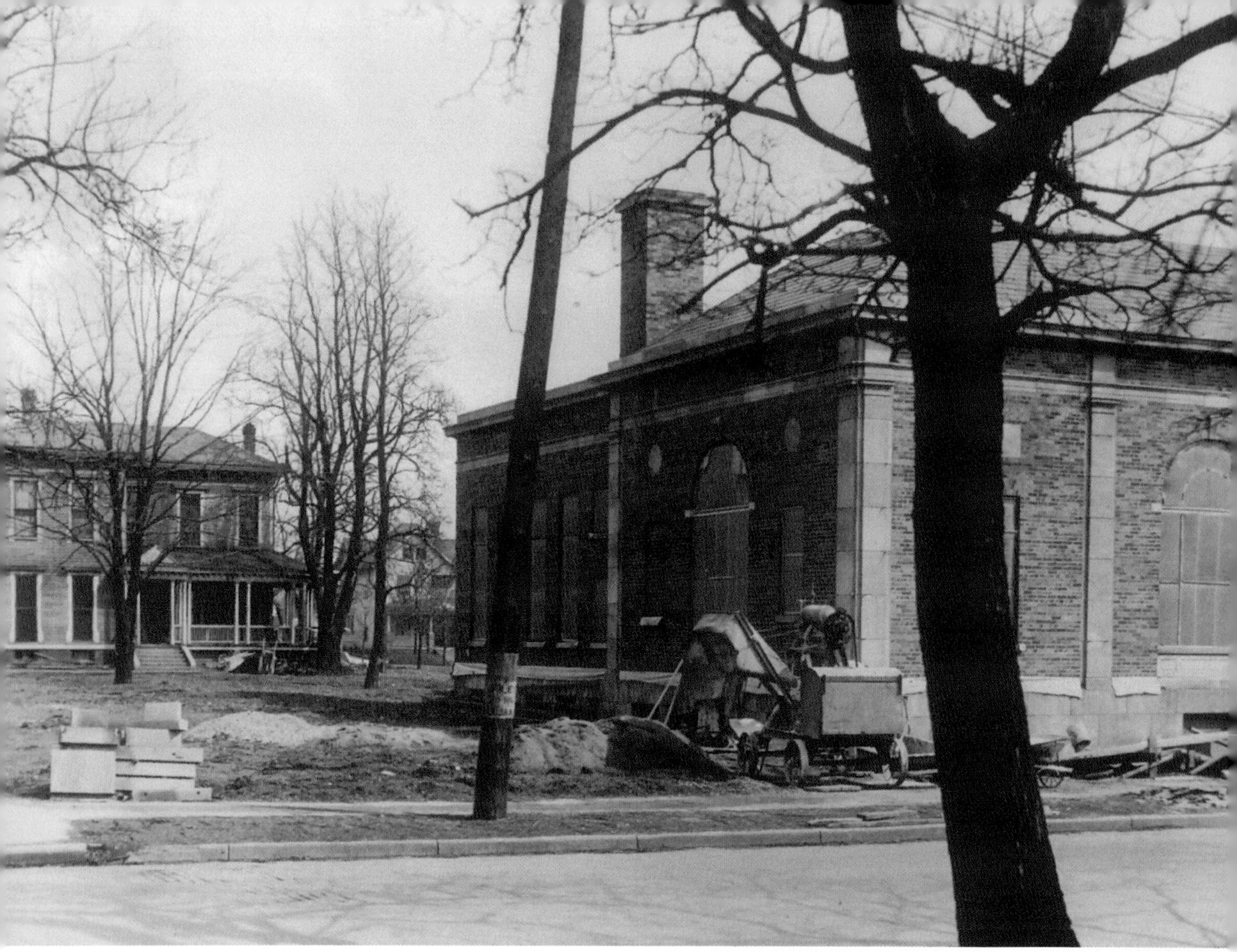

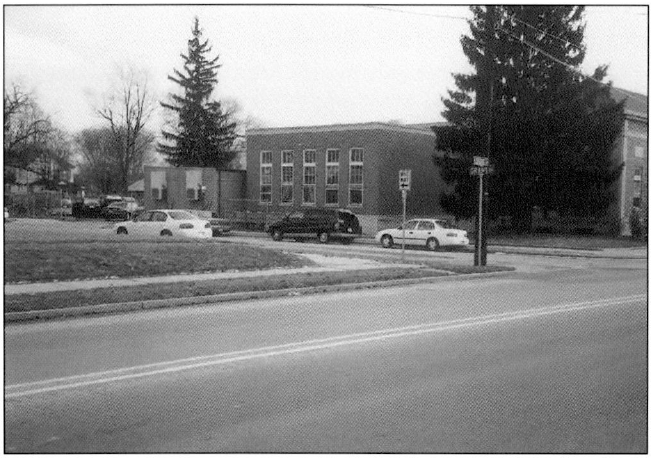

The home of John Ward and Mary Walker was at the rear of a block where the Greenfield Post Office and Central Park now stand. Pott's Ditch ran across part of the front of the property. The design for a new post office necessitated tearing down the old house in 1931. This post office remains in use today. (Photo Courtesy of Tom Williams.)

The 1874 Hancock County Jail with the courthouse heating plant behind the building is seen here. The D.H. Goble Printing building is shown to the left. The portion of the Goble building showing the slope of a gable roof is in truth the original building of the Greenfield Christian Church. The old heating plant and the Goble building have both been torn down. The wall exposed from the church is still shared with the old Why Not Theater, later known as the Riley Theater building. A modern addition has been added to the jail. The earlier of the photographs was taken in November of 1967. The jail is now the prosecutor's office, and a new jail has been built behind it facing Main Street.

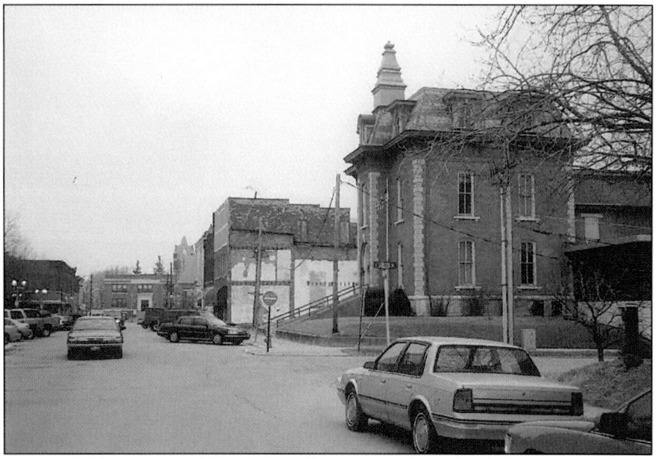

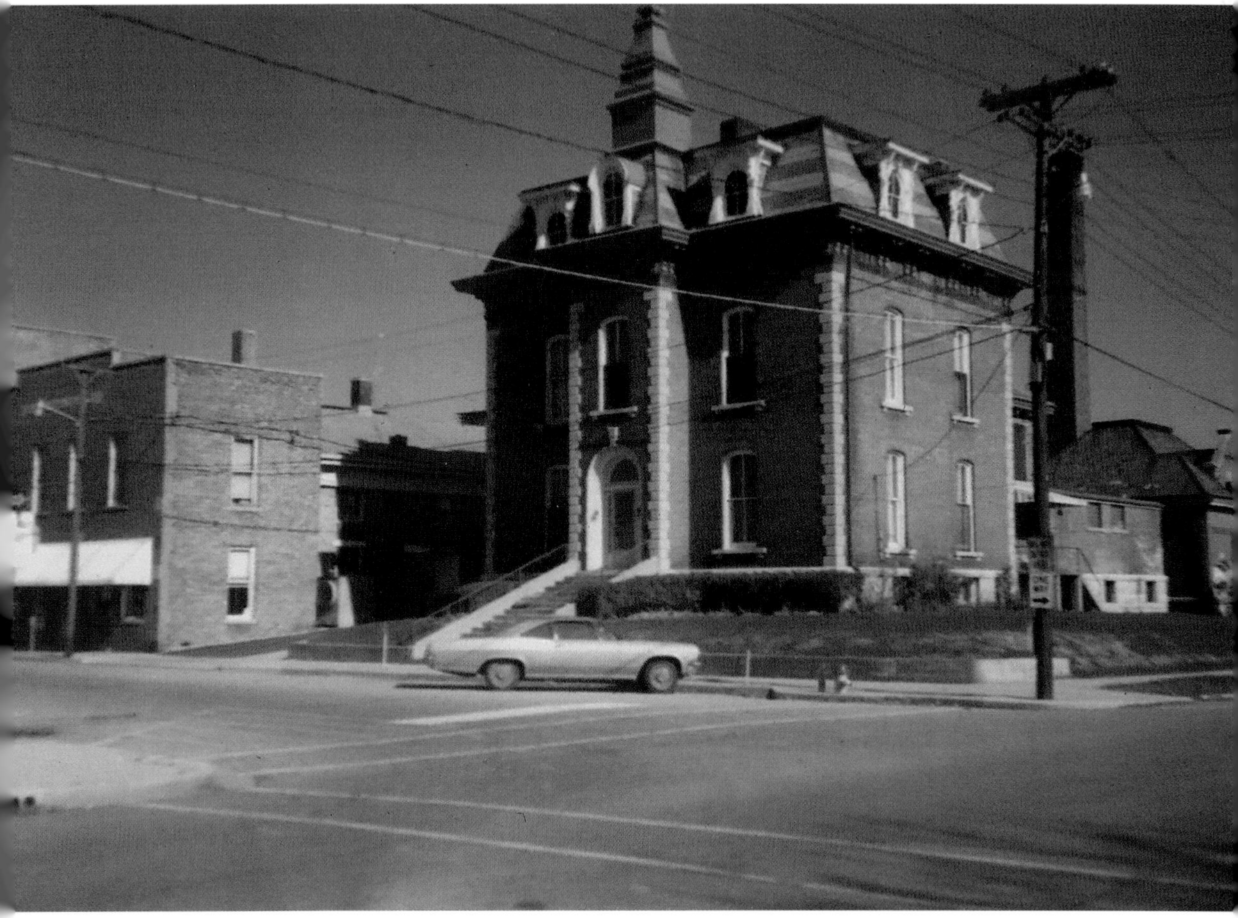

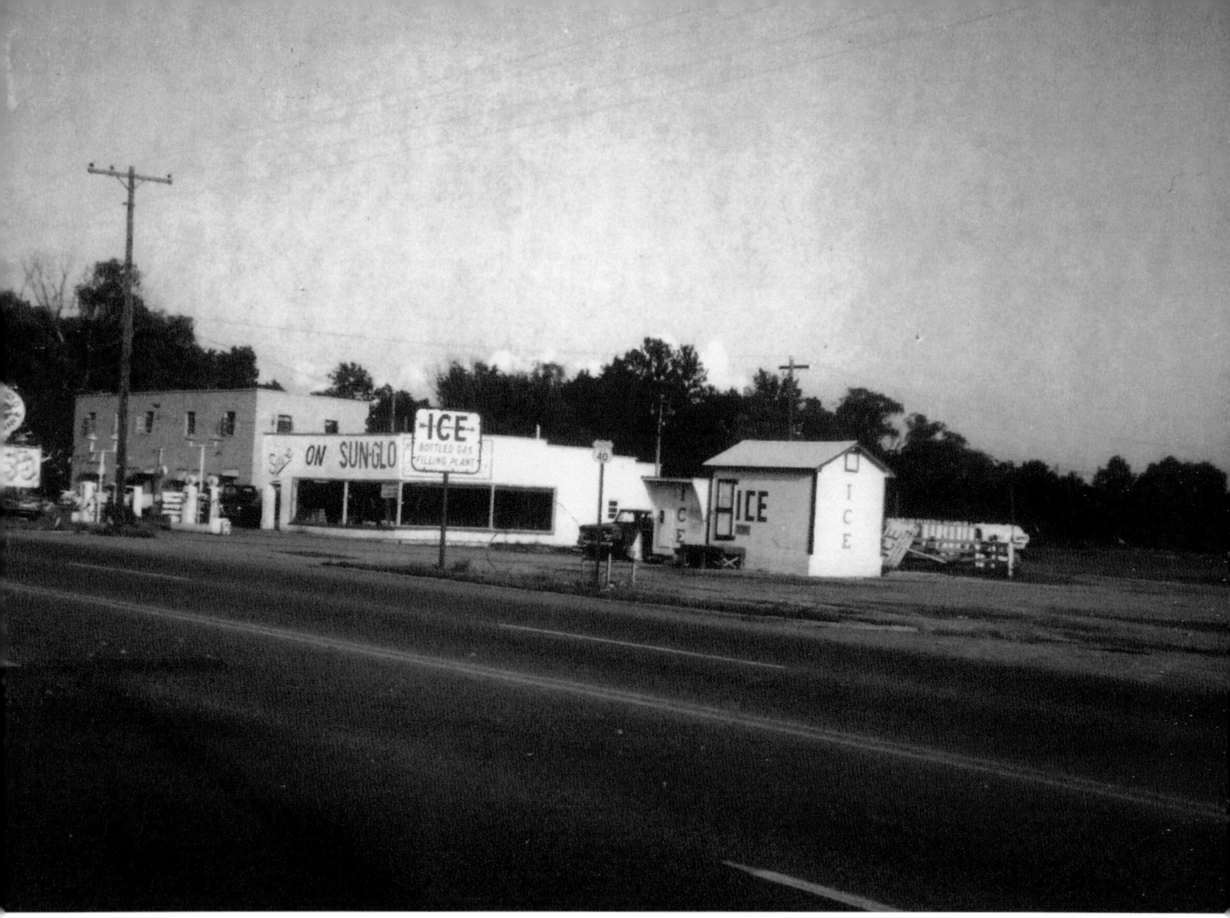

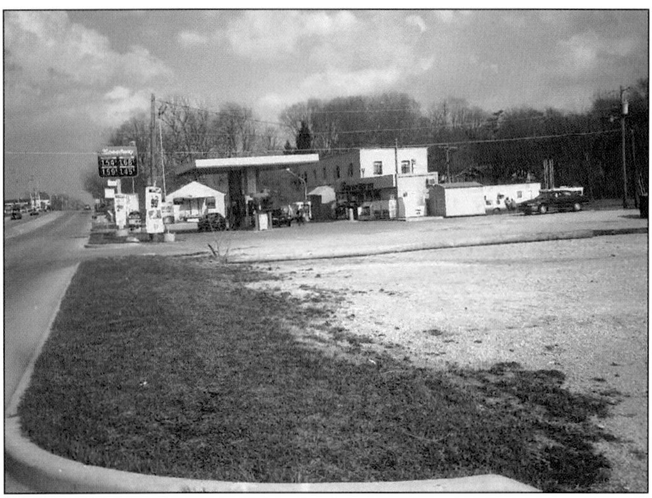

The Speedway Station across U.S. 40 from Riley Park now occupies this site. Jim Baker's father Burt Baker owned the station for several years in the 1960s to the 1970s. The original picture dates *c.* 1960s, when the George Wilfong's Sunglo brand was used at this location for gas and oil. The building housed a Studebaker dealership for many years until that brand of automobile was no longer manufactured. When major interstate traffic was diverted from the area the station became a less desirable location for awhile. The nearby park continues to add to the business traffic to this day, as does the increased flow of local traffic on U.S. 40.

Greenfield Granite has provided monuments for the local area for many years. There work graces most, if not all, of the cemeteries in Hancock County that have been active the last 50 years. The early photo is *c.* 1965, and gives testimony that the northeast corner of Franklin Street and Main Street has not changed much in the intervening years.

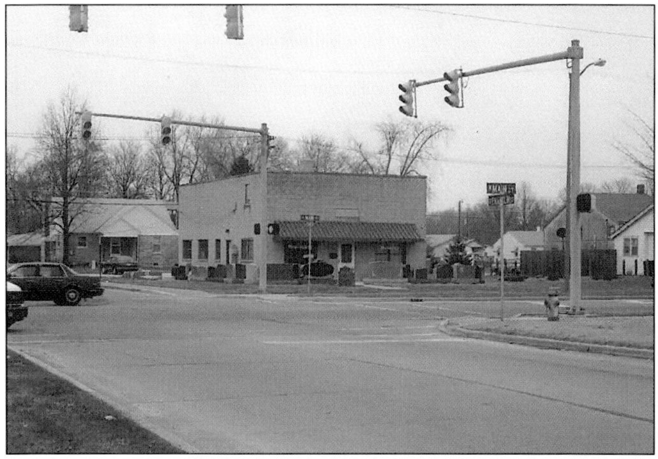

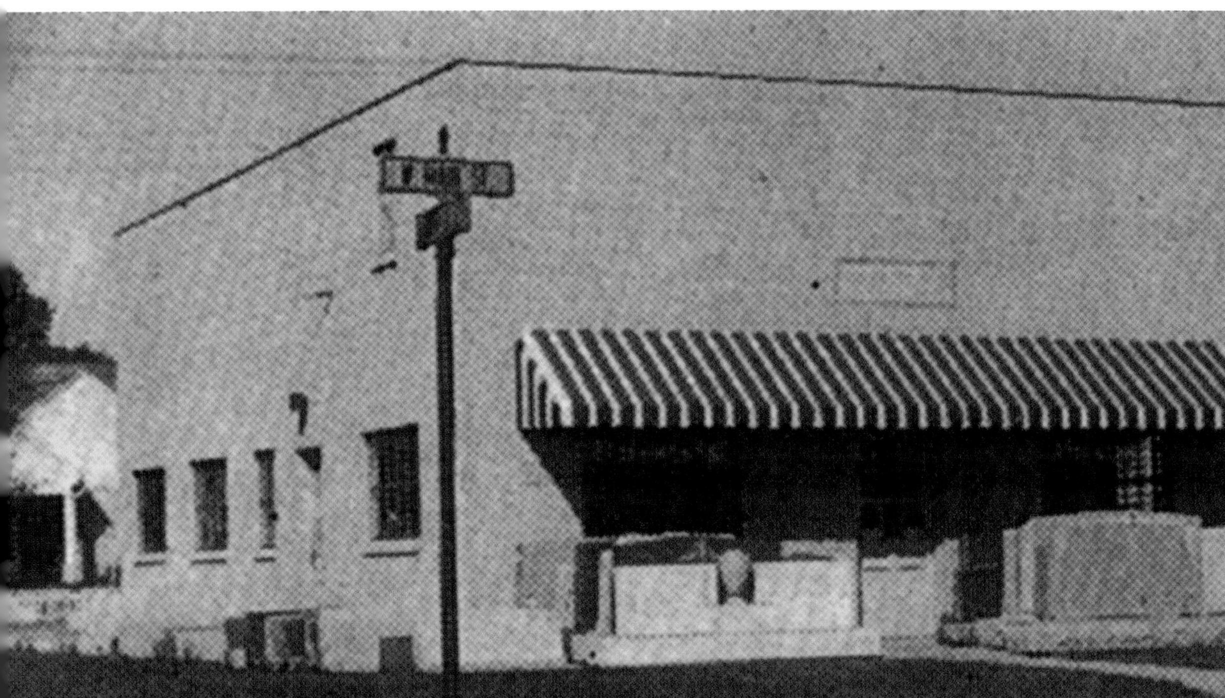

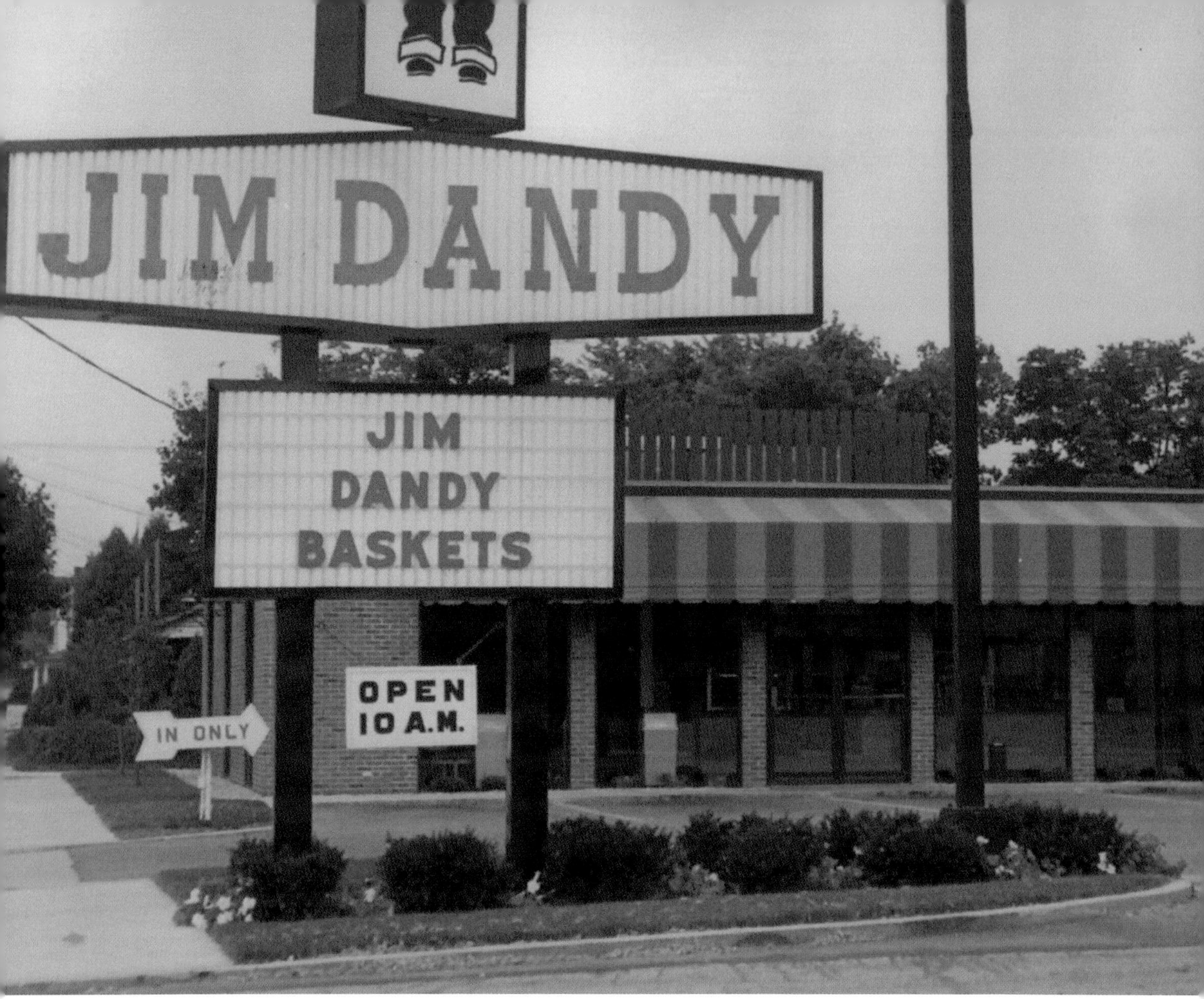

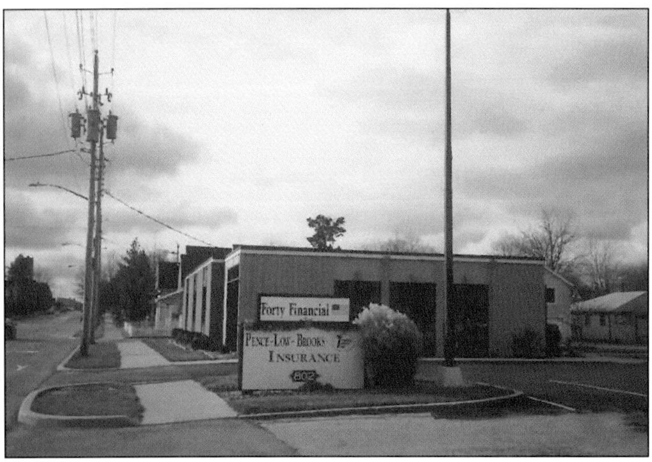

The former Jim Dandy Restaurant next to the Riley Park entrance built in 1969 was later replaced by a new restaurant on the north side. The "old" building became the home of a local insurance agency founded by Lawrence Wood in the early 1900s. The current name is reflected in the sign Pence-Low-Brooks. The facility was remodeled to modern office space, and the exterior was toned down to reflect more conservative business needs in the 1990s. The location on US 40 next to Riley Park remains through the years an excellent commercial location.

The picture dates from the late 1940s or early 50s. The site was home to a number of businesses over the years including Shadley Implement, a Kaiser Frazier dealership. Located on E. Main Street next door to Riley Park, the structure was torn down to make way for the Riley Park Drive-In. During the 1950s and 60s, it was one of the restaurants that catered to people in their late 10s and early 20s. The business became a "hot" meeting place for the younger set who were cruising town nightly. They usually drove a route from this drive-in to Crider's on the west of Greenfield and back making a detour through the Dairy Queen parking lot. The Riley Park operation became a part of a chain operated by Jim Dandy Restaurants and was succeeded by a large indoor restaurant on the lot next door to the west in the fall of 1969. Years later the business moved to the north end of town taking a new site on McKenzie Road on the south edge of the Marsh Plaza.

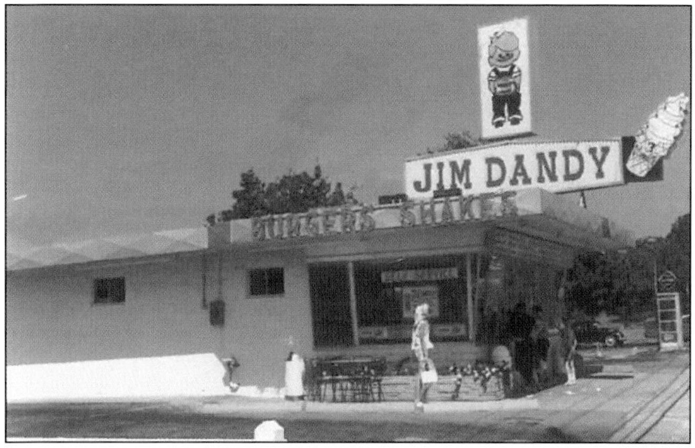

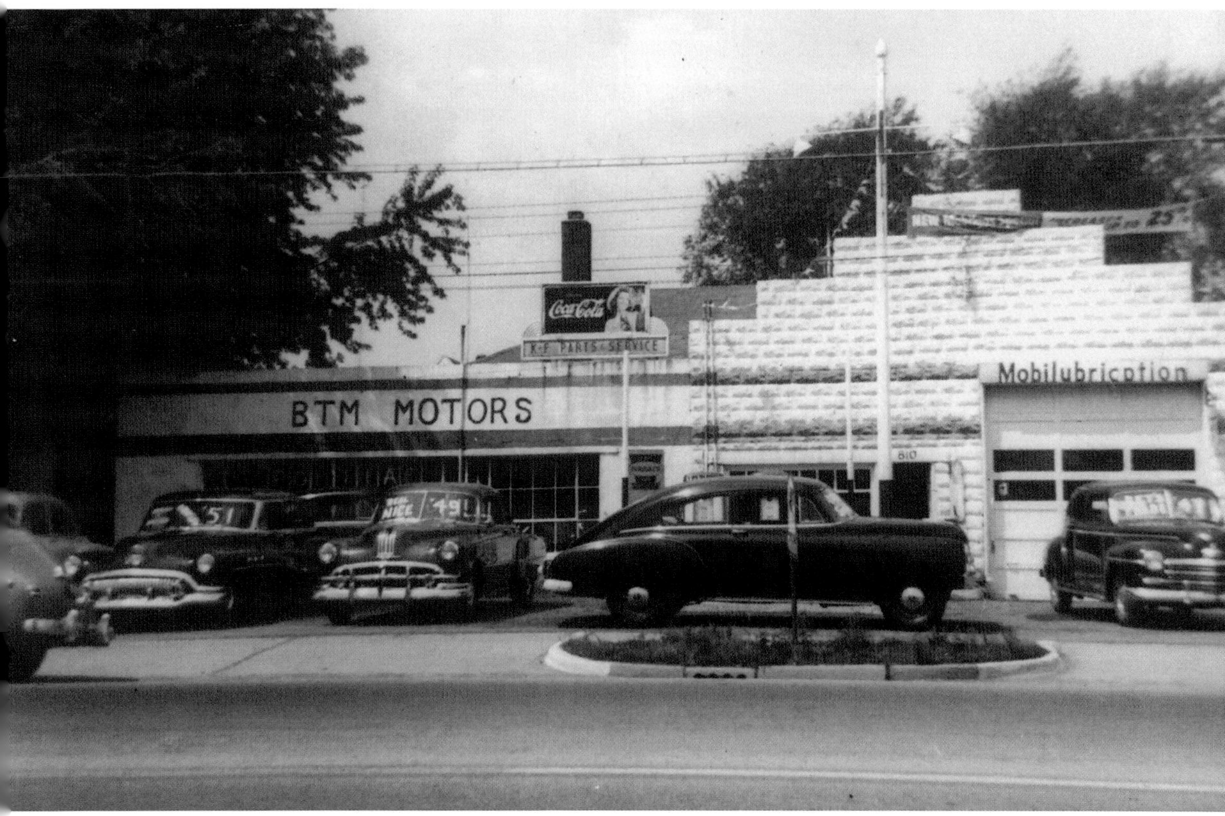

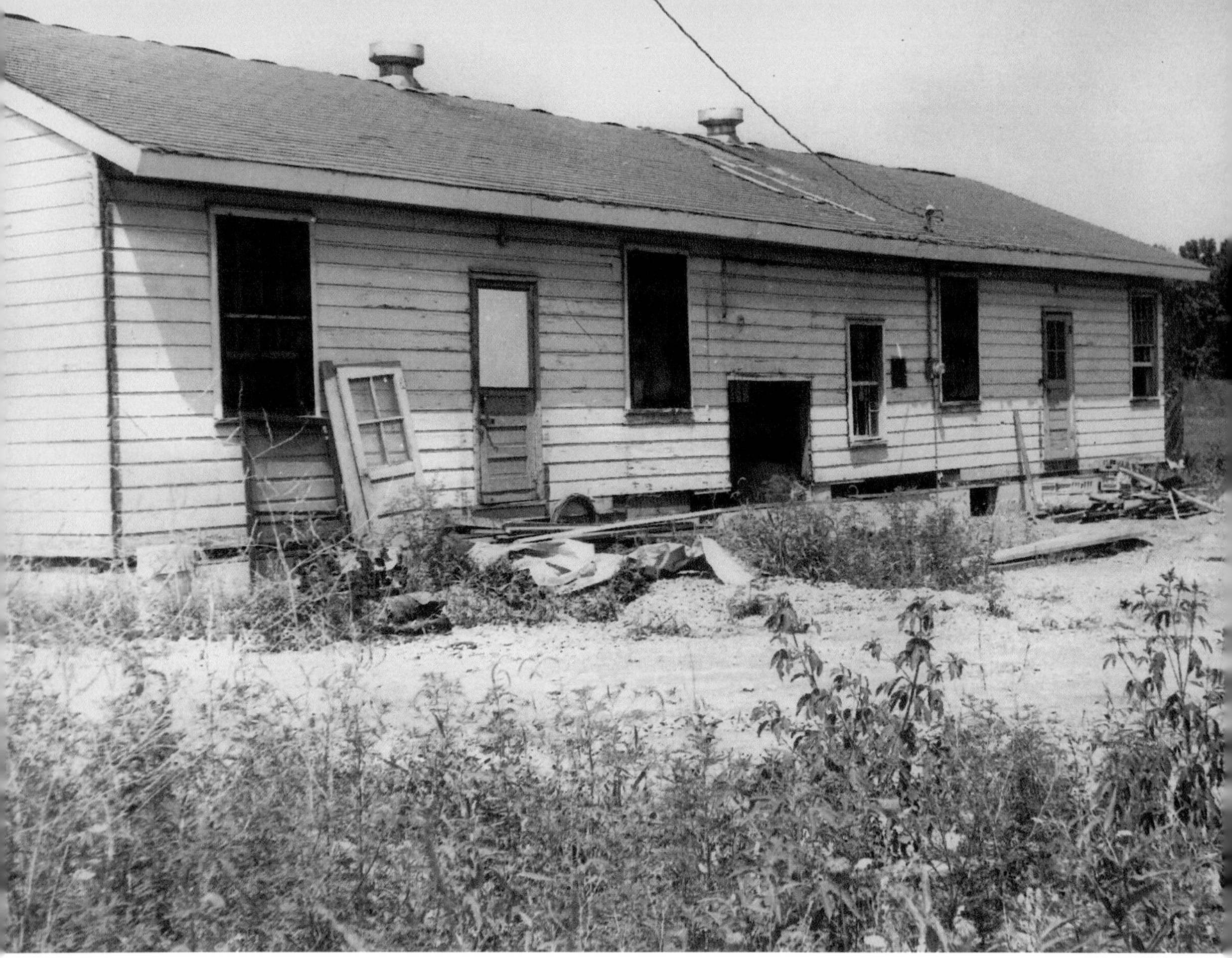

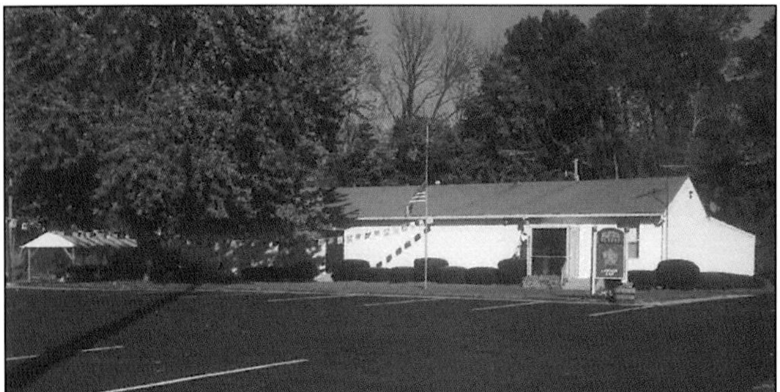

This former military barracks was moved from Camp Atterbury to Greenfield and sat on a lot on 100 South just west of the Brandywine Bridge. The building probably was originally built around the late 1930s or early 1940s. The structure was disposed of after the camp was closed. A renovation and an addition to provide a hall for the local lodge of the Fraternal Order of Police #140 followed the move to Greenfield. By the year 2000, the hall looked very much at home on its site and was a credit to the hard work of the members who have made a tremendous improvement in the building over the years. Additions to the structure have made the structure more appropriate for the organization's needs in the intervening years.

The original Greenfield Christian Church was built in 1854 on the east side of the Courthouse Square at the location of the D.H. Goble Printing Co. The bricks from the first brick courthouse were purchased for $250 and used in the construction. The current Christian Church was begun in early 1895, and on 9 July 1895 the cornerstone was laid. The last services in the old building were held on 26 January 1896. The new church lot on the southeast corner of North and East Street was purchased for $1,250. On Feb. 23, 1896, the current Christian Church was finished at a cost of $20,000. In 1905, the congregation burned the mortgage. John Felt is said to have been the architect. Many years later a classroom addition was added to the south side and years later the two houses to the left were cleared. The early picture is *c.* 1958, showing a parade in progress. In order to show the dramatic change, the second picture is taken from the opposite direction. It highlights the modern yet sympathetic blending of architectural style for their recent classroom and multipurpose room addition.

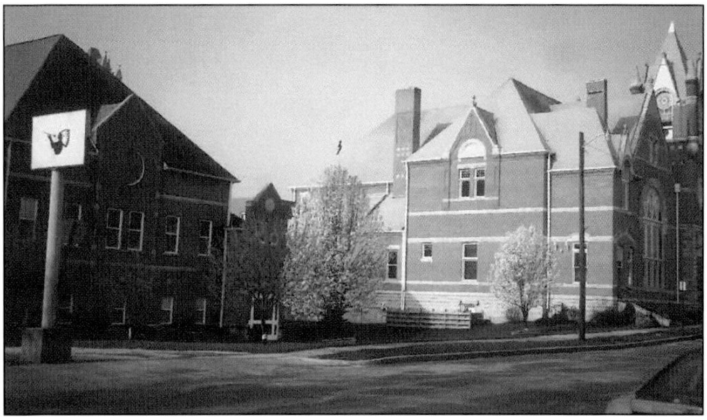

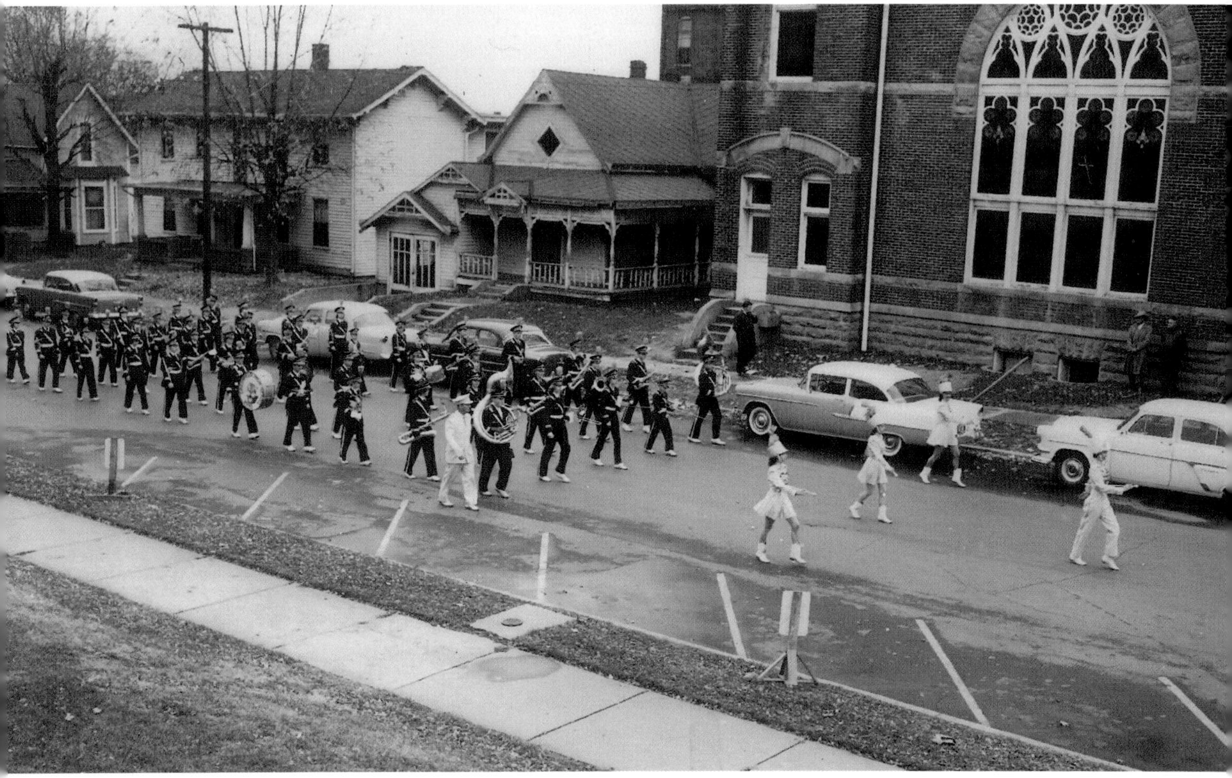

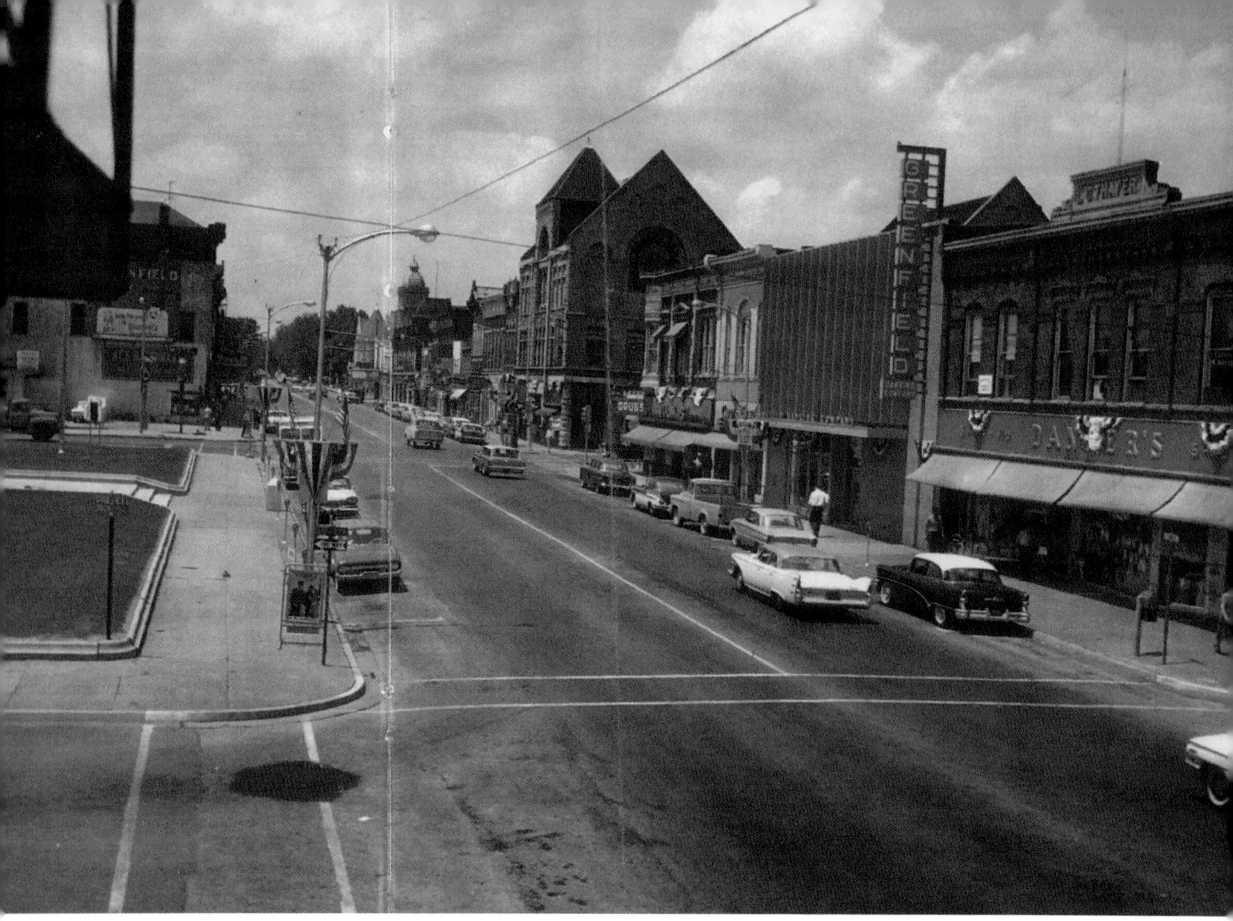

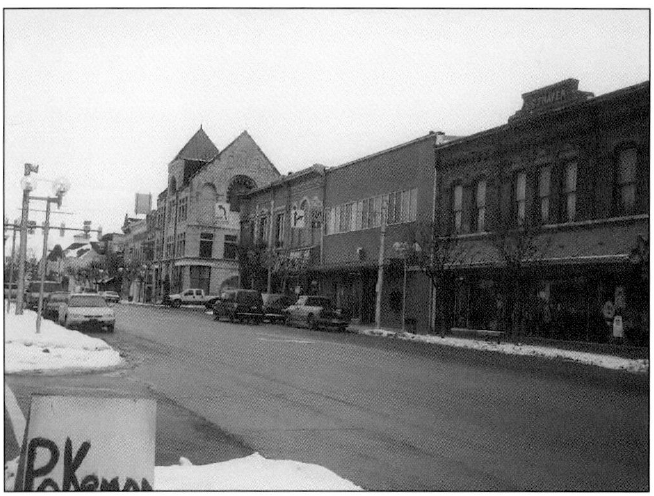

Downtown Greenfield's business buildings are full in this 1960 photograph. Thomas's Drug Store is in operation as is CarrMac's Clothing and Danner's 5 and 10. The original belfry still crowns Bradley Methodist Church. Greenfield Ice Cream is advertised on the Ace Hardware once known as Gambles. The original storefront on the Danner's (Thayer) building was replaced with the modern glass in the late 1950s.

Greenfield Banking's Main Office had received an "ultra" modern front a few years earlier. Contrast this with the present day photo and note the changes.

In one small town the young lady is standing on a lighted bridge October 1929. The location is at the edge of New Palestine at Sugar Creek. Our small towns were a bridge to the outside world for our rural inhabitants of Hancock County's Townships. They were church, general store, doctor, and club associations for the community. In our modern age, the small town has lost much of its significance to the regional mall, medical center, and outlet stores.

Chapter 3

OTHER TOWNS AND COMMUNITIES

Hancock County to this day is made up of a series of small communities. Some of them were planned while others just grew on their own. Fortville is the largest town in Hancock County. It began as Phoebe Fort's Corner, but was also called Walpole. In 1865, it was incorporated under the name of Fortville. Cumberland, the second largest town which until recently was entirely located in Marion County. In 1865, Urias McCord laid out McCordsville which developed into a sizable community. Shirley straddles the Hancock and Henry County lines. Several factories were located in Shirley between 1897 and 1921. In 1910, 1,519 people lived there. Spring Lake was incorporated in the 1920s. Wilkinson was platted in 1883, and incorporated in 1913. It grew as a result of the railroad, and later interurban development. Wilkinson became more important than Warrington, and eventually the township high school was moved from Warrington to Wilkinson. Charlottesville was platted in 1830, and incorporated in 1867. It lost its charter in a financial problem over school construction. In 1838, Jonathan Evans platted land on Brookville Road and then called the town Palestine. But the post office was called Sugar Creek. In 1871, the town was incorporated as New Palestine. Finly, or Carrollton, in Brandywine Township has also been called Kinder in 1847, Reedville, and Tailholt. Other towns were Cleveland (originally Portland 1834), Eden 1835, Gem 1871, Maxwell (June 1881), Mohawk 1883, Mount Comfort 1840s, Philadelphia 1838, Stringtown, Westland 1852, Warrington 1834, Woodbury, and Willow Branch.

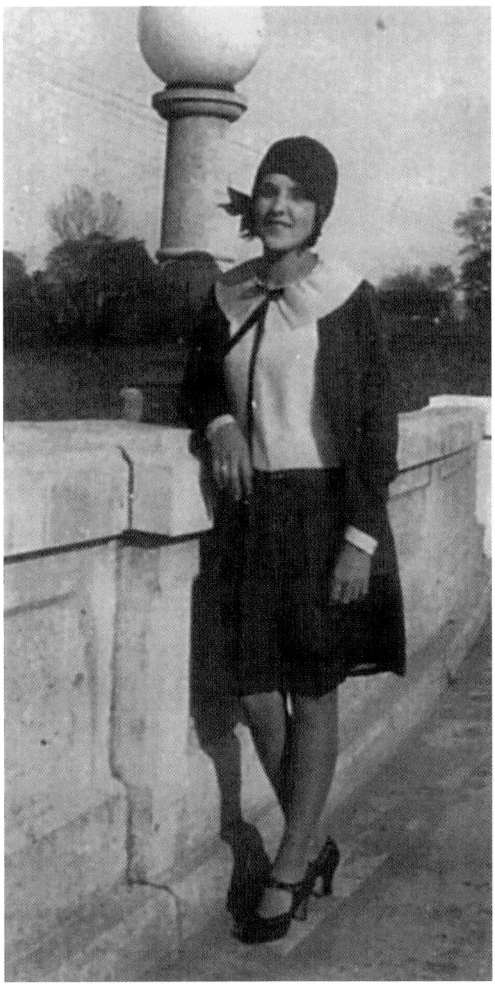

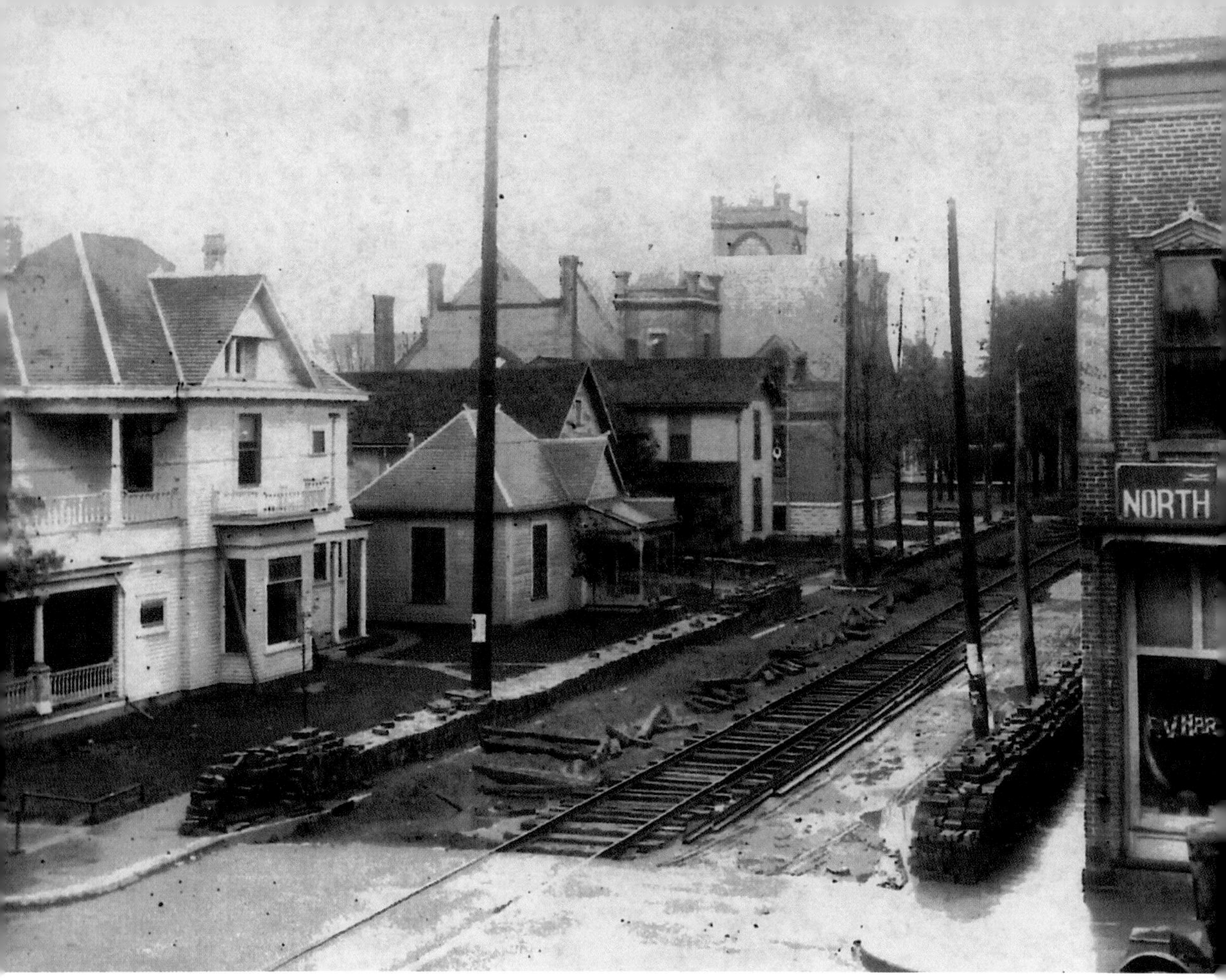

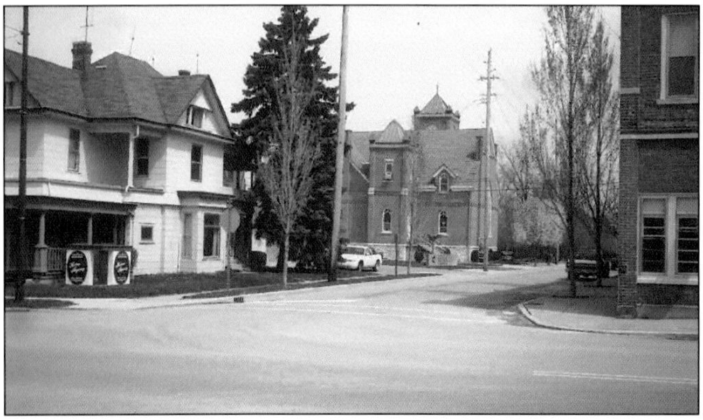

In the background you can see the Fortville Methodist Church, and in the foreground the construction on an interurban line that connected the town with Indianapolis on the south and Anderson to the north. The picture is *c.* 1902, and shows the Helms property and other homes in the area. Three of the homes have been cleared in years past to make way for a church parking lot and for space at the back of the Helms property.

Don't miss the rear end of the antique car in front of the store building. The interurban lines closed *c.* 1930–37 and the rails, cars, and other equipment were mostly sold for scrap. (Photo courtesy of Randy Sorrell.)

The old Fortville library still stands, and it has found other uses for its old walls. Library services have grown beyond the ability of early facilities like this one to continue to provide for their communities. Some communities have enlarged and added to facilities of this type with excellent results. In Fortville, a building that was formerly a corporate office became available and it made sense to the community to renovate that structure for future use. The larger area serves the community well on the north side of State Road 67 at the edge of town. The first major move toward developing a library in Fortville began in the spring of 1915. The proponents petitioned for a public library and reading room with 60 or more signatures. They filed their petition with the clerk of the Hancock Circuit Court showing money was subscribed and available for the purpose creating a library. Judge Sample found in their favor and appointed a library board. Application was then made to Andrew Carnegie for aid to build a library.

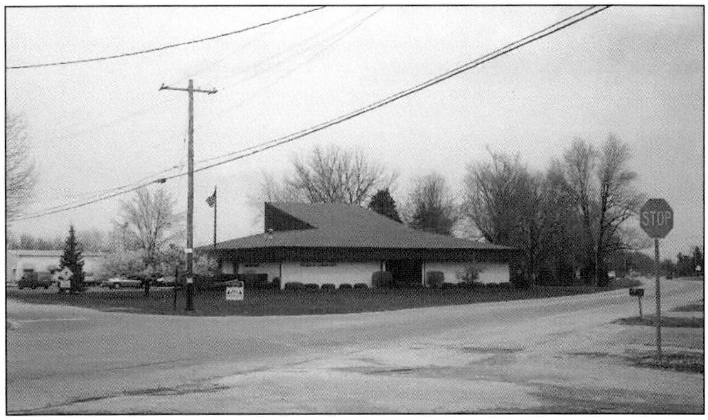

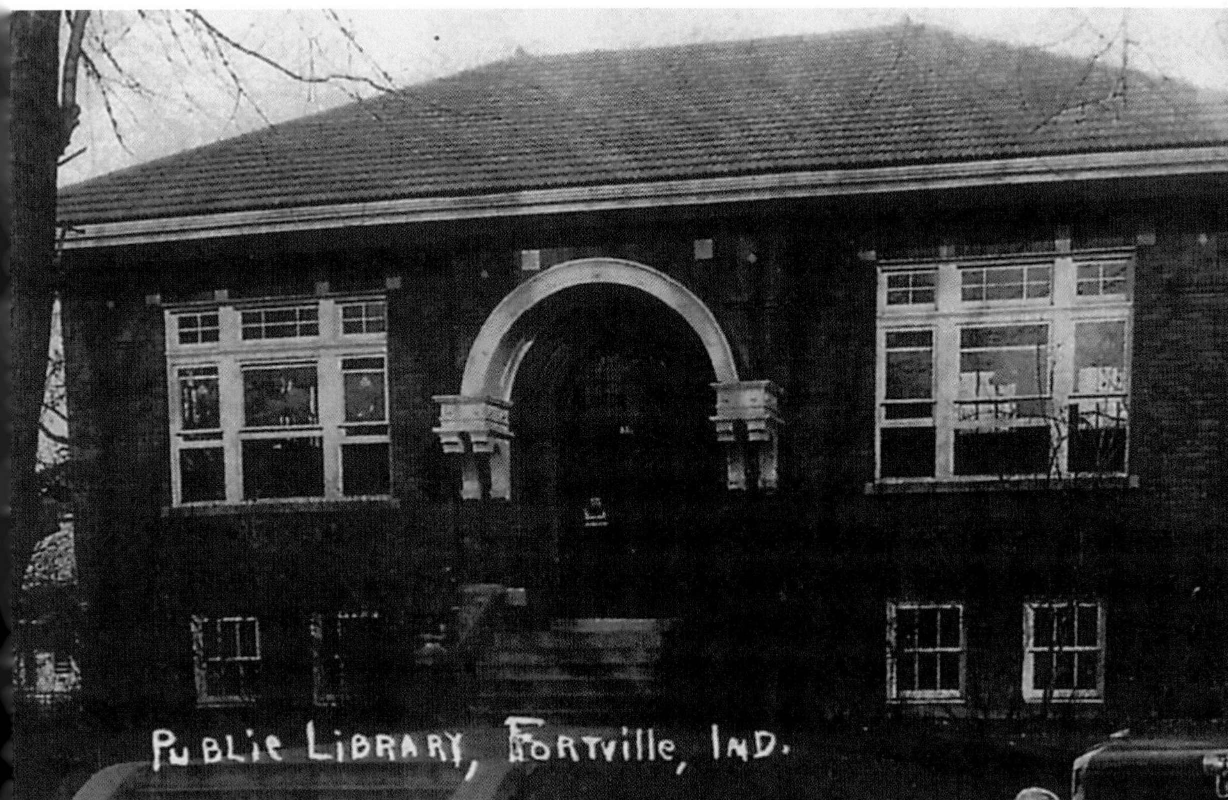

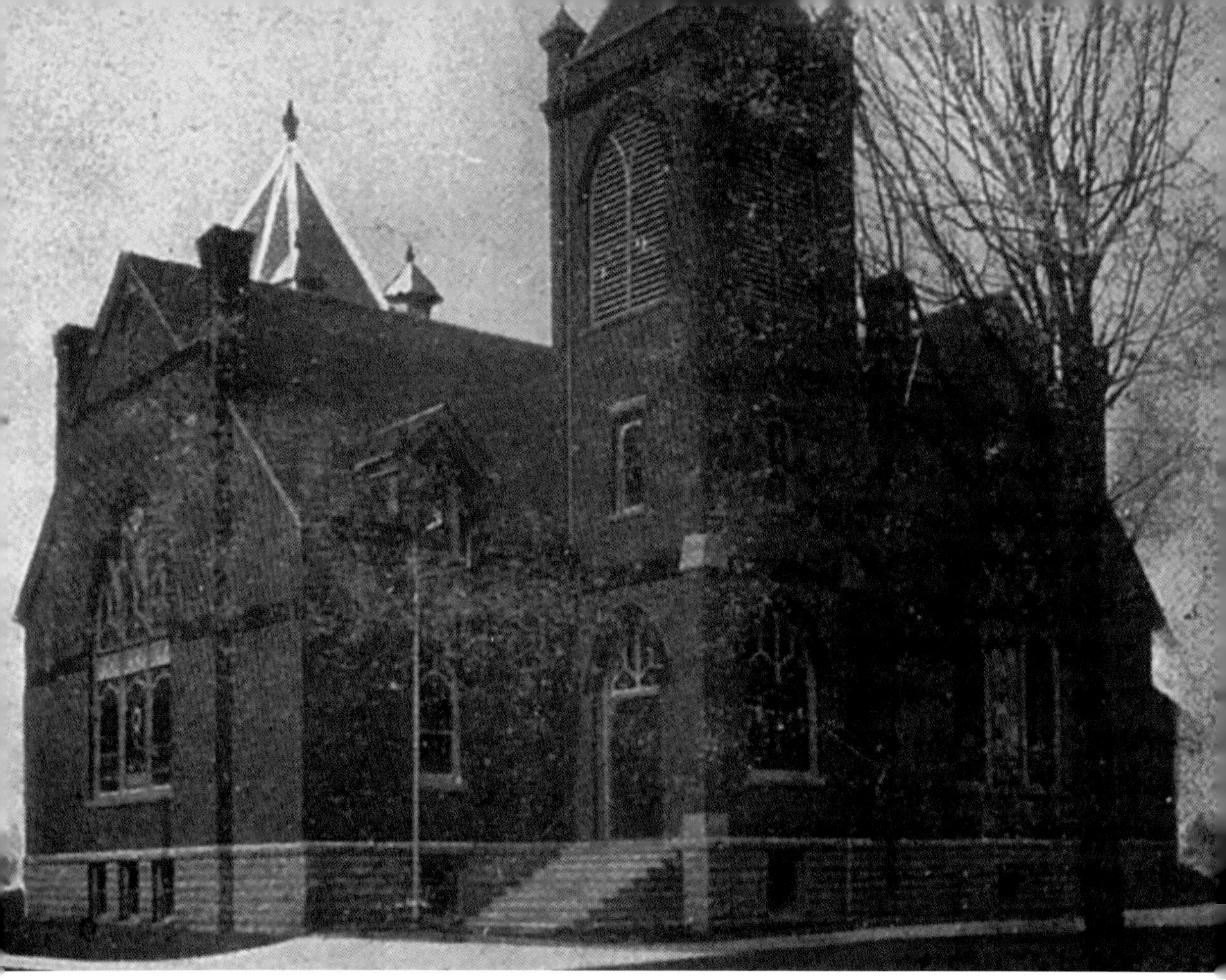

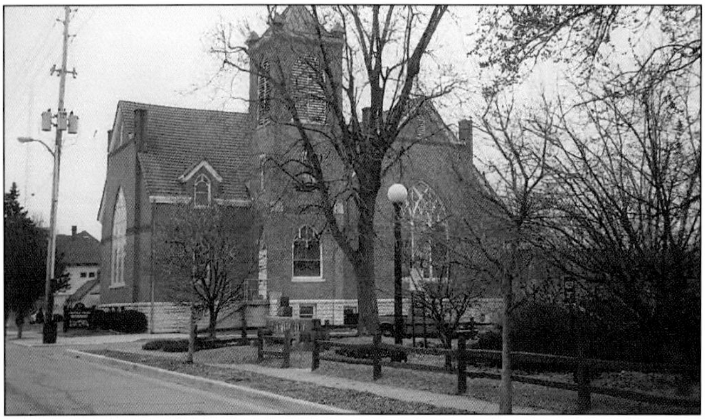

The Fortville Methodist Church is located next to Landmark Park, the former location of Fortville High School.

The picture is dates to 1914. Before 1856, there was a log church called Staat's Cemetery Church located about a mile north of Fortville. They were reorganized after a revival in 1856, and met in Staat's barn for awhile after being renamed the Fortville Methodist Episcopal Church. The movement that resulted in the present church building began after Christmas Day of 1900. The corner stone was laid in July of 1901. The building has been well maintained over the 100 years that have passed since its construction.

This structure was erected in 1900 by Mr. Fatout and a building committee composed of Henry Hiday, Frank Hunter, the Rev. Kerr, and L.W. Crouch. The building now serves as the home of the Fortville Baptist Church, although it originally served the Fortville Christian Church. Except for the closing of a door to the west and a window to the rear of the building, and the addition of a stoop as protection from the weather, the original building is largely unchanged. A large addition has been made to the rear to augment the facilities.

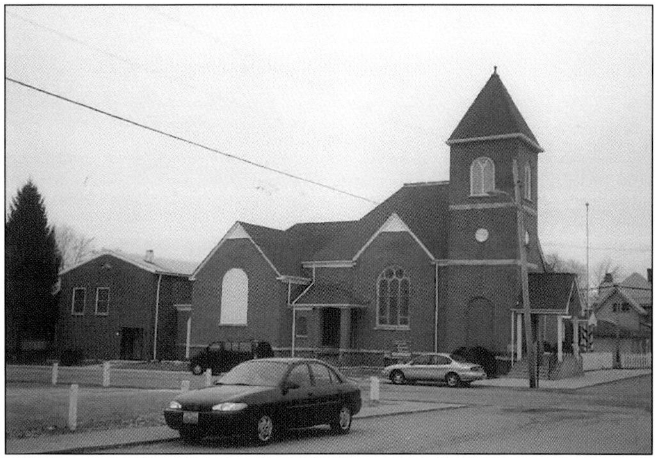

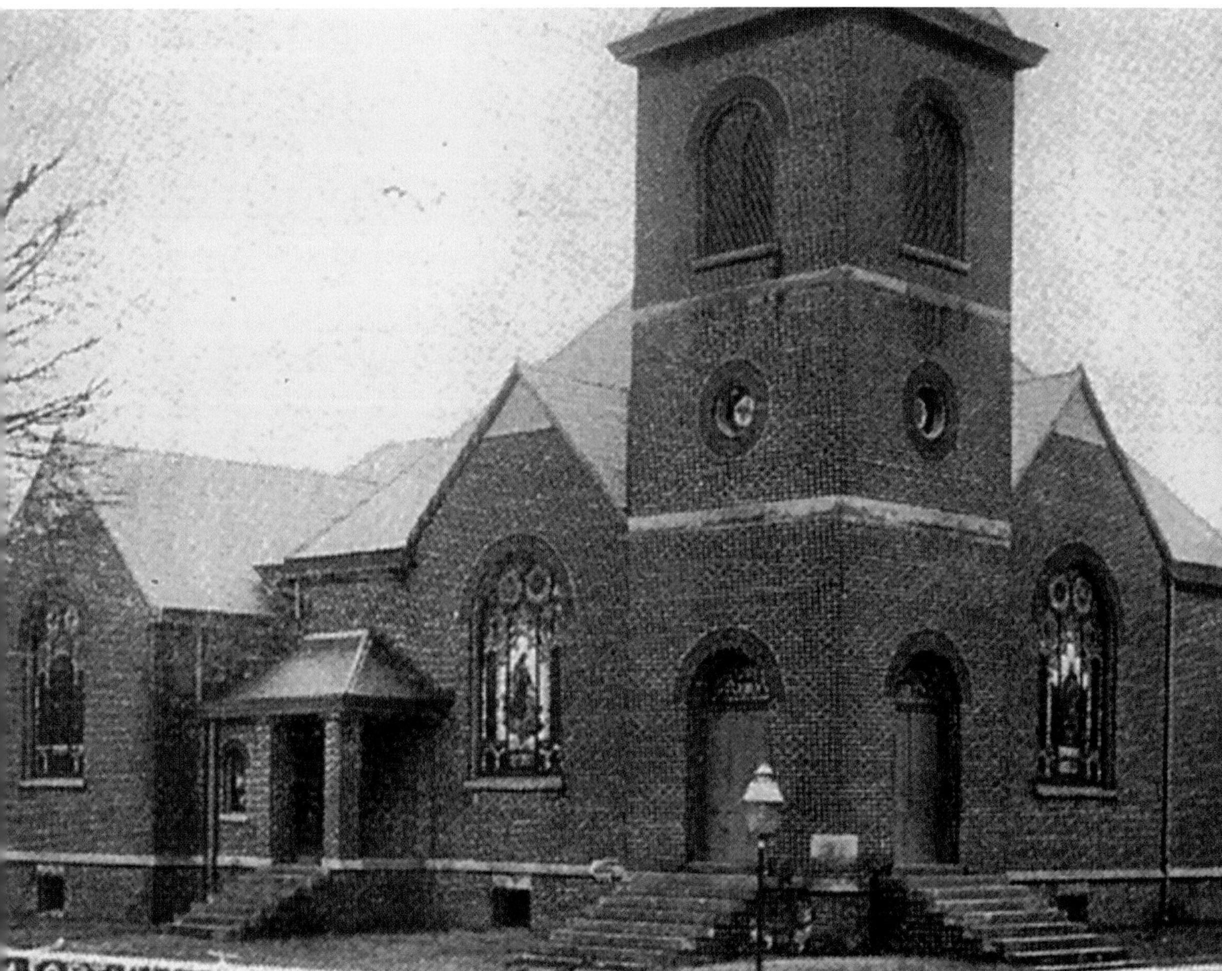

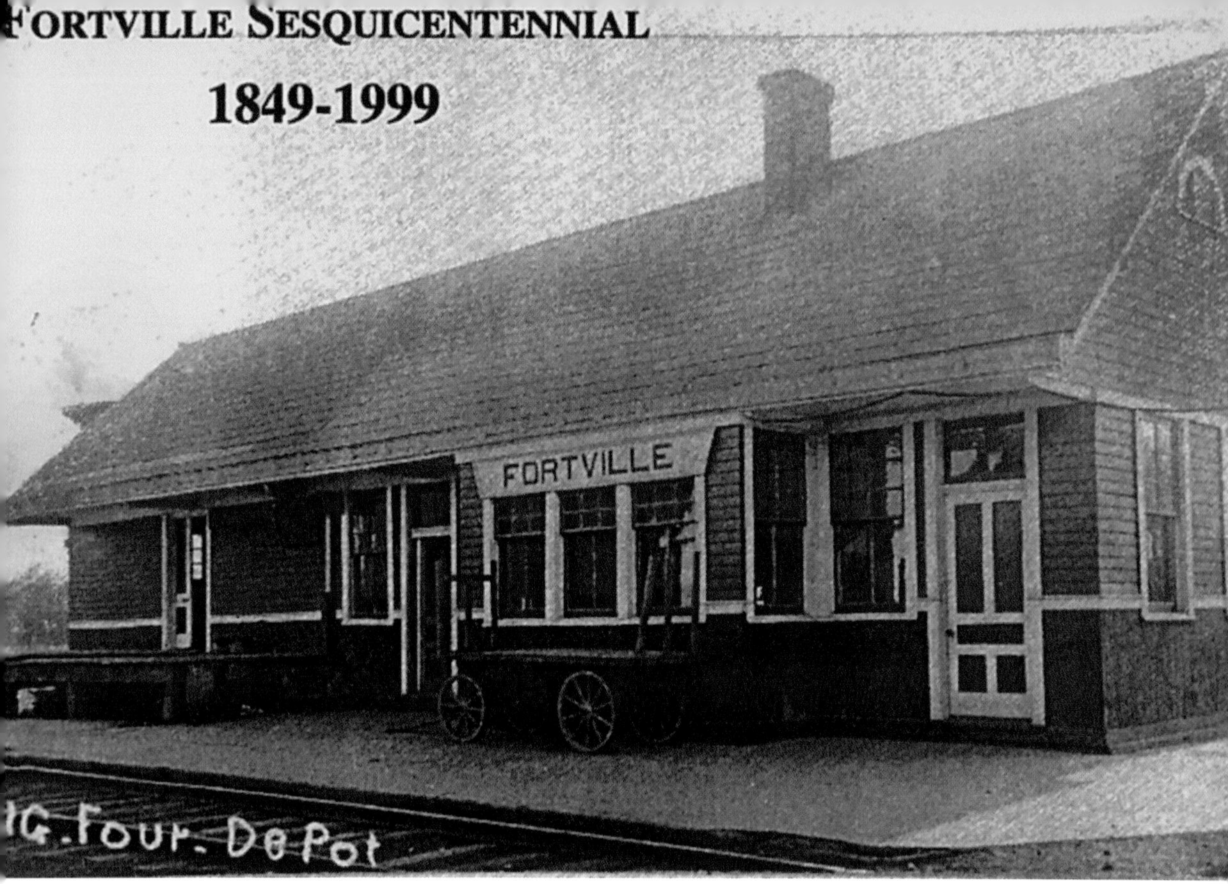

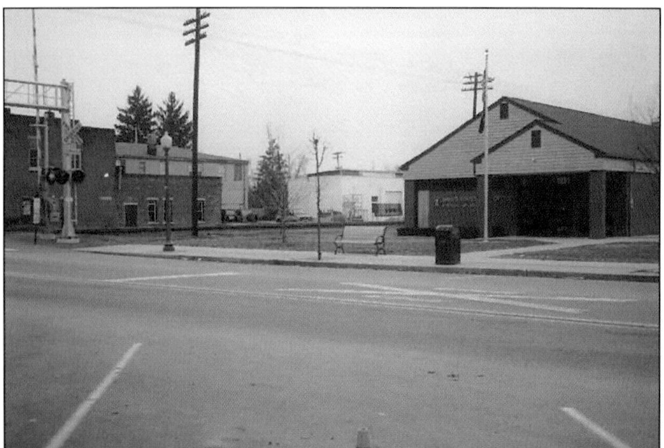

This is the Big Four Depot in Fortville *c.* 1905. The tracks were originally laid about 1852, and the post office was moved to the vaccinate from Walpole and continued using that name while the railroad station was named Fortville in honor of Cephas Fort. The development was slow, but a sizable community has grown in the 150 years that has passed. Now the new post office occupies a location near the site of railroad's old station. The town's improvements included coal oil lamps that were replaced by natural gas, and electric streetlights were installed in 1913.

This is Fortville's I.O.O.F. hall, which no longer stands in the form seen in the original picture due to a fire.

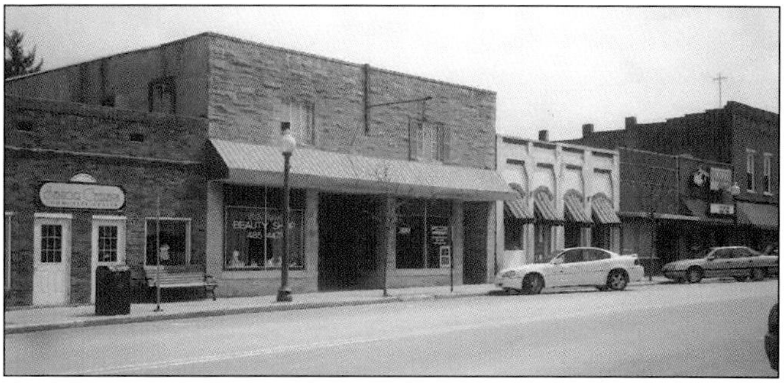

The current structure is a reconstruction using the original walls to an extent, but changing the windows and general style. The International Order of Odd Fellows was very active throughout the area of Indiana. There was at least one hall in most major towns and cities, and one could be found in most small communities. They were a fraternal organization like the Eagles, Elks, or Moose Lodges. The building was located in this area of downtown Fortville across from the Masonic Hall. The Odd Fellows in Fortville first talked of organizing about 1856. The building they took over was near the tracks and burned 1896, destroying their records and property. The building shown here was erected on a vacant lot where a livery stable was once located. They used their insurance money and everything they could raise to build the structure in 1896. A few years later Dr. McCord was active in Fortville, and the lodge knew he was treating a woman with child in a camp of "Mexican Gypsies." The lodge enjoyed an excellent dinner with food left over that cold night, and Charles Merrill and H.T. Baker took what was left to help feed the families in the camp. The Odd Fellows were known for their generosity.

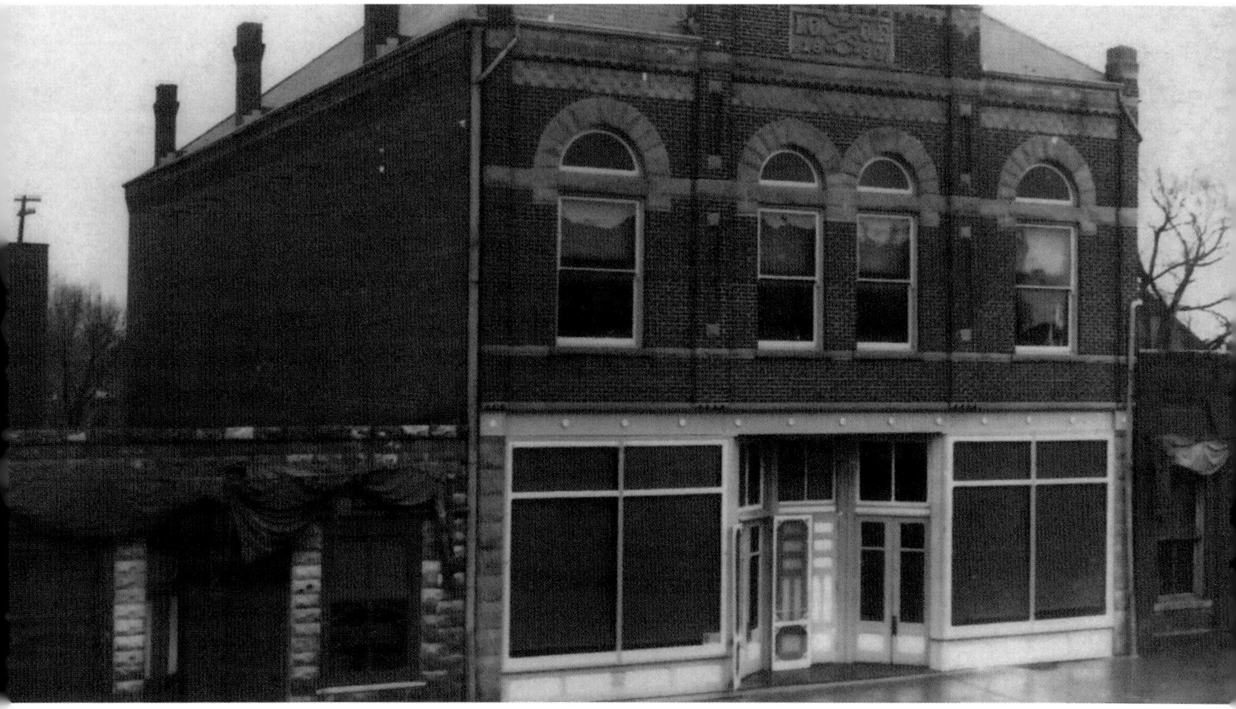

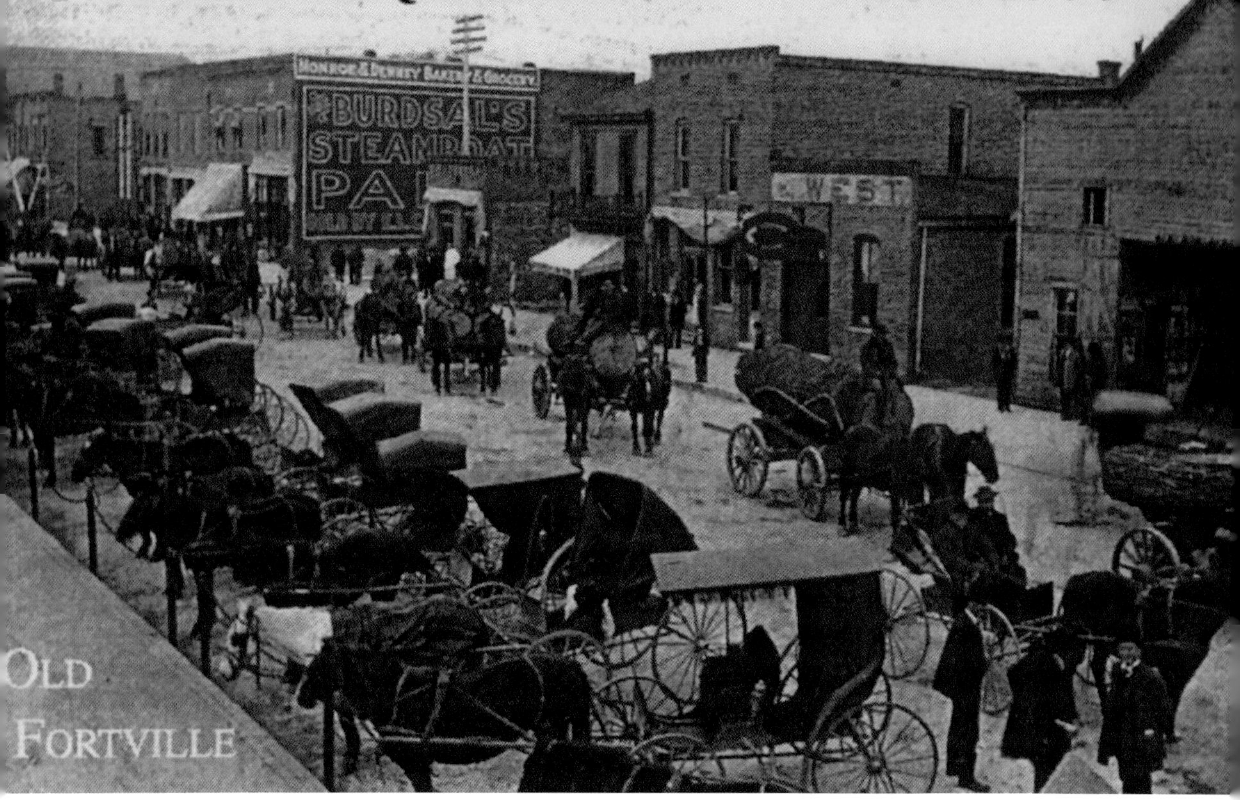

OLD FORTVILLE

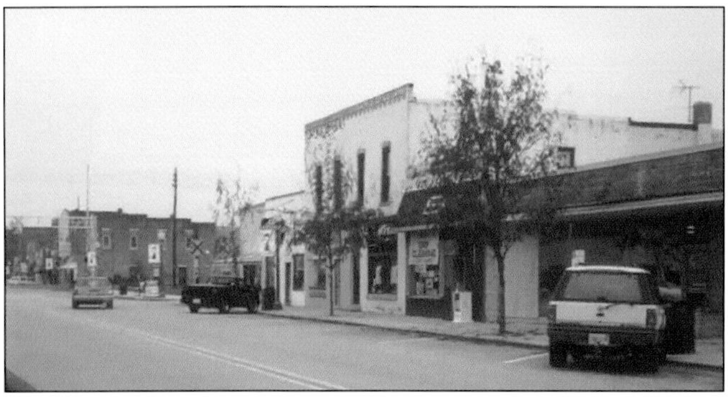

The main business street in Fortville was teaming with activity in this turn of the century picture. Local people had come downtown to purchase their needs and from the amount of activity it might be possible to guess that this could be a Saturday. When you look closely you will notice wagons loaded with huge logs running from the right to the left down the street. Marie Adams father owned the horse carts and she was well known locally because she was a missionary to China. We are looking north along the east side of Main Street. The picture was taken near the fork just north of Highway 67. The livery stable presents a wide open door just across the street. The stable was demolished long ago, but the two bricks just north of it can be seen standing in the new photo. Today commercial activity is drawn to buildings, larger malls, and strip malls in the area on the east edge of Indianapolis. Downtown Fortville remains a pleasant place to conduct business with a local newspaper office, parts store, the VFW, the American Legion, craft shops, offices, and a furniture store. Fortville began as Phoebe Forts corner, and the post office bore the name Walpole. Cephas Fort laid out the town of Fortville in 1849, many years after Phoebe Forts activities.

In 1952, Fortville was a busy town with cars parked along the street north of the railroad crossing. We are looking toward the west side of the street where a pharmacy and a number of other shops conducted business. The next to the last building to the north is the Masonic Hall, which was lucky to survive a devastating fire many years ago. The third story and attic were lost in that terrible disaster. There has been a concerted effort on the part of the town to beautify the area and make it attractive to shoppers. Just north of this location on the east side of the street you would find the office of the Community Shopper, a local newspaper. A petition was circulated in 1865 to officially change the town's name from Walpole to Fortville. The first election of town officers was held in 1865.

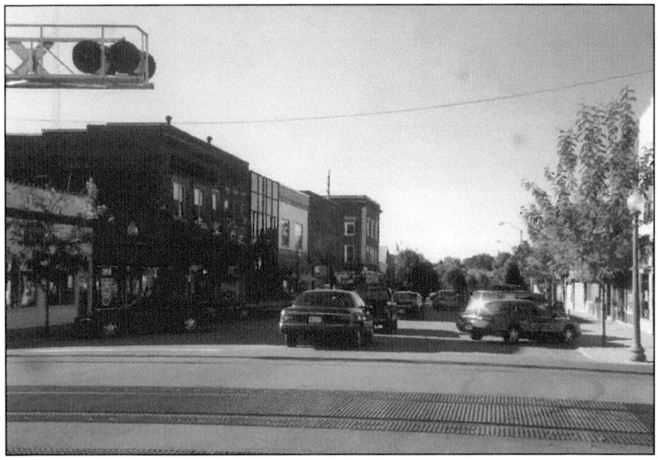

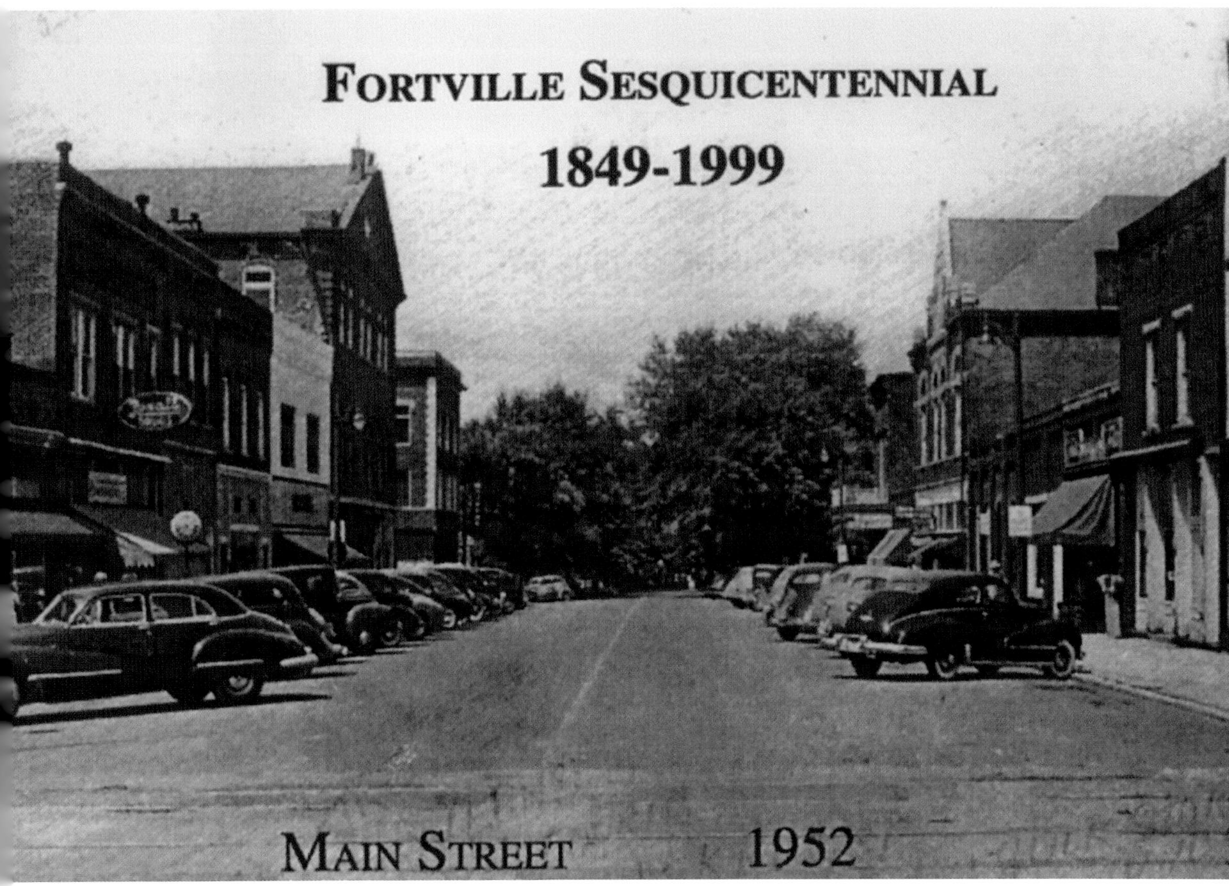

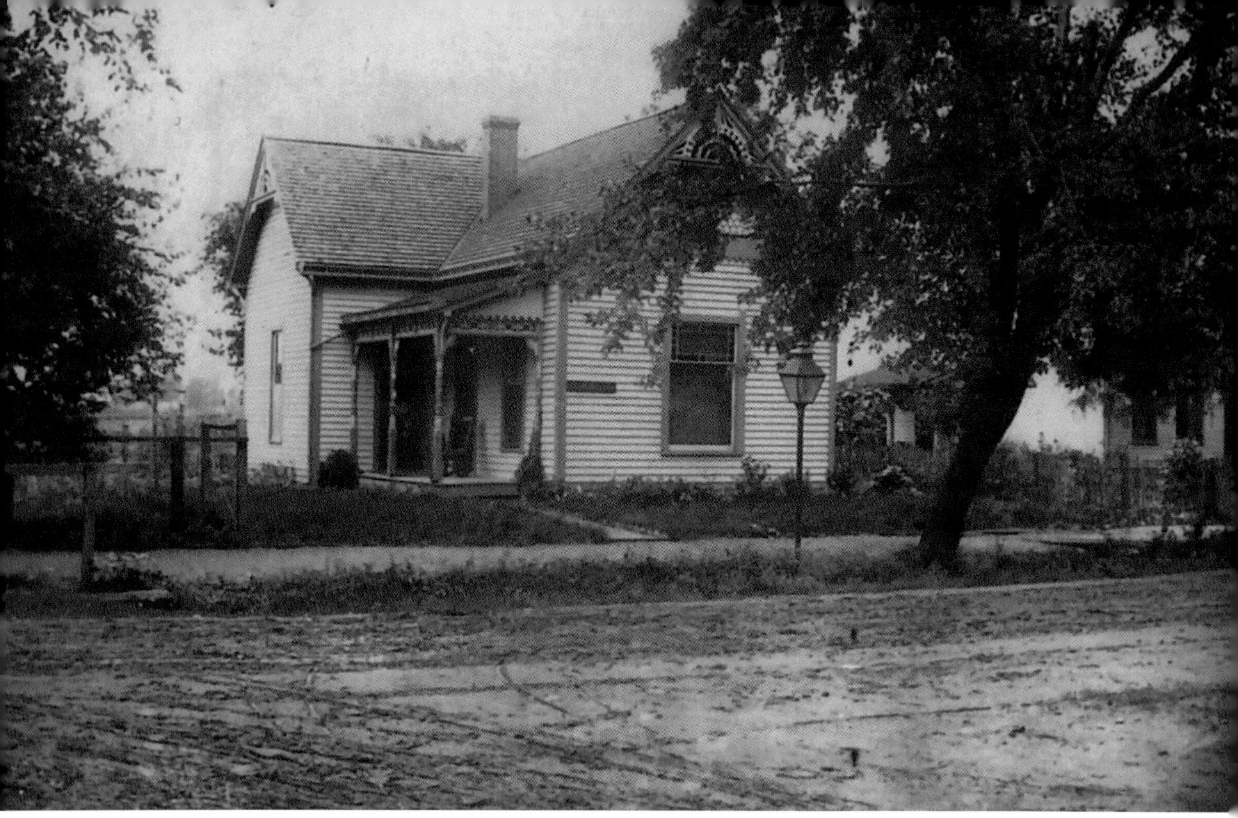

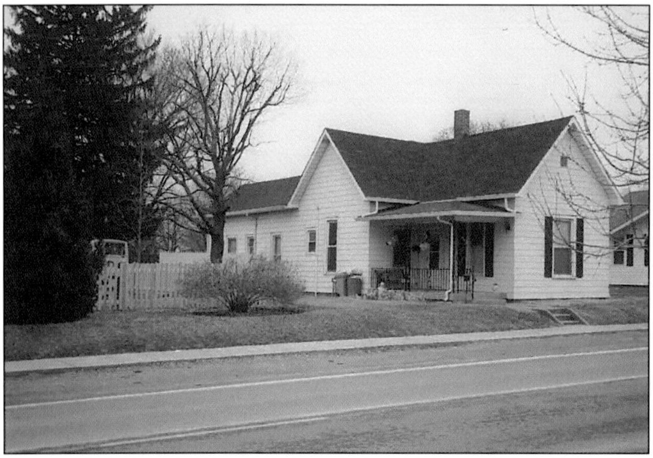

This was the home of Doctor McCord in Fortville. The exact location remains a mystery as various individuals give possible locations of a very similar house on Pearl Street an others on State Street and Michigan Street. The contrasting home is located on Michigan Street. This house is certainly similar in style. Homes of the period were made more elegant by the addition of gingerbread or carpenter's designs that became elaborate trim. Concrete sidewalks had been added to the neighborhood but the street is unpaved. The picture is probably *c.*1910. By the 1950s through the 1990s, homeowners faced with painting deteriorating trim often removed it and used inexpensive metal work in its place. The second house is thought not to be the same house. (Photo courtesy Vernon Township Library—Richard Bell.)

Gilboa is located near the Hoosier Evangelist John T. Hatfield's home. A number of Hatfields are buried in its cemetery. Around 1830, individuals began holding Methodist meetings in homes in this Blue River Township area. An occasional circuit rider visited the flock, providing a connection to other Methodist groups. In 1832, the congregation built a log church on ground donated by James Sample and Benjamin Miller. Rev. Amos Sparks was the first preacher. In 1852, a frame building was constructed. Membership reached 45 in the 1880s. Ten years later only six people remained as part of the membership. In the early 1900s, the building was removed from the site. Today foundation stones that give testimony to the existence of a once thriving country church can still be seen.

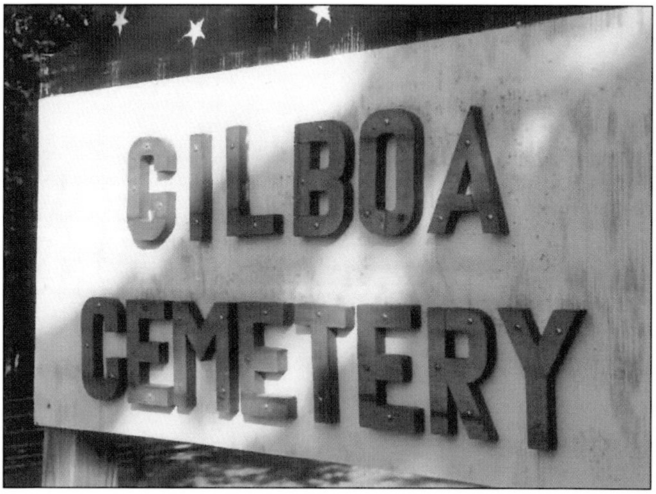

The local Boy Scouts were instrumental in maintaining the Gilboa Cemetery in 2001.

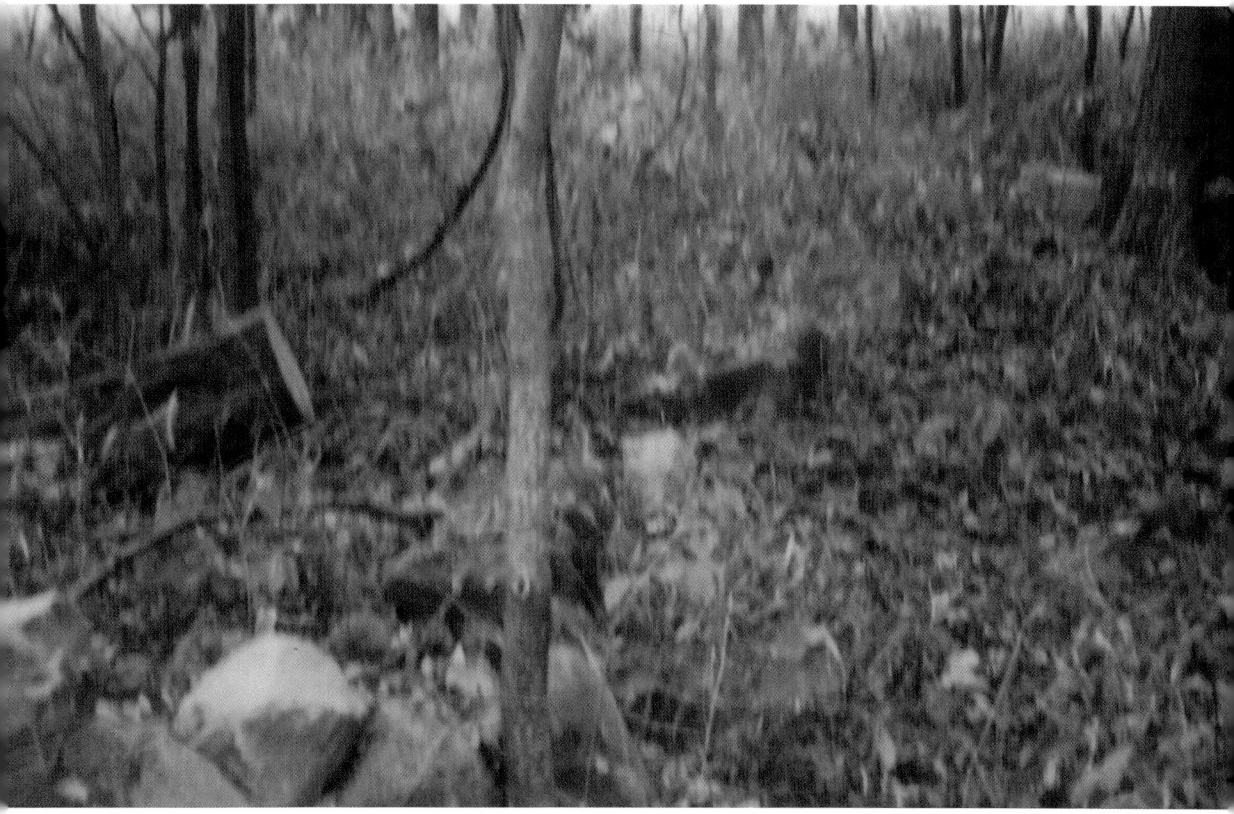

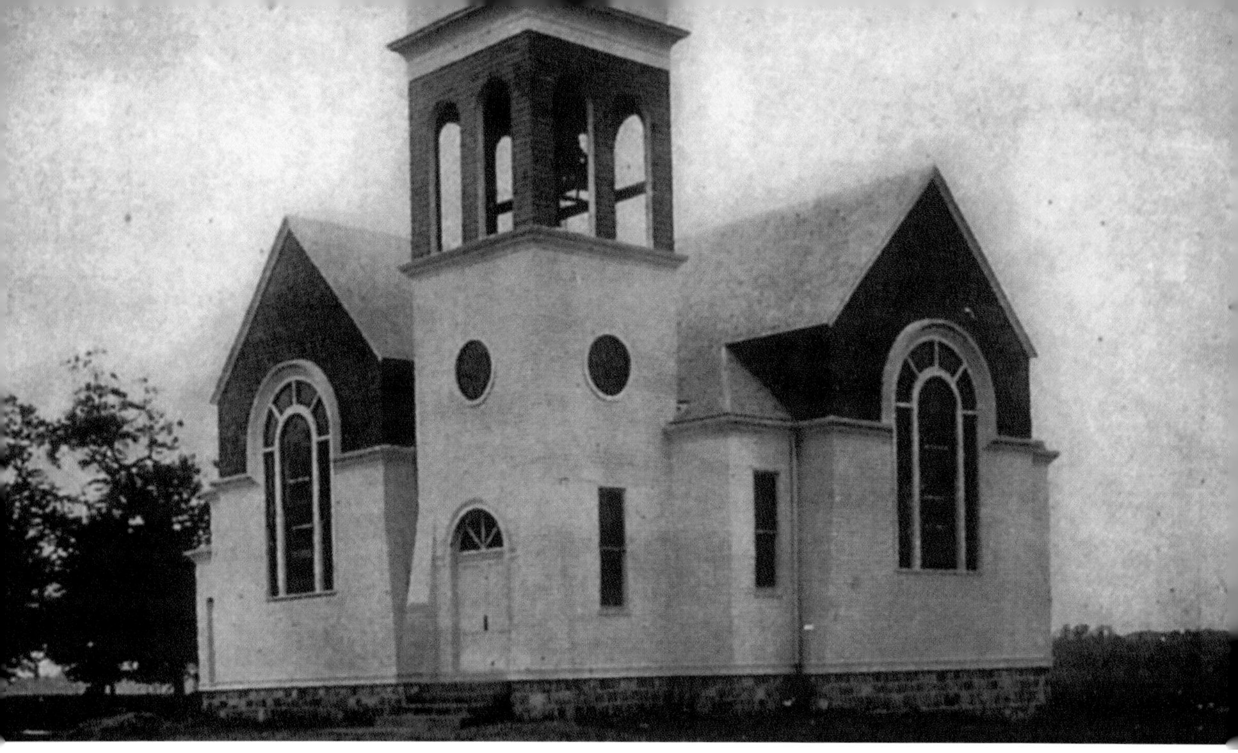

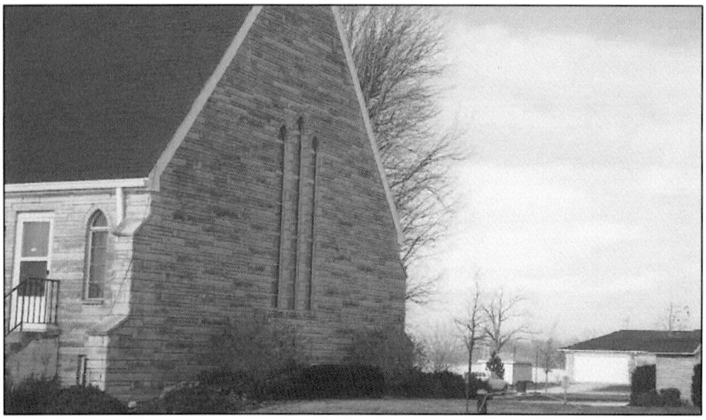

The Nameless Creek Christian Church was founded in a log building after meeting in the homes of members for a time. The place was referred to as the "Union Meeting House." In 1839, a permanent church organization was established as the "Reformed Baptist Church of Christ." The group went through several name changes. In 1853, a frame building was erected to replace the original log structure. The members were over the years influenced by the teachings of Alexander Campbell and others that brought a more enlightened view of the scriptures. Many such churches including Nameless Creek became involved with that movement through the Disciples of Christ and similar groups. Campbell taught on several occasions in central Indiana at Rushville and other sites. In 1904, the church built a wonderful new structure that served the community well until a disastrous fire in the late 1940s. The congregation met at Charlottesville School for awhile until a new parsonage and basement church could be erected. The present church was added later. The building stands in tribute to the hard work of past members and their families many of whom were laid to rest at the end of their days in Simmons Cemetery.

The Charlottesville Methodist Church is one of the older churches of Hancock County dating from 1838. The early photograph of the church is *c.* 1912. The town dates from 1830, and Jackson Township dates from 1831. This congregation at Six-Mile Cemetery north of Charlottesville constructed the earliest church building. Several years ago, the Cleveland Methodist Church joined with the Charlottesville congregation and they constructed a parsonage between the two towns. The current building has been modernized and the belfry has been removed. This gives the structure a somewhat different look.

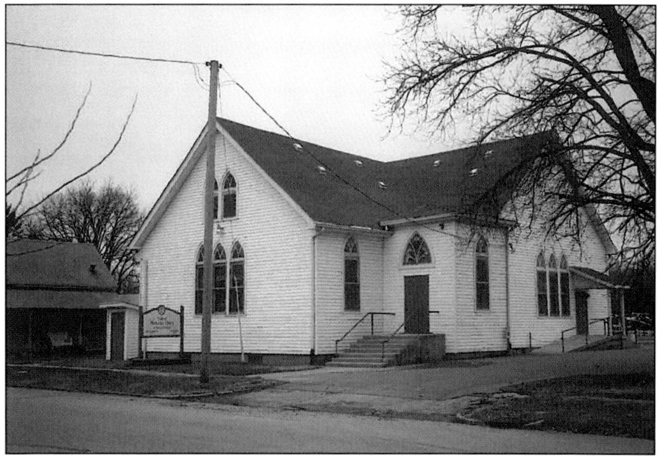

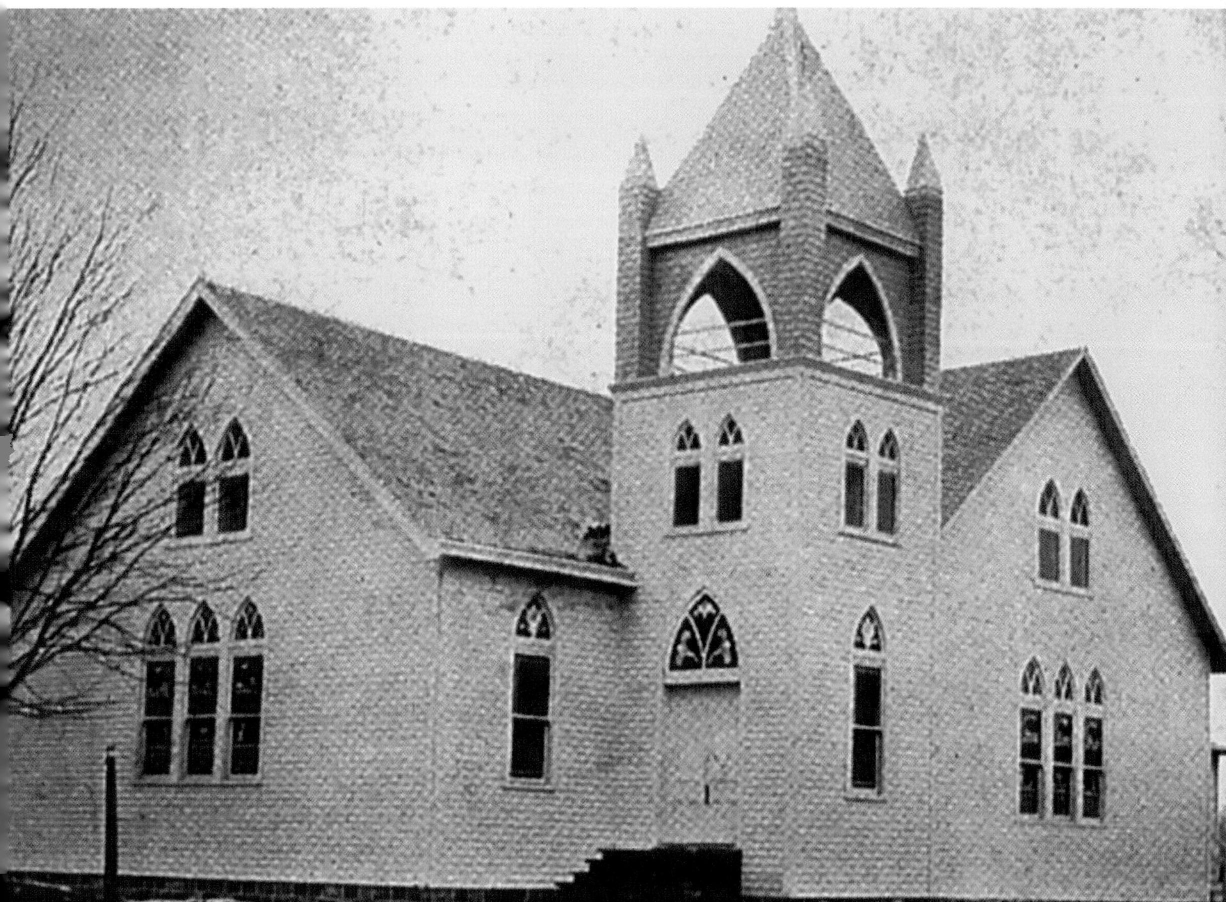

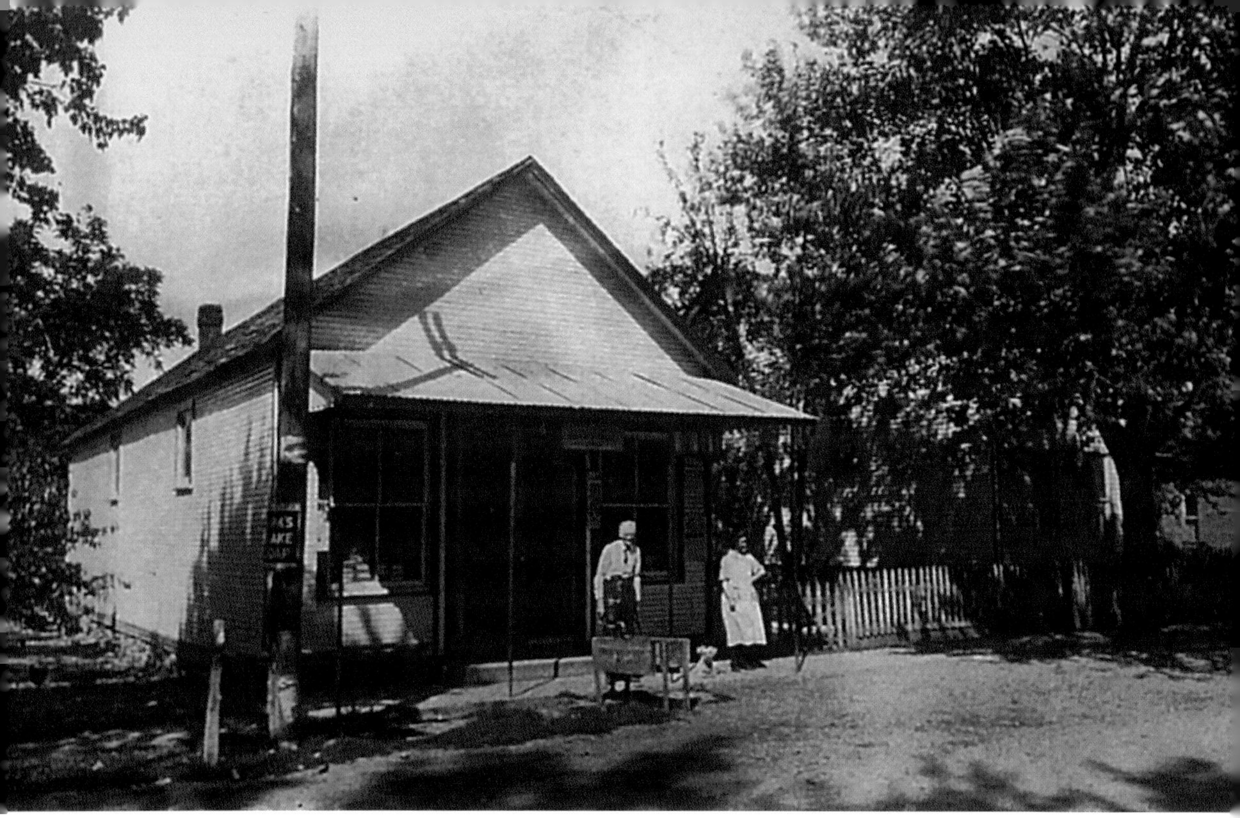

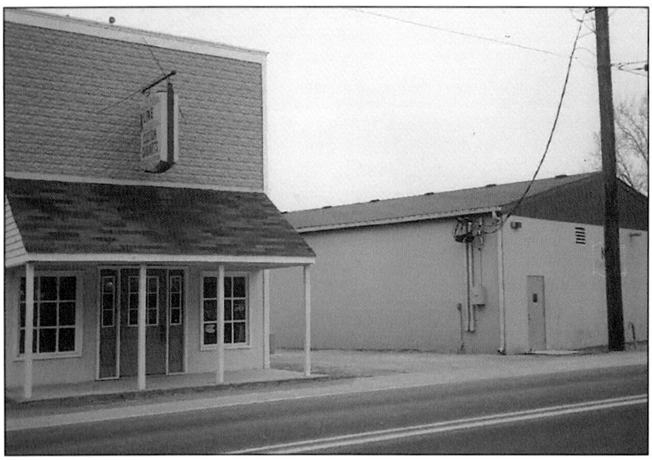

Elijah Cooper operated his store in this old building south of Jackson Street in Maxwell. His store served local residents for many years. When it was torn down, a window from the building was placed on display at the Old Log Jail Museum in Greenfield. The town of Maxwell was surveyed in August of 1881 by Massa Apple, and was first called Junction. The construction of the railroad at the time was instrumental in its founding. The modern building on the right probably stands near the location of the Cooper Store and the railroad right-of-way. The older building on the left is the home of Kline Custom Cabinets.

The large brick building on the right still stands and has been the location of the Maxwell Post Office, a general store, and many other businesses with apartments located upstairs. Just behind it you can see the old Maxwell Train Station and the tracks. A frame store stands just beyond the tracks then you can see a large brick structure that is long since gone. If you look closely beyond that building, partially obscured by the trees is the steeple of the old Maxwell Methodist Church that was organized in 1886. The older picture is *c.* 1900. The outline of the current Maxwell Methodist may be seen beyond the car lot in the modern photograph.

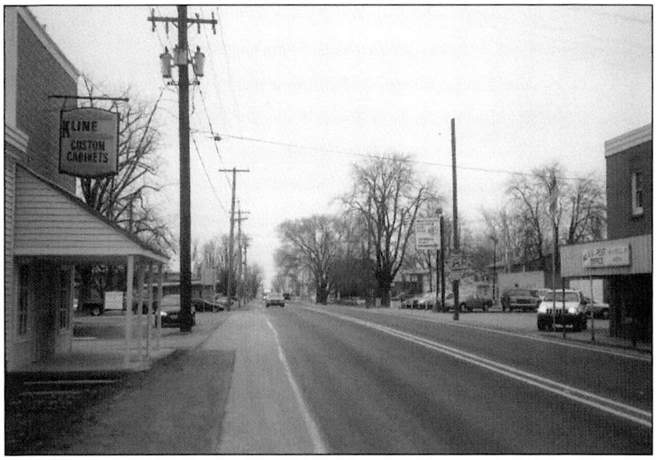

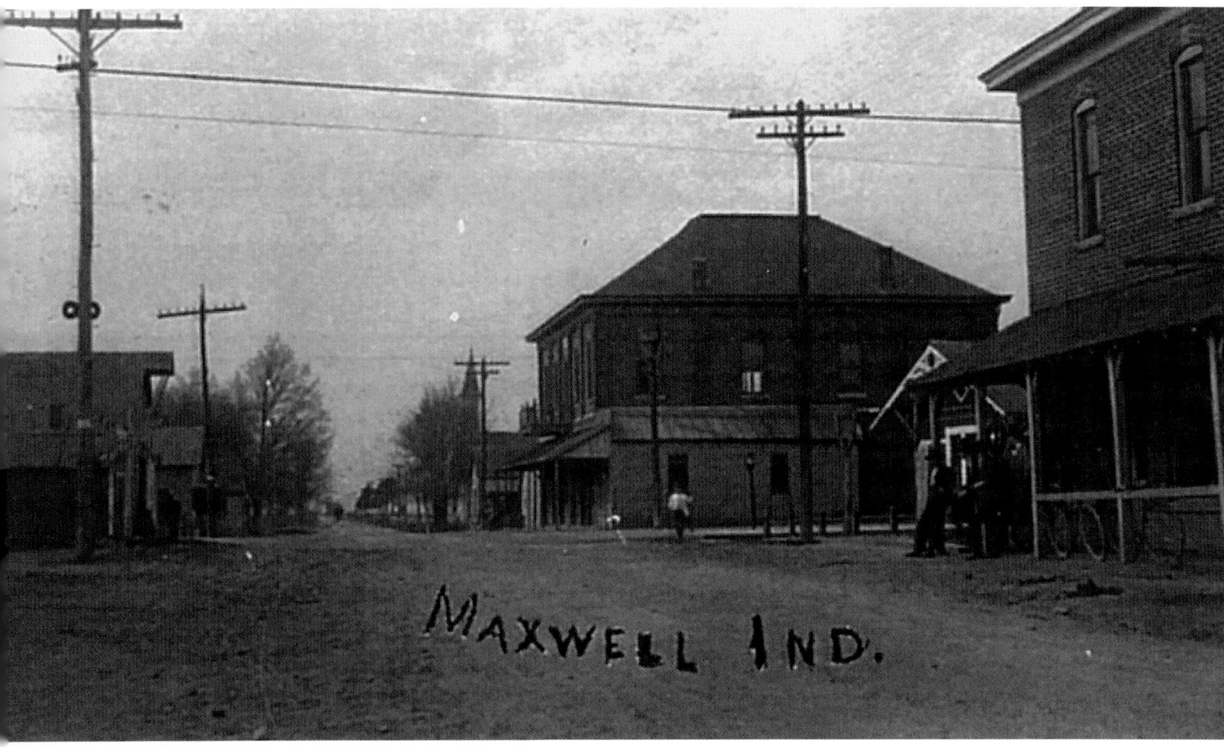

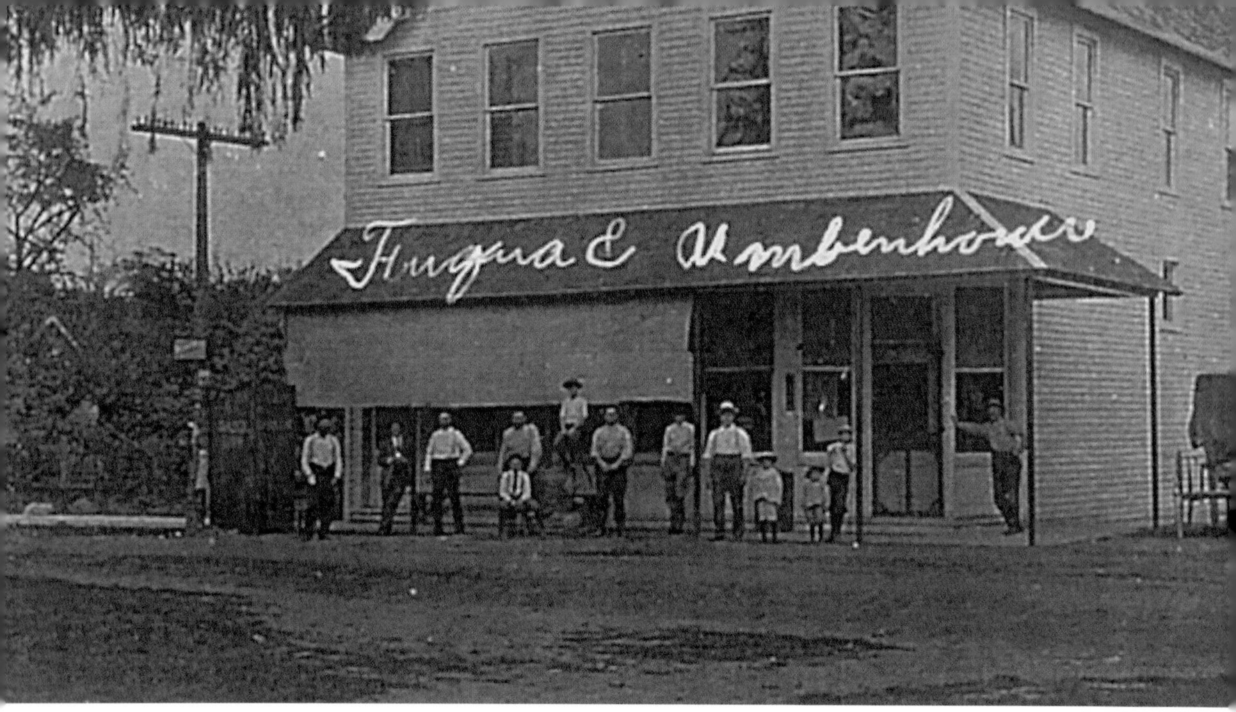

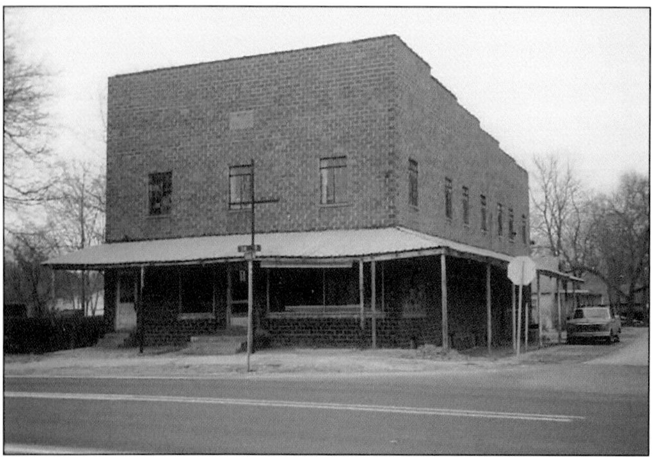

The old frame general store in Eden operated by Fuqua and Umbenhower stood at the main intersection on the northeast side of the street *c.* 1890. This building was replaced by a more modern structure sometime in the late 20s or early 30s. The upstairs was originally the home of the Eden Masonic Lodge. In 2001, the building was no longer being used for anything other than possible storage. Eden was originally platted as Lewisburg in August 1835. Green Township was first organized in September 1832.

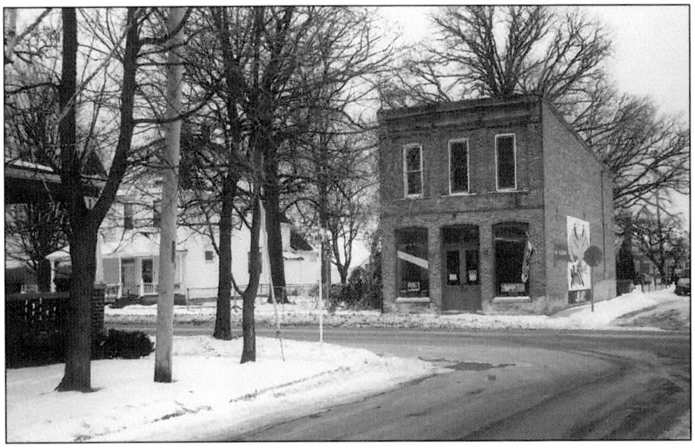

This structure was called Legion Hall and is now the library at New Palestine. It was constructed *c.* 1900 at the corner of Main and Depot Streets in New Palestine. Harry Nichols owned a general store there for several years and later Elsworth Phares sold furniture, groceries, and dry goods in the building. The local post office was located here for several years. John Ashcroft also ran a grocery store at this location. The building has had many different uses before and after Mrs. Nichols gave the building to the American Legion.

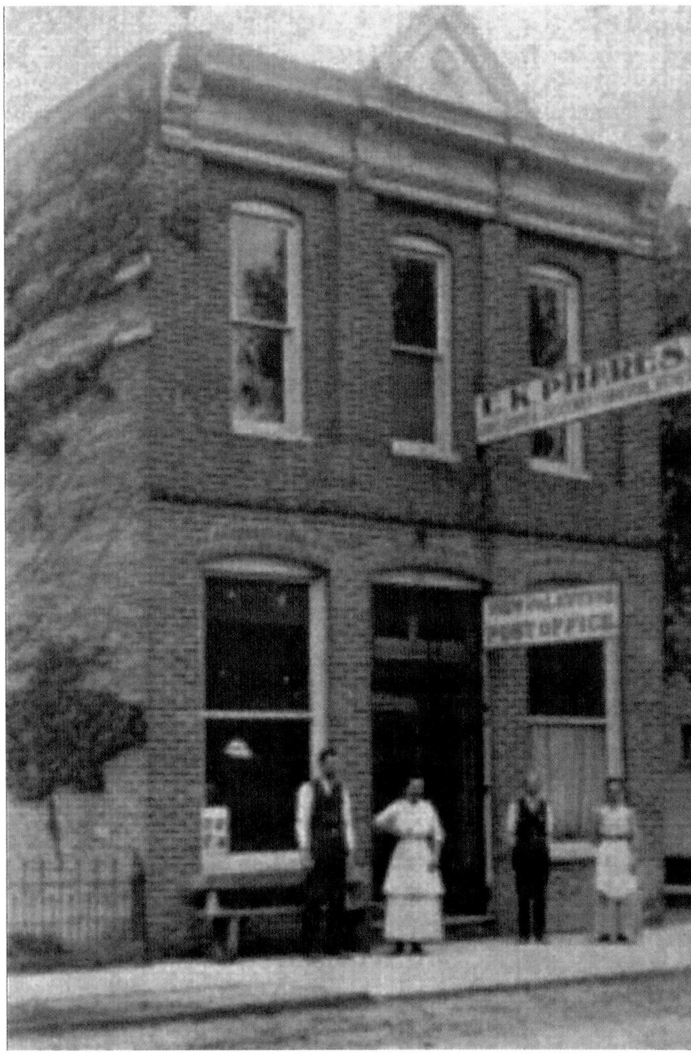

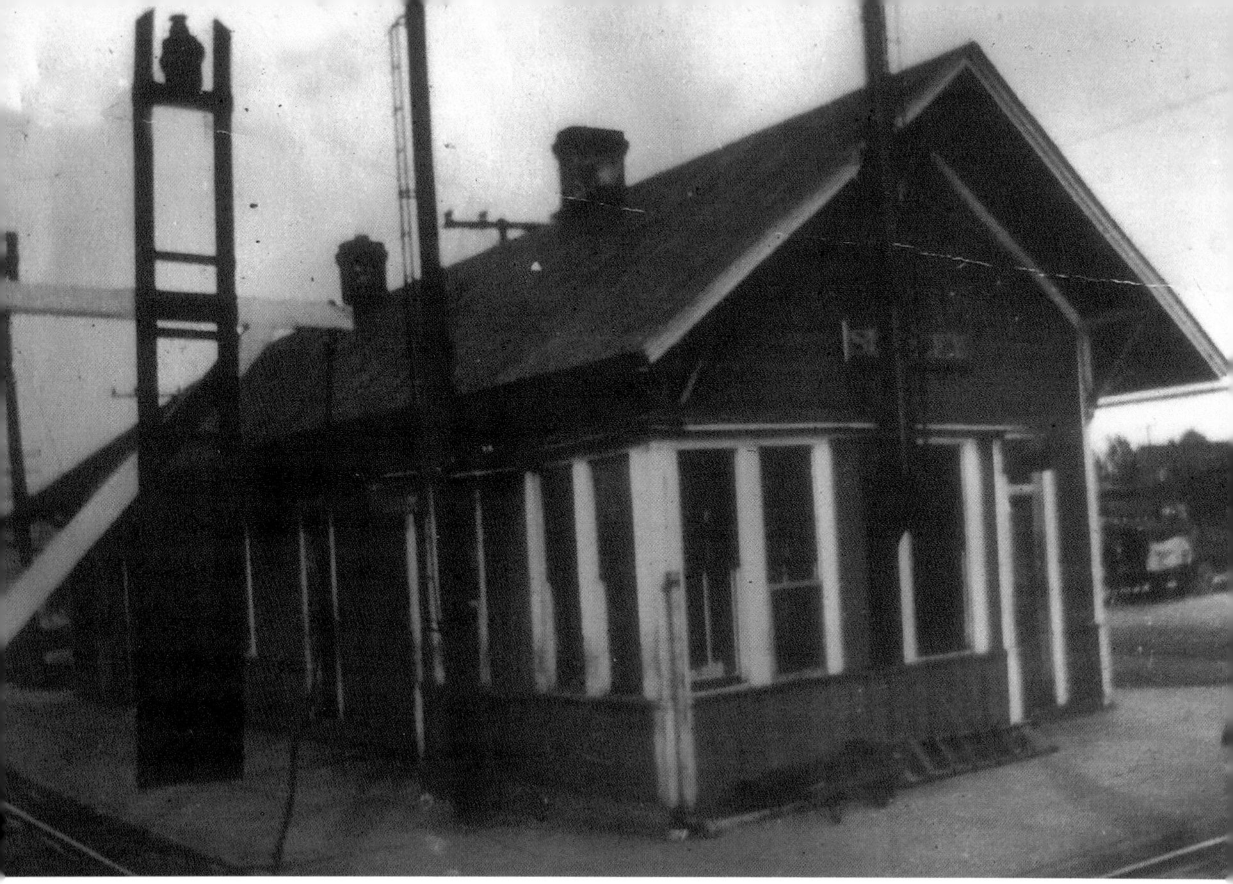

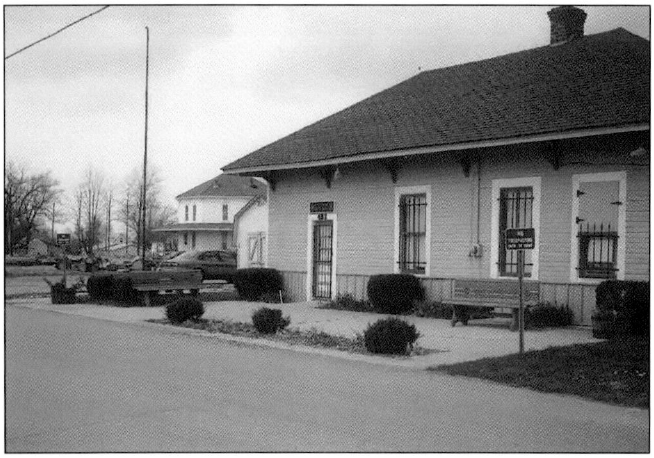

This is a *c.* 1900s rail depot at Shirley. The contrasting photo is of the surviving depot located on the east west rail route through town that is now a historical museum for the community. Shirley became a rail center when the Cincinnati, Wabash, & Michigan railway, once called the Big Four, was constructed across the east end of Brown Township. The original survey was done in 1890, and the community grew fast because another railway angled north and east through Willow Branch, Wilkinson, and Shirley. The town developed numerous factories several bars of note and a good number of churches. One that no longer stands is the Mother of God Catholic Church. Since Shirley and Wilkinson set so close to one another there has always been both a sense of community and a rivalry between the two. Shirley's Main Street sets astride the Hancock-Henry County line.

This is the home of Gary and Marcia Hunt on U.S. 40 just east of Charlottesville. The photo was taken just after the tornado on 3 April 1974. The house originally belonged to John Craft and is a fairly early structure. This is an excellent example of how time heals the wounds and ravages of storms and the like.

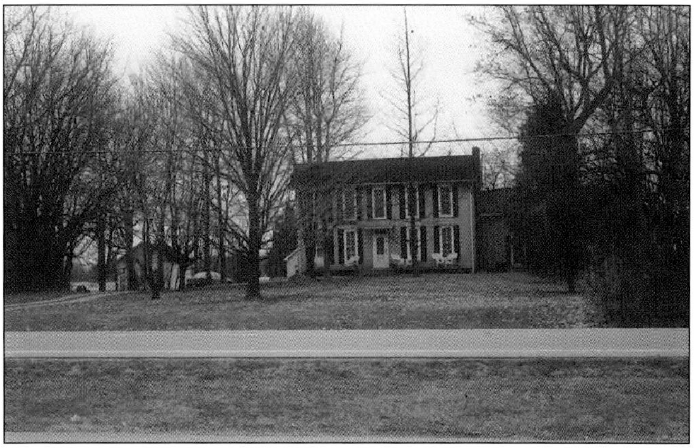

Hancock County has weathered a number of terrible storms over the period of its history, including a number in the 19th and 20th centuries. One referred to as a cyclone blew down a chain factory in Maxwell and destroyed many homes and barns across Hancock County, generally between Greenfield and 600 North. It even interrupted calling at a home funeral, and some are said to have taken refuge under feather ticks. One young boy was left exposed to the weather when the house lifted off the cellar where his family took shelter. He was left to face the wind, rain, and the hail that poured down.

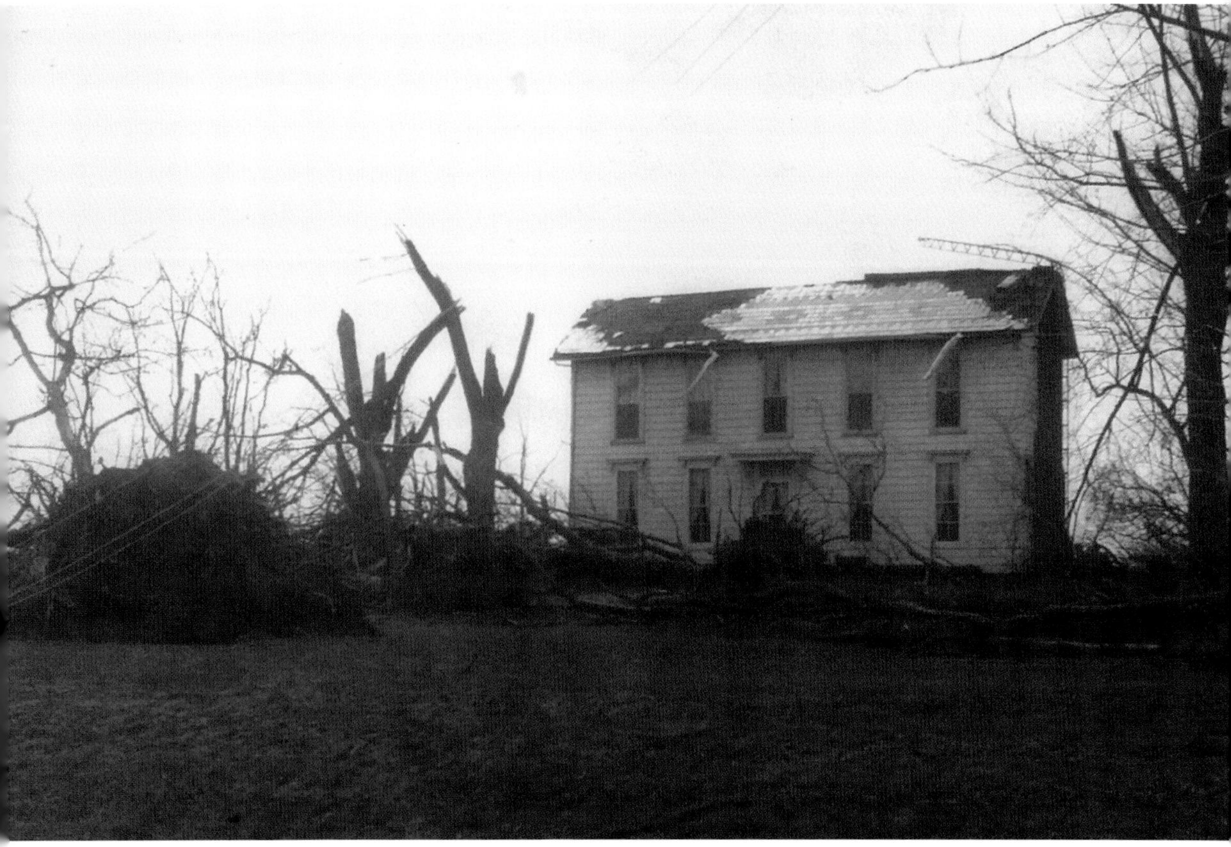

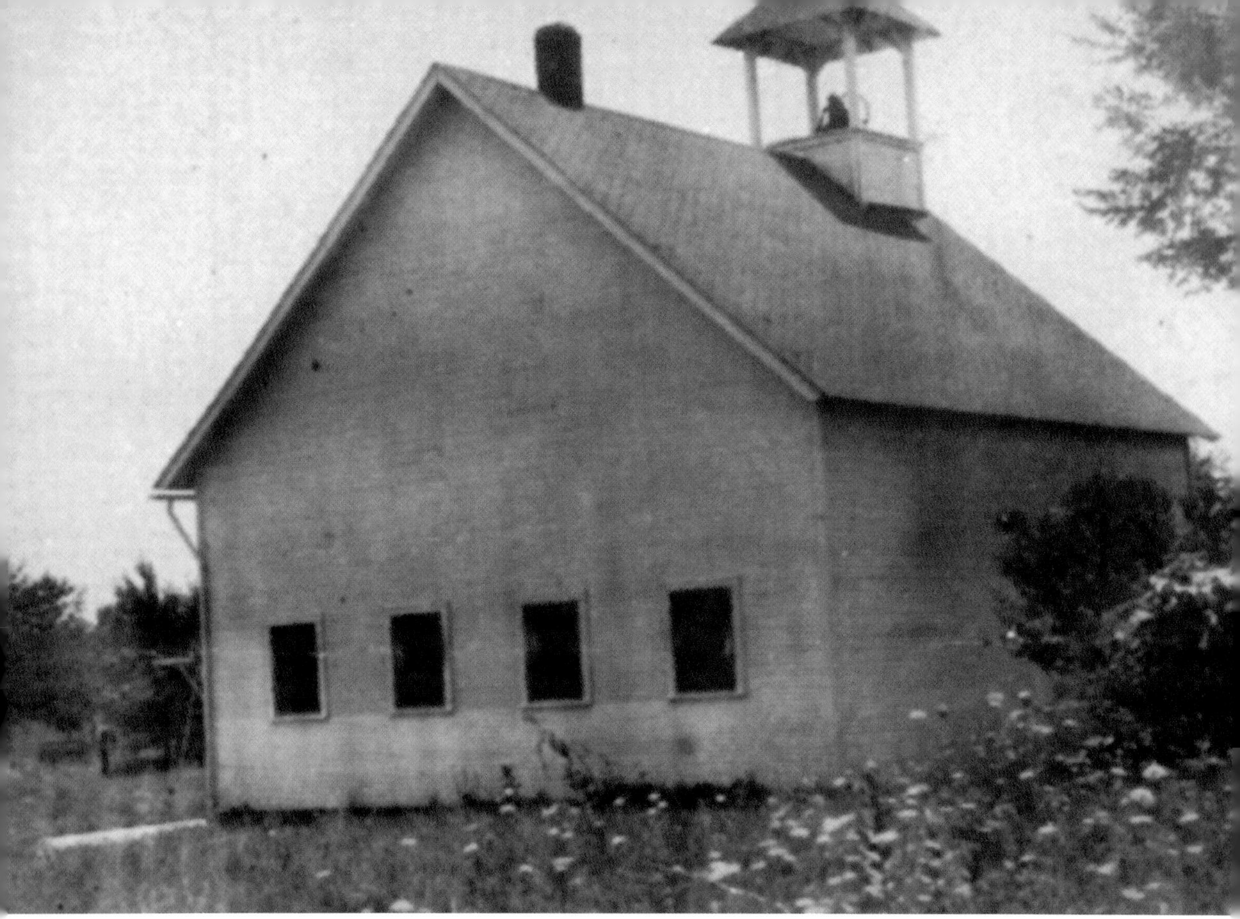

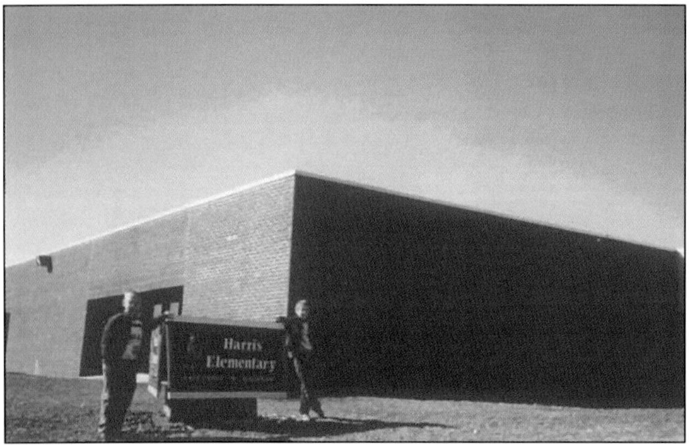

The architectural style as well as size of school buildings has changed over the years. In 1908, local teacher Mrs. Ada New asked for a new schoolhouse in East Greenfield. The school board would not consent at first. Mrs. New was persistent, and a plain frame one room building was soon erected. In 1948, the East Greenfield School was abandoned as the last one-room school. The new Harris School was officially opened in 1954, and was named for Captain Leo O. Harris who was James Whitcomb Riley's teacher. The school is located next to the middle school on Park Avenue. The school board had overseen its construction at a cost of $180,000. The building has been added to and extensively remodeled to meet current needs.

Chapter 4
SCHOOLS

The Old School House at New Palestine was known as "Union Hall" during the Civil War Period. It was the center of many of the communities meetings as well as the educational building it was meant to be. Torn down later to make way for more modern facilities, it had disappeared long before 1900. The picture dates *c.* 1870. In 1915, there were only 30 one-room schools in Hancock County, as students began to move to the larger township schools in the leading towns. No townships at that time had consolidated their one-room schools completely into the central township school except for Blue River. The state finally dealt with the issue by providing aid for transportation to the townships central location. Thus, the tradition of the one-room school began its final days in Indiana. The last one-room school in Hancock County was closed in East Greenfield in 1948. People gradually favored moving to the larger systems, and in time those schools were thought to be too small to provide all the opportunities that were needed. Blue River and Jackson Township consolidated their schools after a major fire at Westland School in 1947. Maxwell (Center Township) and Eden consolidated after a major fire at Maxwell in the 1950s. Strong competition still slowed the merger of the high schools. In 1956, voters turned down a proposal to merge Hancock Central and Greenfield City Schools. But in 1959, the Indiana School Reorganization Act required that districts having 1,000 students or more be formed. A local committee drew up several plans, and new boundaries were considered. In the end Brown, Jackson, and Blue River made up the Eastern District and Green, Center, and Greenfield made up the Greenfield-Central District. On the west side of the county in the north Buck Creek, Vernon, and Fortville made up the Mt. Vernon District and in the South Brandywine, and Sugar Creek made up the Southern Hancock School Corporation. In this manner, the county's schools were formed as they exist today.

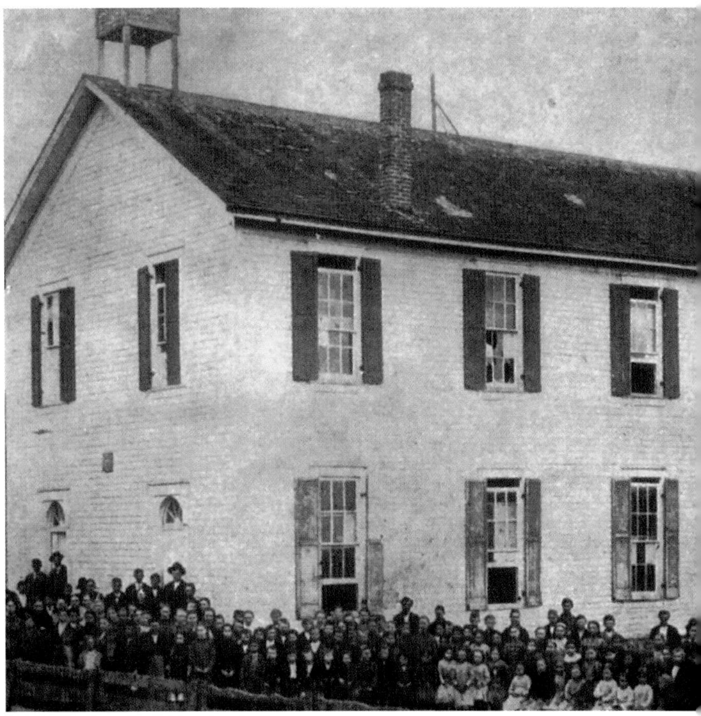

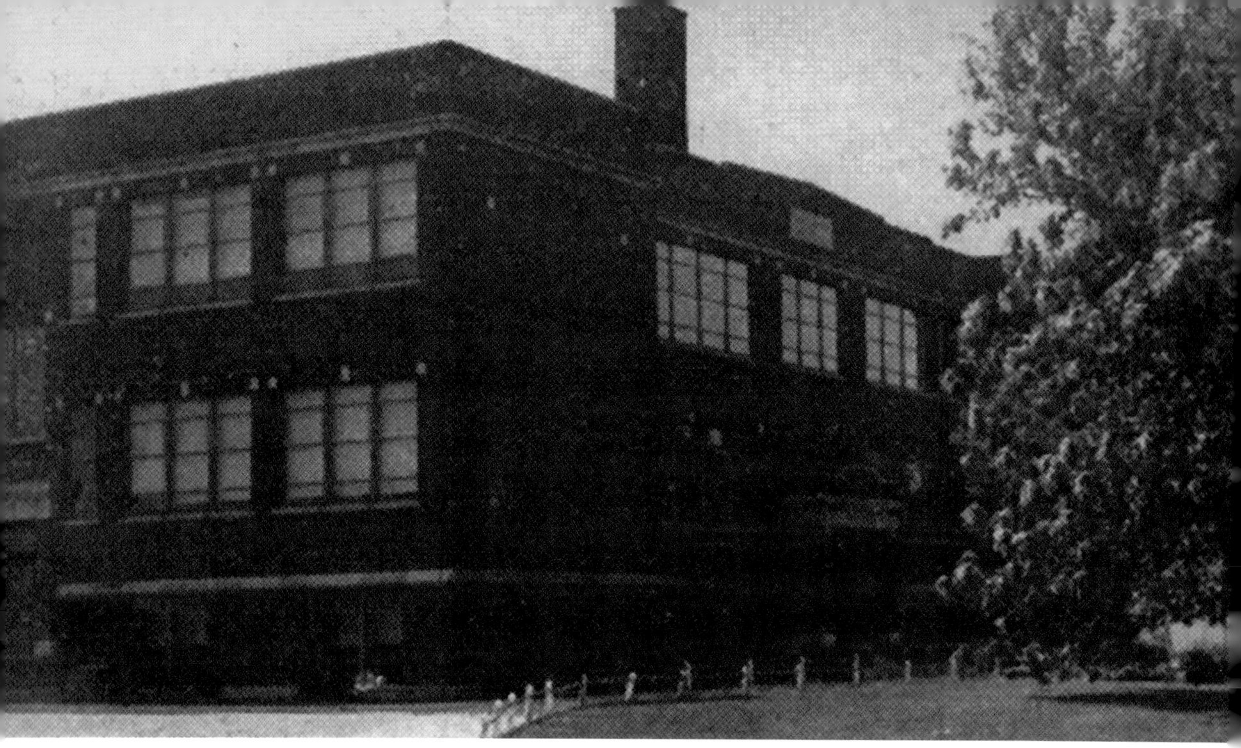

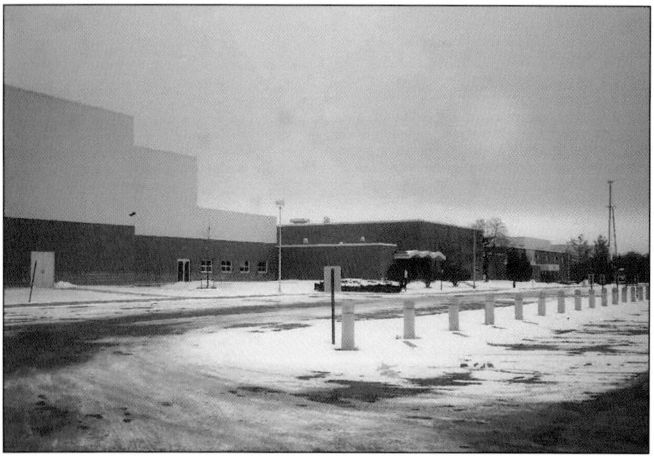

New Palestine High School is shown here, as is its replacement on its original site. The older building was built in 1919, and torn down just a few years ago to make room for new facilities including an auditorium. A much earlier frame building was replaced by the first brick structure that was a joint venture between town and township in 1884. A systematic high school course of study was added in 1895. In 1914-1915, there were 40 students in high school and 253 in the elementary grades. New Palestine was consolidated with Brandywine Township as a result of the 1960s school consolidation. Brandywine had only ran an elementary school previous to that time and the students of high school age went to surrounding township high schools.

In 1905, Jackson Township had eight schools. Six of these were one-room schools. Charlottesville had a combined grade and high school. A devastating fire destroyed the Charlottesville building in 1935. In August of 1936, the cornerstone was laid for a new school building. The cost would be $125,000 for a large brick and stone structure with a 500-seat gym. Thomas Walker's "History of Jackson Township Schools" was placed in the cornerstone. Irwin Schultz, a Charlottesville resident and professor of psychology at Butler University, spoke at the dedication. After the Westland School fire on 24 January 1947, the Jackson-Blue River Consolidated School Corporation was formed. Later, the building housed a Christian academy. It is now used as a warehouse.

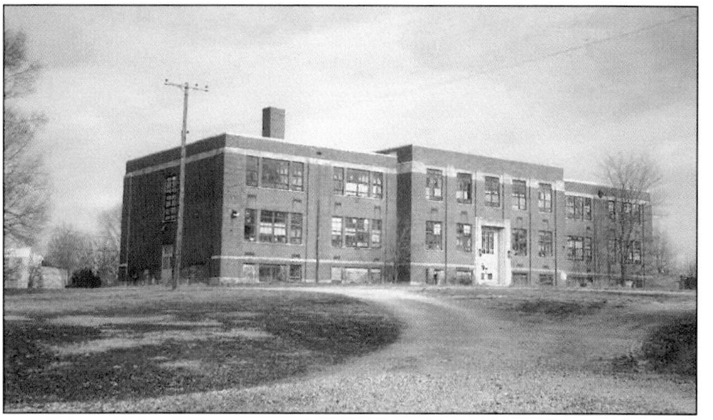

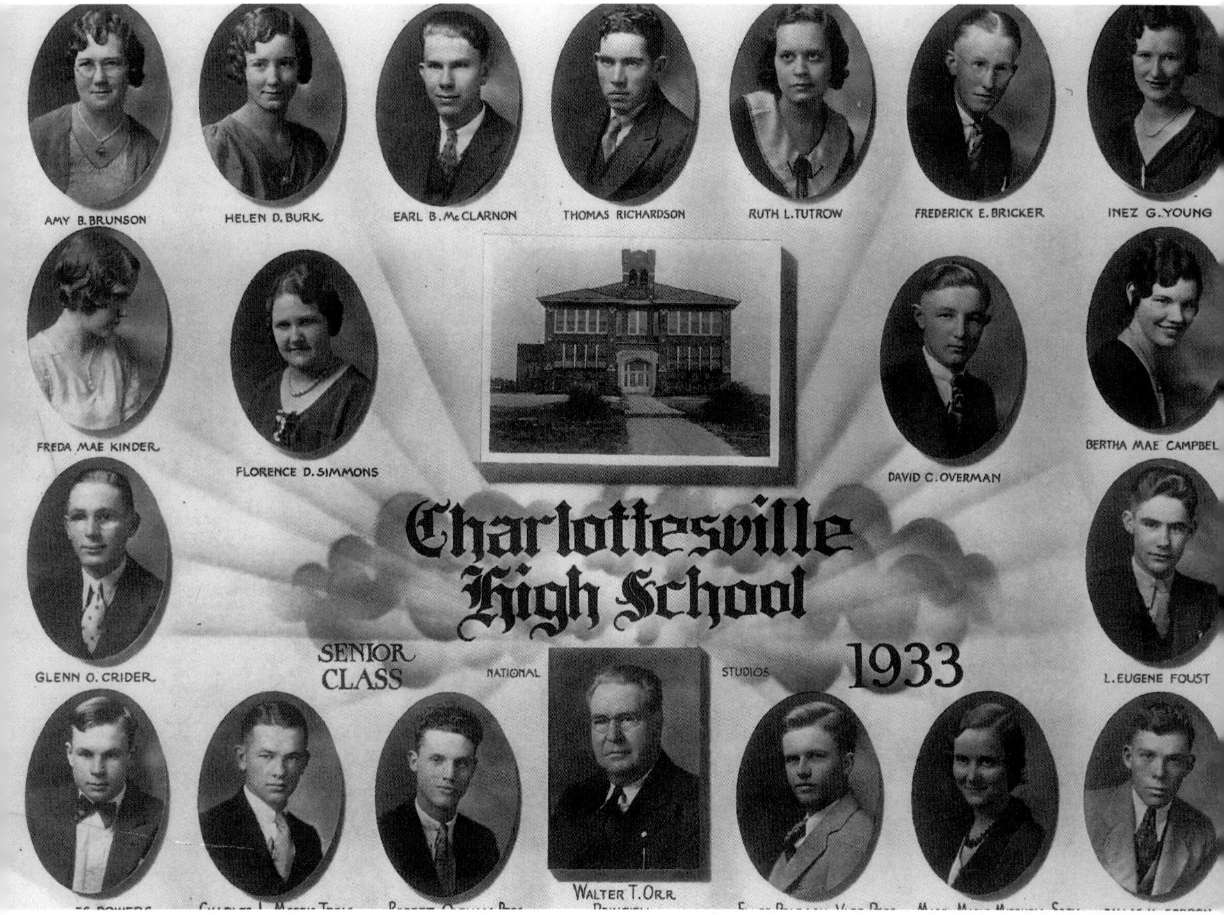

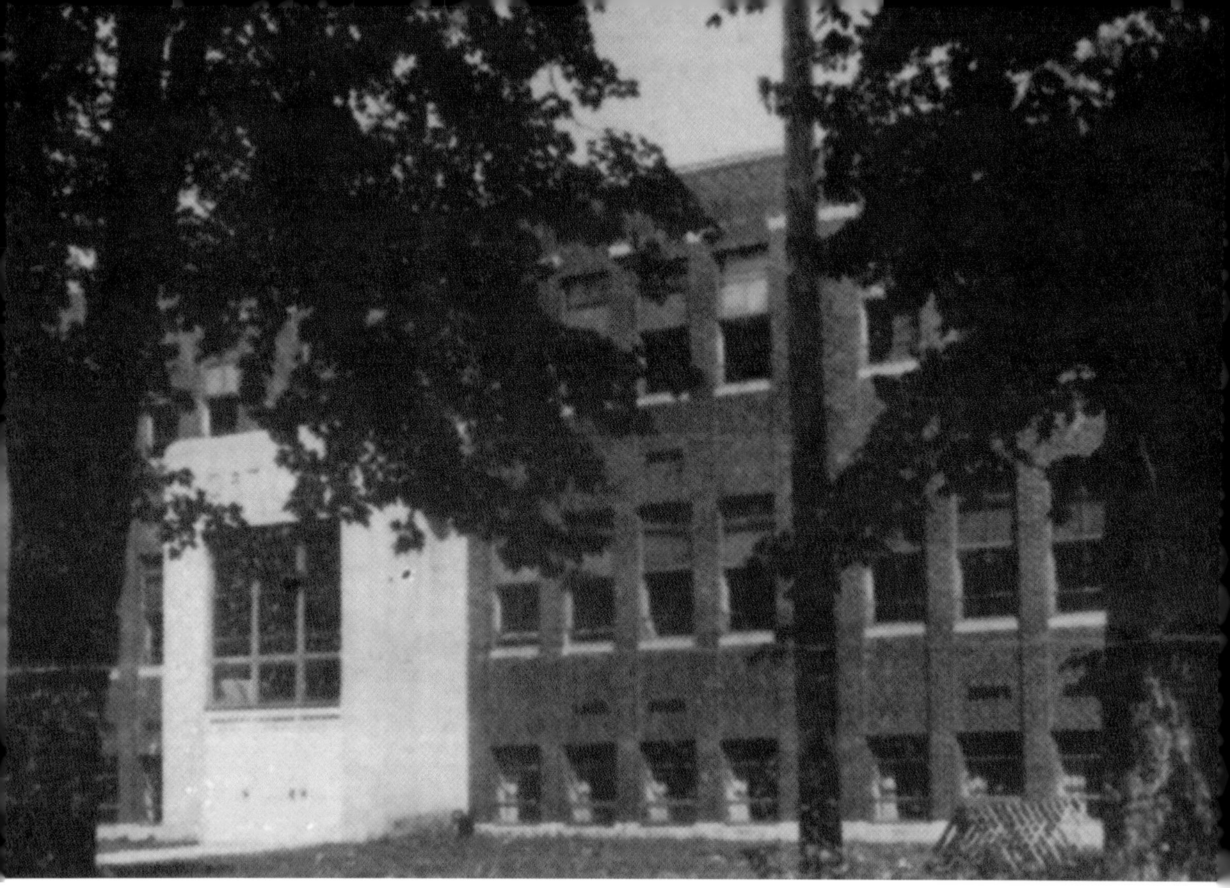

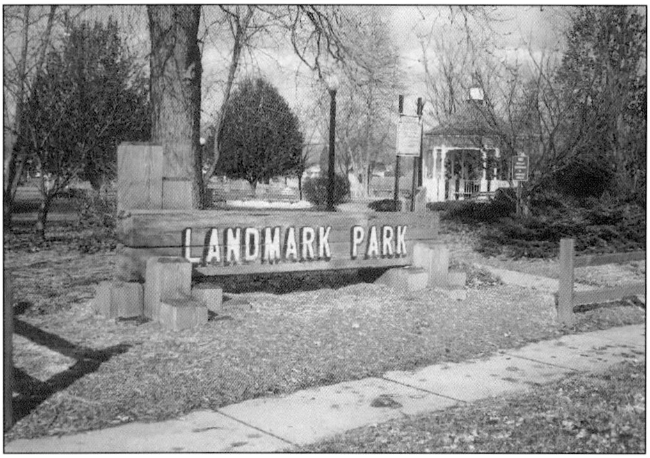

The Fortville School was constructed in 1938 on a site near the downtown area and next to the Methodist Church. One of the first school houses in Vernon Township was located one mile south of McCordsville. Another was located where Fortville now stands. Currently, Landmark Park stands at the site of Fortville High School. The park provides a pleasant place of retreat for local residents with a gazebo and appropriate landscaping, and you would not guess a large brick building once occupied the area.

Green Township constructed the Eden School in 1922. The old Eden School was constructed in 1889, to which additional rooms were added in 1900, so that the township could have a high school. In 1923, Eden High School won the Hancock County Basketball Tournament, but Mt. Comfort eliminated them in the Sectional Tournament. For years the school was considered second to none among the township high schools. The old building was eventually demolished and replaced in the 1920s. A modern structure that is part of the current building was added in the 1950s. When Center Township district joined with Green Township in August 1955, the former 12-grade school at Eden was converted into a grade school, and the high school was moved to Maxwell. A disastrous fire at Maxwell had brought about the change.

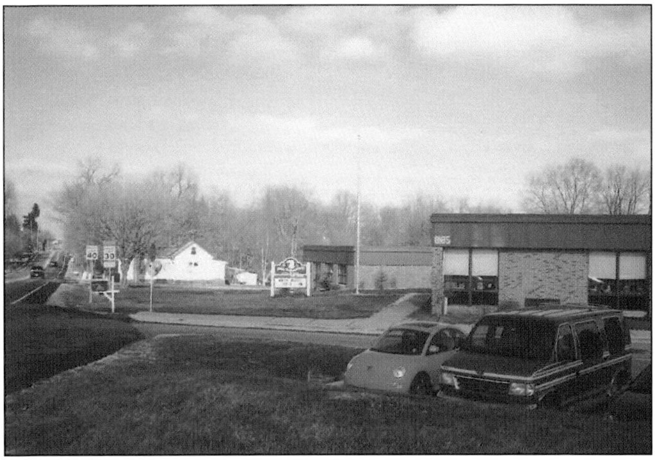

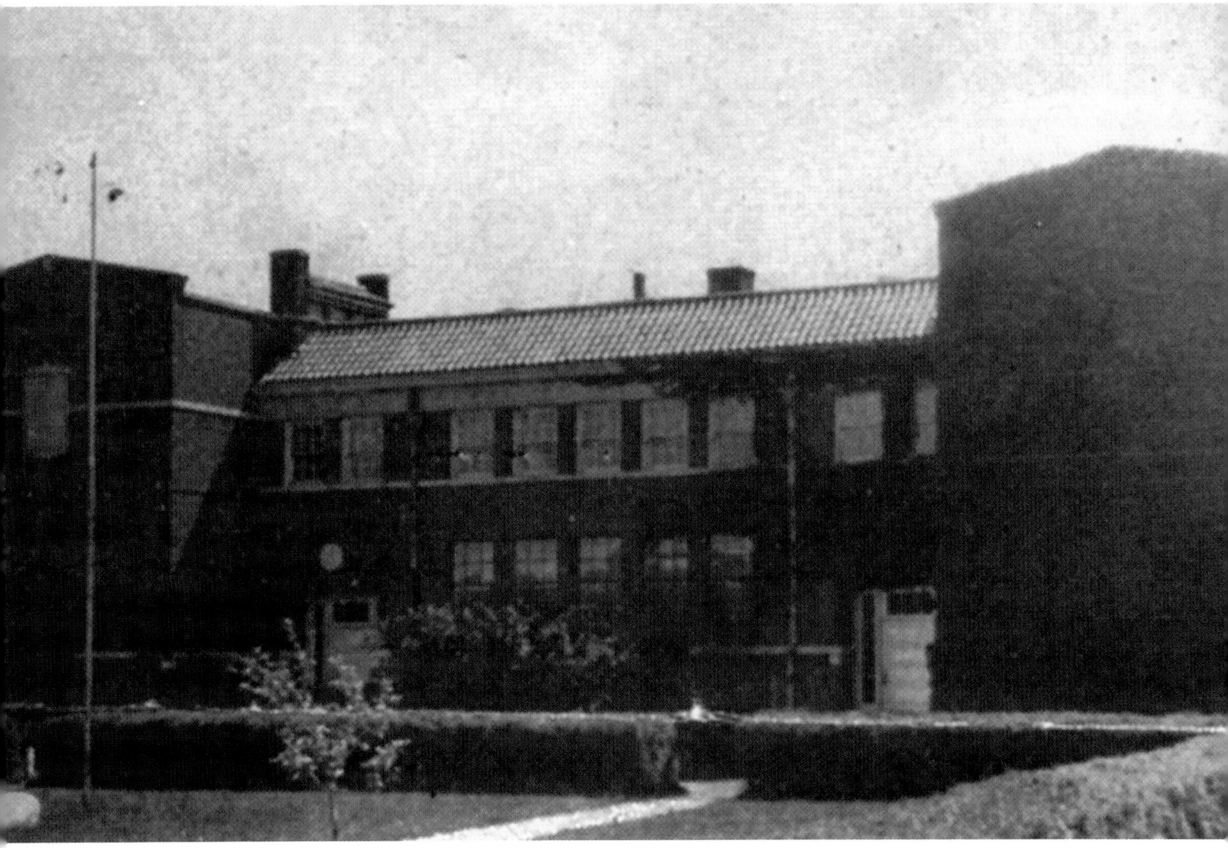

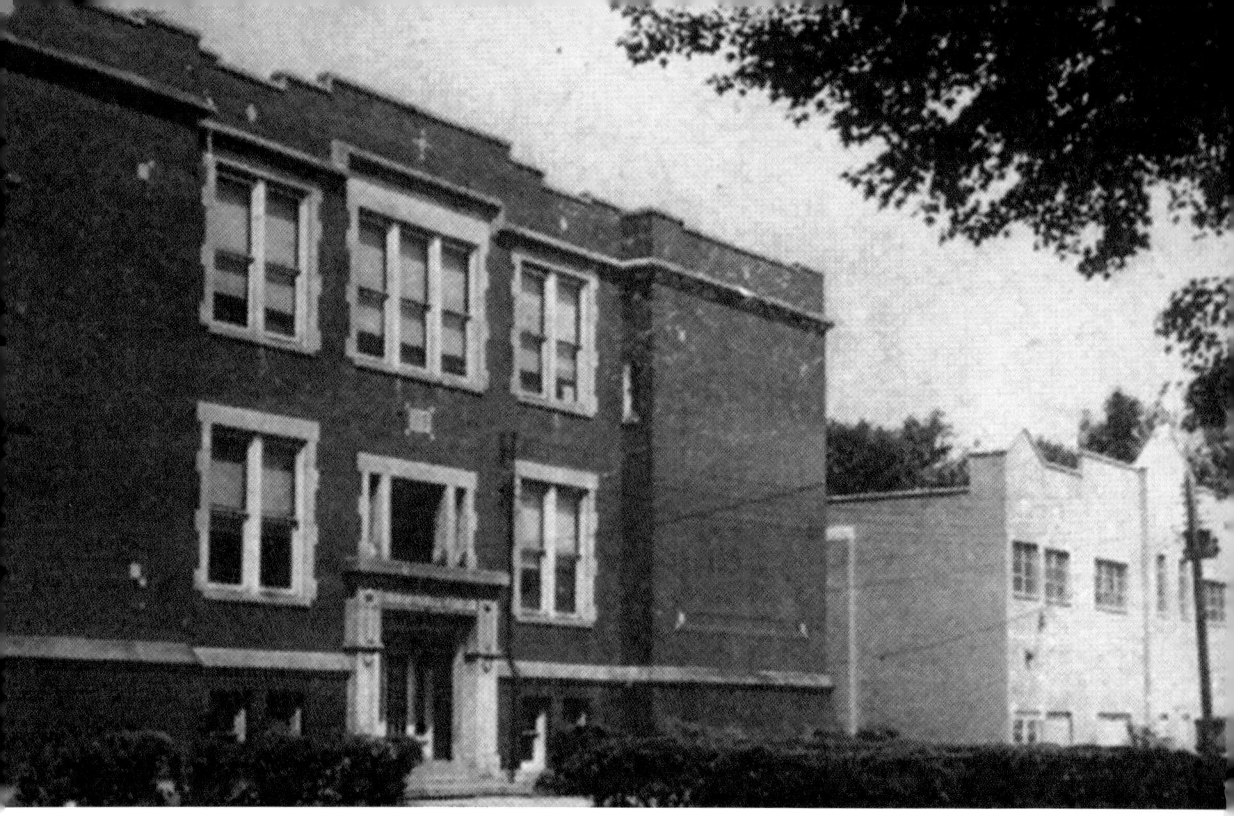

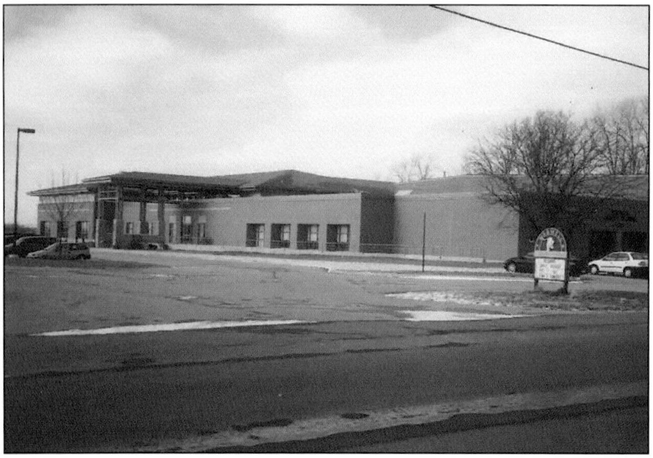

The old Maxwell school burned *c.* 1955, although an elementary building behind the main structure was saved, as was the gym, which was demolished years later. As a result of the fire, Center Township joined with Green Township to form the Hancock Central School District in August 1955. New additions were added to the gym and elementary at Maxwell, and that became the location of the high school and some junior high classes. On Election Day 5 May 1964, Greenfield Schools and the Hancock Central School District were joined together in the Greenfield-Central Community School Corporation by a vote of 1,294 to 1,211. The old gym was later demolished at Maxwell, and a new facility replaced the gym. Later the former elementary was demolished and a new larger structure replaced the middle school that has occupied the site since the merger of the high schools in the fall of 1969. Hancock Central and Greenfield combined to form the Greenfield-Central Community School Corp. and joined their high schools in 1969.

In 1905, Vernon Township had three schools. A combined grade and high school was located in McCordsville. It had seven teachers. The other two were one-room grade schools. The township constructed this McCordsville School in 1902, after a fire destroyed the previous building. In 1925, this building also burned. In 1926, Vernon Township constructed a new building which also burned, and after the formation of the Mt. Vernon School Corporation the site was cleared for a park with the entry of the last building placed on an angled mound. McCordsville was the first certified high school in Hancock County.

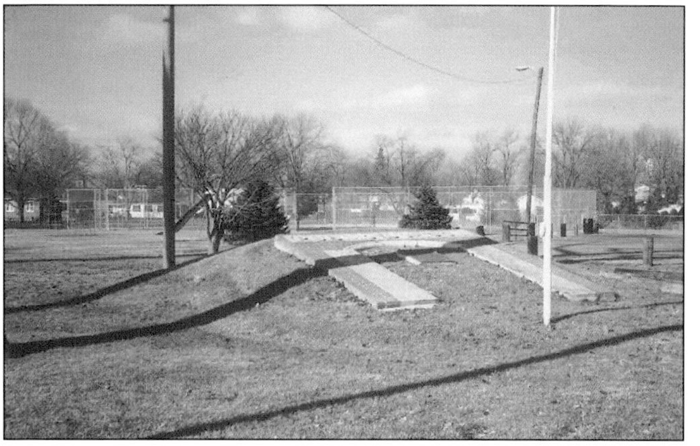

Before consolidation in the 1960s Mt. Comfort maintained a high school for Buck Creek Township. The Mt. Vernon system maintains an elementary school on the site to this day.

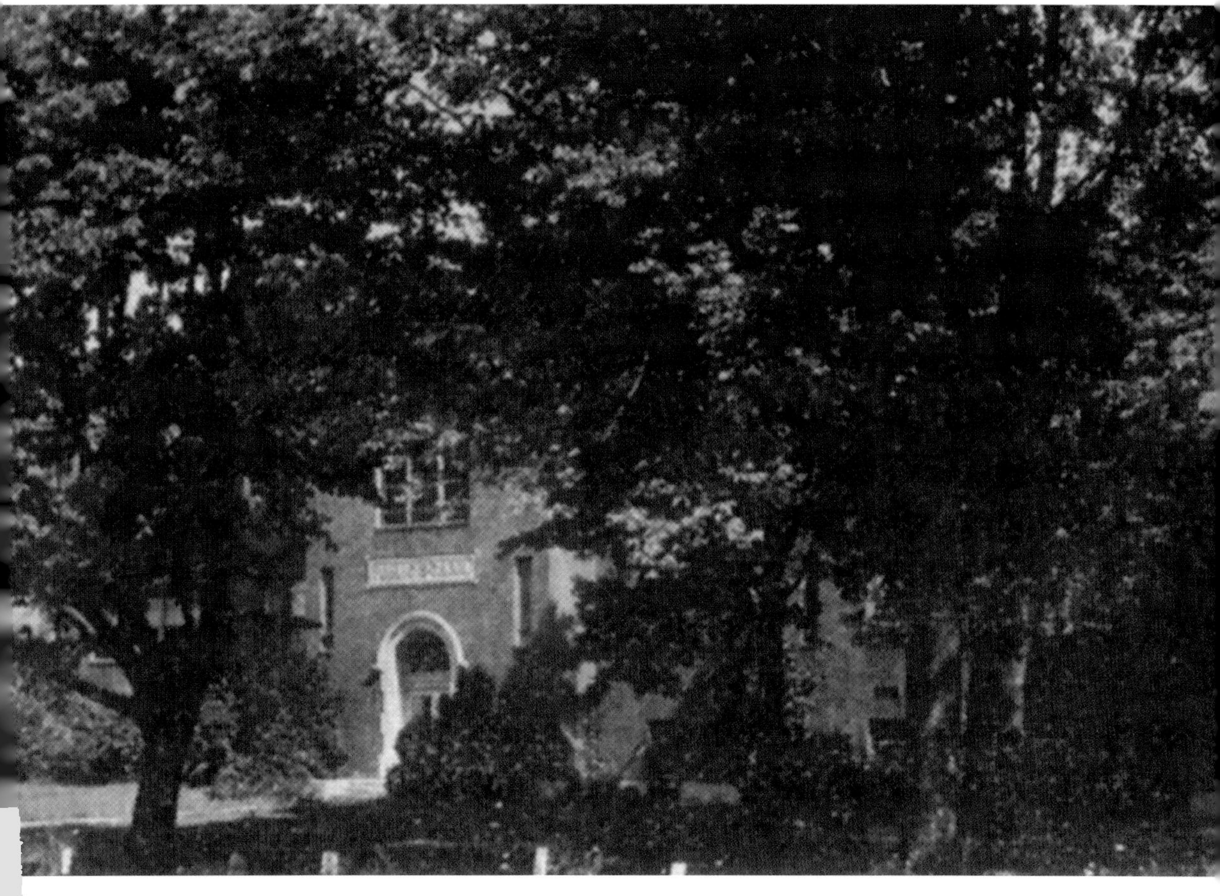

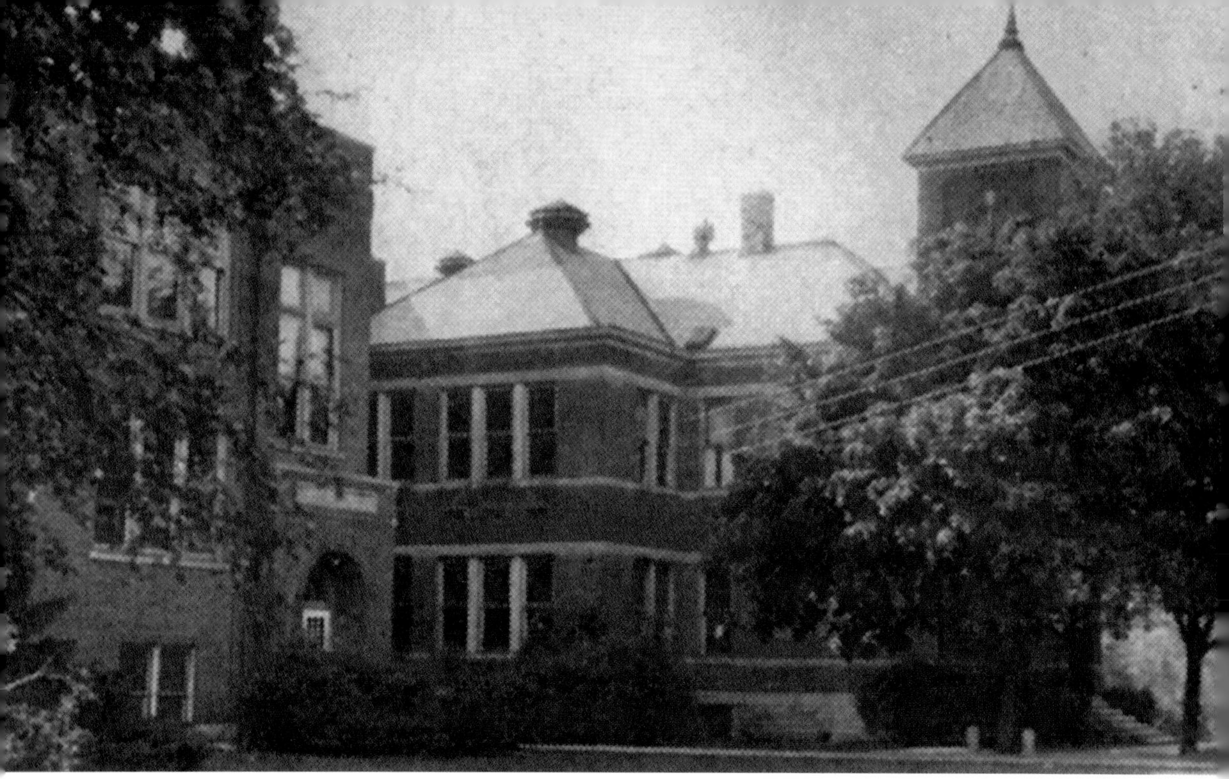

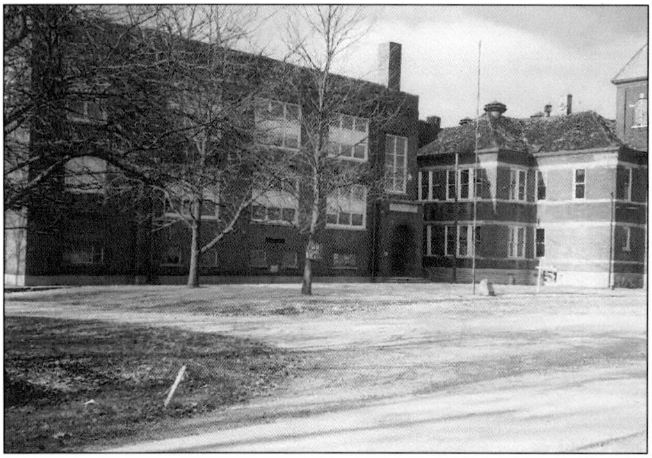

Brown Township constructed the Wilkinson School building in 1904. In the fall of 1911, the question of the location of the high school became acute, and the trustee and advisory board had to make a decision as to whether it would remain at Warrington or be moved to Wilkinson. It was finally moved to Wilkinson. In 1922, an extensive addition was added to the building. From the fall of 1911 until the fall of 1964, both elementary and high school students were housed in the Wilkinson building. The Wilkinson structure still exists and periodically has been used by various business enterprises in the community. There has been a hardware store, restaurant, and a storage facility housed in the old school building. The structure is currently deserted, but it still looks better than you might expect.